Realidades A

realidades.com

Digital Edition

Peggy Palo Boyles
OKLAHOMA CITY, OK

Myriam Met
ROCKVILLE, MD

Richard S. Sayers
LONGMONT, CO

Carol Eubanks Wargin

PEARSON

Boston, Massachusetts I Chandler, Arizona
Glenview, Illinois I Upper Saddle River, New Jersey

WE DEDICATE THIS BOOK TO THE
MEMORY OF OUR ESTEEMED COLLEAGUE,

Carol Eubanks Wargin.

Front cover, left: Teen boy
Center left: Incan ruins at Machu Picchu, Peru
Center right: Young women wearing traditional flamenco dress at the April Fair, Seville, Spain
Right: Handmade bowls in Chichen Itza, Mexico

Acknowledgments appear on pages 292–293, which constitute an extension of this copyright page.

PEARSON

ISBN-13:   978-0-13-319962-8
ISBN-10:   0-13-319962-2
11 17

Realidades Authors

Peggy Palo Boyles

During her foreign language career of over thirty years, Peggy Palo Boyles has taught elementary, secondary, and university students in both private and public schools. She is currently an independent consultant who provides assistance to schools, districts, universities, state departments of education and other organizations of foreign language education in the areas of curriculum, assessment, cultural instruction, professional development, and program evaluation. She was a member of the ACTFL Performance Guidelines for the K–12 Learners task force and served as a Senior Editor for the project. She currently serves on the Advisory Committee for the ACTFL Assessment for Performance and Proficiency of Languages (AAPPL). Peggy is a Past-President of the National Association of District Supervisors of Foreign Language (NADSFL) and was a recipient of ACTFL's K–12 Steiner Award for Leadership in K–12 Foreign Language Education. Peggy lives in Oklahoma City, OK with her husband, Del. Their son, Ryan, works at the University of Texas at Arlington.

Myriam Met

For most of her professional life, Myriam (Mimi) Met has worked in the public schools, first as a high school teacher in New York, then as K–12 supervisor of language programs in the Cincinnati Public Schools, and finally as a Coordinator of Foreign Language in Montgomery County (MD) Public Schools. She is currently a Senior Research Associate at the National Foreign Language Center, University of Maryland, where she works on K–12 language policy and infrastructure development. Mimi Met has served on the Advisory Board for the National Standards for Foreign Language Learning, on the Executive Council of ACTFL, and as President of the National Association of District Supervisors of Foreign Languages (NADSFL). She has been honored by ACTFL with the Steiner Award for Leadership in K–12 Foreign Language Education and the Papalia Award for Excellence in Teacher Education.

Richard S. Sayers

Rich Sayers has been an educator in world languages since 1978. He taught Spanish at Niwot High School in Longmont, CO for 18 years, where he taught levels 1 through AP Spanish. While at Niwot High School, Rich served as department chair, district foreign language coordinator, and board member of the Colorado Congress of Foreign Language Teachers. Rich has also served on the Board of the Southwest Conference on Language Teaching. In 1991, Rich was selected as one of the Disney Company's Foreign Language Teacher Honorees for the American Teacher Awards. Rich has served as a world languages consultant for Pearson since 1996. He is currently the Curriculum Specialist for Pearson in the Mountain Region.

Carol Eubanks Wargin

Carol Eubanks Wargin taught Spanish for 20 years at Glen Crest Middle School, Glen Ellyn, IL, and also served as Foreign Languages department chair. In 1997, Ms. Wargin's presentation "From Text to Test: How to Land Where You Planned" was honored as the best presentation at the Illinois Conference on the Teaching of Foreign Languages (ICTFL) and at the Central States Conference on the Teaching of Foreign Languages (CSC). She was twice named Outstanding Young Educator by the Jaycees. Ms. Wargin passed away in 2004.

Contributing Writers

Eduardo Aparicio
Chicago, IL

Daniel J. Bender
New Trier High School
Winnetka, IL

Marie Deer
Bloomington, IN

Leslie M. Grahn
Howard County Public Schools
Ellicott City, MD

Thomasina Hannum
Albuquerque, NM

Nancy S. Hernández
World Languages Supervisor
Simsbury (CT) Public Schools

Patricia J. Kule
Fountain Valley School
   of Colorado
Colorado Springs, CO

Jacqueline Hall Minet
Upper Montclair, NJ

Alex Paredes
Simi Valley, CA

Martha Singer Semmer
Breckenridge, CO

Dee Dee
Drisdale Stafford
Putnam City Schools
Oklahoma City, OK

Christine S. Wells
Cheyenne Mountain
   Junior High School
Colorado Springs, CO

Michael Werner
University of Chicago
Chicago, IL

National Consultants

María R. Hubbard
Braintree, MA

Patrick T. Raven
Milwaukee, WI

Getting Started with REALIDADES

Why Study Spanish?

Congratulations on your decision to study Spanish! Did you know that more than 425 million people in Spain, 18 Latin American countries, Puerto Rico, Equatorial Guinea, the Philippines, and the United States speak Spanish? It is the second most common language in the United States and the third most commonly spoken language in the world.

Learn to communicate When you study Spanish, you will be able to communicate with the many people in your community and across the globe who speak Spanish. You can bargain in a market, read information on the Internet, and watch television shows. ▶

◀ **Understand culture** The Spanish-speaking world is rich in music, food, art, literature, and everyday traditions. Learning about culture helps you understand other people's perspectives, patterns of behavior, and contributions to the world at large.

Expand career opportunities In today's increasingly global community, your employment and career options expand greatly when you have the right job skills *and* proficiency in Spanish. ▶

◀ **Improve language skills** Studying Spanish improves your first language skills: vocabulary, grammar, reading, and writing. Research shows your test scores may even improve!

Online Resources with realidades.com

REALIDADES includes lots of online resources to help you learn Spanish! You can easily link to all of them when you log on to your Home Page within realidades.com. Your teacher will assign some activities, such as the ones in the workbooks. Others you can access on your own.

You'll find these resources highlighted on the pages of your print or online Student Edition with technology icons. Here's a list of the different icons used.

 Bilingual Visual Dictionary Links to additional vocabulary words presented visually

Reference Atlas Quick links to the countries in the online atlas

 Mapa global interactivo Links to GIS showing locations across the Spanish-speaking world

 Videos

Videocultura Cultural overview of each theme

Videohistoria Vocabulary video to help present the new vocabulary

GramActiva Grammar explanations to help present the new grammar

Grammar Tutorials Clear explanations of grammar with comparison to English

Animated Verbs Animations that highlight verb conjugations

 Modelo *Videomodelos*
Video models of speaking activities

 Audio Audio files for vocabulary, listening practice, and pronunciation

 Canciones de hip hop Songs to help practice new vocabulary and grammar

 Flashcards Practice for the new vocabulary

 RealTalk! Speak-and-record tool for speaking activities

 GramActiva **Activity** Extra practice for the *GramActiva* video

Más práctica GO **Online practice**

Instant Check Short activities that check your progress right away

Guided Workbook Step-by-step vocabulary and grammar practice

Core Workbook Vocabulary and grammar exercises

Communication Workbook Listening, video, and writing activities

Cultural Reading Activity Questions for the *Lectura* reading

Puzzles End-of-chapter games

Getting Started on realidades.com

At the beginning of the year, you'll want to get registered on realidades.com. Your teacher will help you get started. If you log on to realidades.com using a non-school computer, be sure to check out the System Requirements to make sure you are using compatible browsers and have the needed software.

realidades.com Home Page

After you register, you'll land on your realidades.com Home Page. Here you'll be able to access assignments, grades, and study resources. You'll also be able to communicate with your teacher.

 You'll find everything that's in the book online as eText.

RealTalk!

You'll be able to record many of your speaking activities using RealTalk! You can use the microphone in your computer or a headset with microphone. If you want, you can download and save your recording.

Mapa global interactivo

Build your geography skills and learn about more locations throughout the Spanish-speaking world. You can download .kmz files from realidades.com and link to sites using Google Earth™ or other geographic information systems.

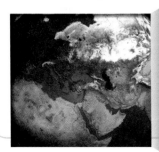

Tabla de materias

Tema 1 Mis amigos y yo

Tema 2 La escuela

Tema 3 La comida

Tema 4 Los pasatiempos

Apéndices

México

Ciudad de Guanajuato, México

El Zócalo, México, D.F.

México

Capital: México, D.F.

Population: 113.7 million

Area: 761,606 sq mi / 1,972,550 sq km

Languages: Spanish (official), Nahuatl, various Mayan and other indigenous languages

Religions: Roman Catholic, Protestant

Government: federal republic

Currency: *peso mexicano*

Exports: manufactured products, oil and oil products, silver, coffee, cotton

ESTADOS UNIDOS

Tijuana

Baja California

Golfo de California (Mar de Cortés)

SIERRA MADRE OCCIDENTAL

Ciudad Juárez

Río Bravo del Norte

Chihuahua

Nuevo Laredo

Río Grande

Monterrey

SIERRA MADRE ORIENTAL

Golfo de México

30° N

Trópico de Cáncer

20° N

Guadalajara

Querétaro

Mérida

Península de Yucatán

Paracutín ▲

Ciudad de México ✪ ▲ Iztaccíhuatl
● Puebla
Popocatépetl

Veracruz

BELICE

Oaxaca

ISTMO DE TEHUANTEPEC

Acapulco

SIERRA MADRE DEL SUR

GUATEMALA

EL SALVADOR

OCÉANO PACÍFICO

110° O

100° O

LEYENDA
Elevación

Metros	Pies
3,000	9,840
2,000	6,560
1,000	3,280
500	1,640
200	656

— Frontera nacional
✪ Capital
● Ciudad
▲ Volcán o montaña

0 — 200 Millas
0 — 200 Kilómetros

Proyección cónica conforme de Lambert

N
O — E
S

Sierra Tarahumara

México xiii

América Central

Guatemala

Capital: Ciudad de Guatemala

Population: 13.8 million

Area: 42,043 sq mi / 108,890 sq km

Languages: Spanish (official), Quiche, Cakchiquel, Kekchi, Mam, Garifuna, Xinca, and other indigenous languages

Religions: Roman Catholic, Protestant, traditional Mayan beliefs

Government: constitutional democratic republic

Currency: *quetzal*, U.S. dollar *(dólar)*

Exports: coffee, sugar, petroleum, clothing, textiles, bananas, vegetables

Honduras

Capital: Tegucigalpa

Population: 8.1 million

Area: 43,278 sq mi / 112,090 sq km

Languages: Spanish (official), indigenous languages

Religions: Roman Catholic, Protestant

Government: democratic constitutional republic

Currency: *lempira*

Exports: coffee, bananas, shrimp, lobster, meat, zinc, wood

El Salvador

Capital: San Salvador

Population: 6.1 million

Area: 8,124 sq mi / 21,040 sq km

Languages: Spanish (official), Nahua

Religions: Roman Catholic, Protestant

Government: republic

Currency: U.S. dollar *(dólar)*

Exports: offshore assembly parts, equipment, coffee, sugar, shrimp, textiles, chemicals, electricity

El Canal de Panamá

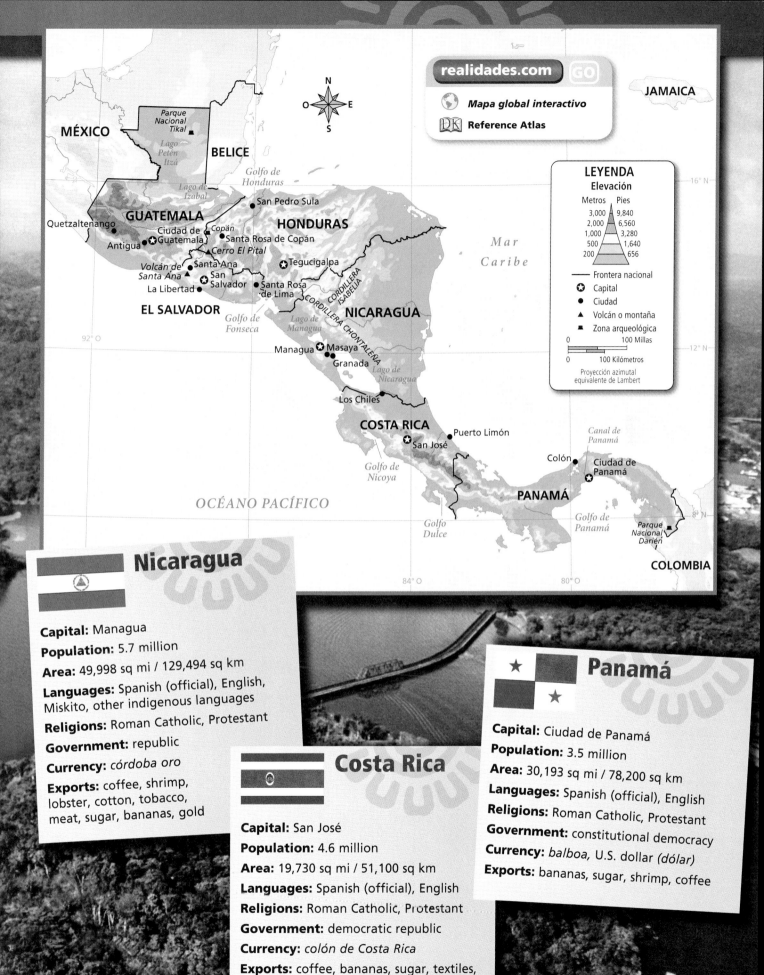

JAMAICA

MÉXICO

Parque Nacional Tikal

BELICE

Lago Petén Itzá

Golfo de Honduras

Lago de Izabal

San Pedro Sula

GUATEMALA

Quetzaltenango

Ciudad de Guatemala
Copán
Santa Rosa de Copán

HONDURAS

Antigua

Cerro El Pital

Volcán de Santa Ana
Santa Ana

Tegucigalpa

La Libertad
San Salvador
Santa Rosa de Lima

CORDILLERA ISABELIA

EL SALVADOR

CORDILLERA CHONTALEÑA

Golfo de Fonseca

Lago de Managua

NICARAGUA

Mar Caribe

Managua
Masaya
Granada

Lago de Nicaragua

Los Chiles

COSTA RICA

Puerto Limón

San José

Golfo de Nicoya

Canal de Panamá

Colón
Ciudad de Panamá

OCÉANO PACÍFICO

PANAMÁ

Golfo Dulce

Golfo de Panamá

Parque Nacional Darién

COLOMBIA

realidades.com GO

Mapa global interactivo

Reference Atlas

LEYENDA
Elevación

Metros	Pies
3,000	9,840
2,000	6,560
1,000	3,280
500	1,640
200	656

—— Frontera nacional
✪ Capital
● Ciudad
▲ Volcán o montaña
■ Zona arqueológica

0   100 Millas
0   100 Kilómetros

Proyección azimutal equivalente de Lambert

16° N
12° N
8° N
92° O
84° O
80° O

Nicaragua

Capital: Managua

Population: 5.7 million

Area: 49,998 sq mi / 129,494 sq km

Languages: Spanish (official), English, Miskito, other indigenous languages

Religions: Roman Catholic, Protestant

Government: republic

Currency: *córdoba oro*

Exports: coffee, shrimp, lobster, cotton, tobacco, meat, sugar, bananas, gold

Costa Rica

Capital: San José

Population: 4.6 million

Area: 19,730 sq mi / 51,100 sq km

Languages: Spanish (official), English

Religions: Roman Catholic, Protestant

Government: democratic republic

Currency: *colón de Costa Rica*

Exports: coffee, bananas, sugar, textiles, electronic components

Panamá

Capital: Ciudad de Panamá

Population: 3.5 million

Area: 30,193 sq mi / 78,200 sq km

Languages: Spanish (official), English

Religions: Roman Catholic, Protestant

Government: constitutional democracy

Currency: *balboa*, U.S. dollar *(dólar)*

Exports: bananas, sugar, shrimp, coffee

El Caribe

El Morro, San Juan,
Puerto Rico

Un arrecife de coral, República Dominicana

ESTADOS
UNIDOS

*Golfo de
México*

ISLAS BAHAMAS

Estrecho de la Florida

La Habana

CUBA

*Isla de la
Juventud*

Santiago
de Cuba

Guantánamo

JAMAICA

OCÉANO
ATLÁNTICO

REPÚBLICA
DOMINICANA

HAITÍ

*Bahía de
Samaná*

Santo
Domingo

PUERTO
RICO
(E.E.U.U.) *VIEQUES*

San Juan ★

Ponce ●

El Yunque

24° N

Trópico de Cáncer

20° N

16° N

12° N

80° O   76° O   72° O   68° O

Mar Caribe

LEYENDA
Elevación

Metros / Pies

3,000 / 9,840
2,000 / 6,560
1,000 / 3,280
500 / 1,640
200 / 656

—— Frontera nacional
✪ Capital
● Ciudad
▲ Volcán o montaña

0   100 Millas

0   100 Kilómetros

Proyección azimutal
equivalente de Lambert

República Dominicana

Capital: Santo Domingo

Population: 10 million

Area: 18,815 sq mi / 48,730 sq km

Languages: Spanish (official)

Religions: Roman Catholic, Protestant

Government: representative democracy

Currency: *peso dominicano*

Exports: ferronickel, sugar, gold, silver, cocoa, tobacco, meat

Puerto Rico

Capital: San Juan

Population: 4 million

Area: 3,515 sq mi / 9,104 sq km

Languages: Spanish and English (both official)

Religions: Roman Catholic, Protestant

Government: democracy (commonwealth of the United States)

Currency: U.S. dollar

Exports: chemicals, electronics, apparel, canned tuna, beverage concentrate, medical equipment

Cuba

Capital: La Habana

Population: 11.1 million

Area: 42,803 sq mi / 110,860 sq km

Languages: Spanish (official)

Religions: Roman Catholic, Protestant, and other religions

Government: Communist state

Currency: *peso cubano*

Exports: sugar, nickel, tobacco, shellfish, medical products, citrus, coffee

América del Sur
(Parte norte)

Colombia

Capital: Bogotá

Population: 44.7 million

Area: 439,736 sq mi / 1,138,910 sq km

Languages: Spanish (official)

Religion: Roman Catholic

Government: republic

Currency: *peso colombiano*

Exports: textiles, petroleum, coal, coffee, gold, emeralds, bananas, flowers, pharmaceuticals, sugar

Ecuador

Capital: Quito

Population: 15 million

Area: 109,483 sq mi / 283,560 sq km

Languages: Spanish (official), Quechua, other indigenous languages

Religion: Roman Catholic

Government: republic

Currency: U.S. dollar (*dólar*)

Exports: oil, bananas, tuna, shrimp, cocoa, gold, tropical wood

Las ruinas de Machu Picchu, Perú

Perú

Capital: Lima

Population: 29.2 million

Area: 496,226 sq mi / 1,285,220 sq km

Languages: Spanish (official), Quechua, (official), Aymara, and other indigenous languages

Religion: Roman Catholic and other religions

Government: constitutional republic

Currency: *nuevo sol*

Exports: gold, zinc, copper, fish and fish products, textiles

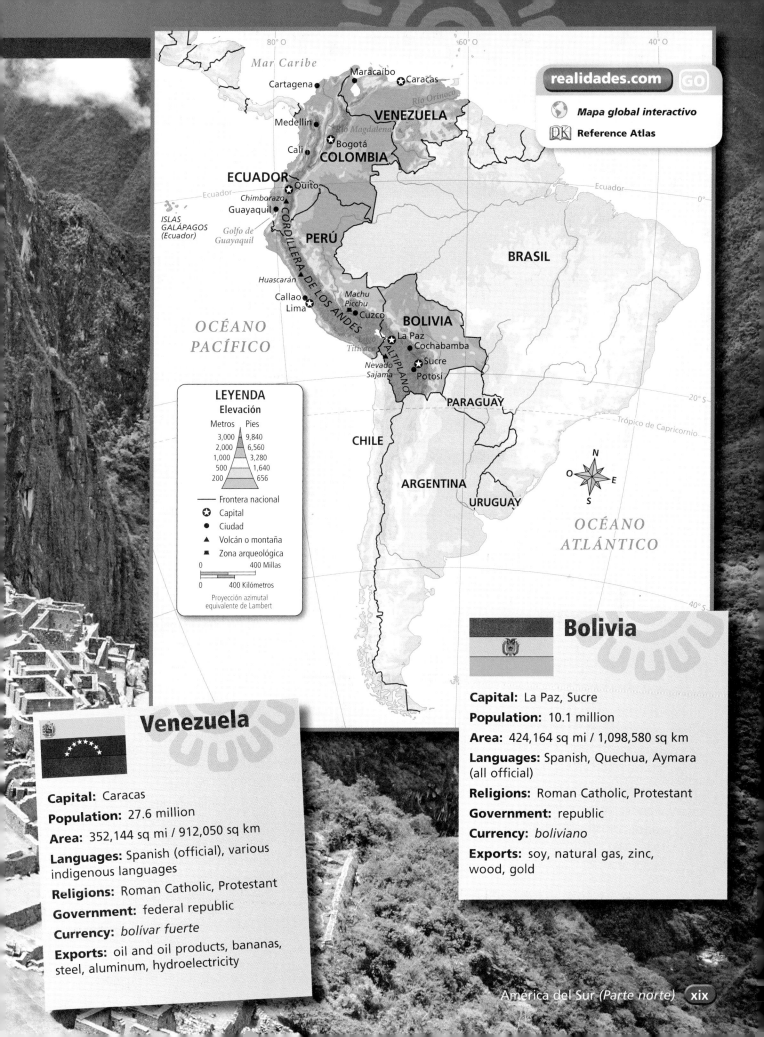

Mapa

Mar Caribe

Cartagena • ★ Caracas
Maracaíbo

VENEZUELA

Medellín •
Río Magdalena
Cali • ★ Bogotá

COLOMBIA

ECUADOR
Quito ★
Ecuador
Chimborazo ▲
Guayaquil

*ISLAS
GALÁPAGOS
(Ecuador)*

*Golfo de
Guayaquil*

PERÚ

Huascarán ▲

Callao • Machu Picchu ■
Lima • Cuzco

**OCÉANO
PACÍFICO**

BOLIVIA

Lago
Titicaca
La Paz ★
• Cochabamba
Nevado
Sajama ▲ ★ Sucre
• Potosí

BRASIL

PARAGUAY

Trópico de Capricornio

CHILE

ARGENTINA

URUGUAY

**OCÉANO
ATLÁNTICO**

realidades.com **GO**

🌐 *Mapa global interactivo*

📖 **Reference Atlas**

LEYENDA
Elevación

Metros	Pies
3,000	9,840
2,000	6,560
1,000	3,280
500	1,640
200	656

—— Frontera nacional
★ Capital
● Ciudad
▲ Volcán o montaña
■ Zona arqueológica

0 — 400 Millas
0 — 400 Kilómetros

*Proyección azimutal
equivalente de Lambert*

Bolivia

Capital: La Paz, Sucre

Population: 10.1 million

Area: 424,164 sq mi / 1,098,580 sq km

Languages: Spanish, Quechua, Aymara (all official)

Religions: Roman Catholic, Protestant

Government: republic

Currency: *boliviano*

Exports: soy, natural gas, zinc, wood, gold

Venezuela

Capital: Caracas

Population: 27.6 million

Area: 352,144 sq mi / 912,050 sq km

Languages: Spanish (official), various indigenous languages

Religions: Roman Catholic, Protestant

Government: federal republic

Currency: *bolívar fuerte*

Exports: oil and oil products, bananas, steel, aluminum, hydroelectricity

América del Sur
(Parte sur)

El Monte Fitz Roy, Patagonia, Argentina

Paraguay

Capital: Asunción
Population: 6.5 million
Area: 157,047 sq mi / 406,750 sq km
Languages: Spanish and Guaraní (both official)
Religions: Roman Catholic, Protestant
Government: constitutional republic
Currency: *guaraní*
Exports: sugar, meat, tapioca, hydroelectricity

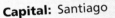

Chile

Capital: Santiago
Population: 16.9 million
Area: 292,260 sq mi / 756,950 sq km
Languages: Spanish (official)
Religions: Roman Catholic, Protestant
Government: republic
Currency: *peso chileno*
Exports: copper, fish, iron, iodine, fruit, wood, paper and pulp, chemicals

Argentina

Capital: Buenos Aires
Population: 41.8 million
Area: 1,068,302 sq mi / 2,766,890 sq km
Languages: Spanish (official), English, French, Italian, German
Religions: Roman Catholic, Protestant, Jewish
Government: republic
Currency: *peso argentino*
Exports: meat, edible oils, fuels and energy, cereals, feed, motor vehicles

LEYENDA

Elevación

Metros	Pies
3,000	9,840
2,000	6,560
1,000	3,280
500	1,640
200	656

— Frontera nacional

✪ Capital

● Ciudad

▲ Volcán o montaña

0   400 Millas

0   400 Kilómetros

Proyección azimutal
equivalente de Lambert

realidades.com GO

🌐 *Mapa global interactivo*

DK Reference Atlas

80° O   60° O   40° O

Mar Caribe

VENEZUELA

COLOMBIA

Ecuador   Ecuador   0°

ECUADOR

PERÚ

BRASIL

OCÉANO
PACÍFICO

ALTIPLANO

BOLIVIA

Río Paraguay

CORDILLERA DE LOS ANDES

GRAN CHACO

PARAGUAY

Asunción ✪   Cataratas
                          del Iguazú   20° S
                                            Trópico de Capricornio

CHILE   Río Paraná

ARGENTINA

Viña del Mar   Rosario ●   URUGUAY
Valparaíso ●✪ Cerro   Montevideo
Santiago   Aconcagua   ✪● Punta del
                  Buenos Aires ●   Este   OCÉANO
            PAMPAS   ATLÁNTICO
                          Río de la Plata
                          Mar del Plata ●

PATAGONIA

40° S

Cerro de
San Valentín ▲

Torres del ▲   TIERRA DEL
Paine   FUEGO
Estrecho de
Magallanes   Cabo de Hornos

Uruguay

Capital: Montevideo

Population: 3.3 million

Area: 68,039 sq mi / 176,220 sq km

Languages: Spanish (official),
Portuñol/Brazilero

Religions: Roman Catholic, Protestant,
and other religions

Government: constitutional republic

Currency: *peso uruguayo*

Exports: foods, vehicles, meat, rice, timber

España
Guinea Ecuatorial

España

Capital: Madrid

Population: 46.8 million

Area: 194,897 sq mi / 504,782 sq km

Languages: Castilian Spanish (official); Catalan, Galician, Basque (official regionally)

Religion: Roman Catholic

Government: parliamentary monarchy

Currency: *euro*

Exports: food, machinery, motor vehicles

El Alcázar de Segovia, Segovia, España

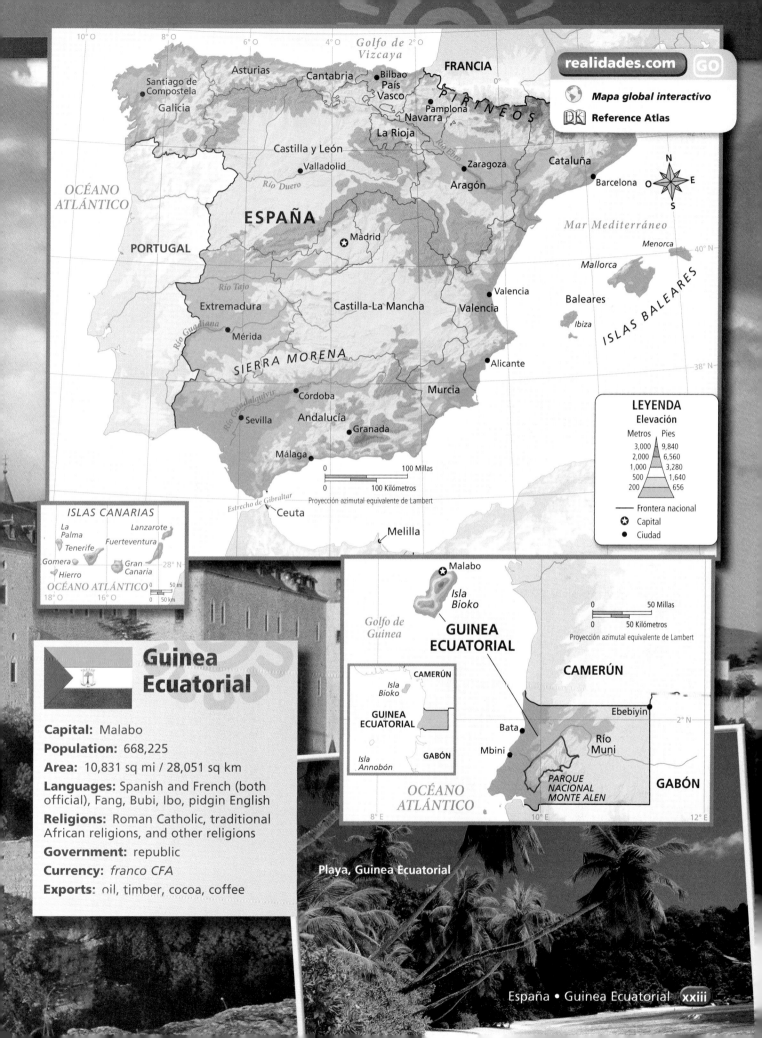

Map Labels

10° O   8° O   6° O   4° O   2° O   Golfo de Vizcaya   0°

FRANCIA

Asturias   Cantabria   Bilbao
País
Vasco

Santiago de
Compostela
Galicia

PIRINEOS

Pamplona
Navarra

La Rioja

Castilla y León

Valladolid

Río Duero

Zaragoza   Cataluña

Aragón   Barcelona

OCÉANO
ATLÁNTICO

ESPAÑA

Río Ebro

N
O   E
S

Mar Mediterráneo

⊛ Madrid   40° N

Menorca

PORTUGAL

Mallorca

Río Tajo

Valencia

Baleares

ISLAS BALEARES

Extremadura   Castilla-La Mancha

Valencia

Ibiza

Mérida

Río Guadiana

38° N

Alicante

SIERRA MORENA

Murcia

0   100 Millas

LEYENDA
Elevación

Córdoba

0   100 Kilómetros

Metros   Pies

Río Guadalquivir

Andalucía

Sevilla   Granada

Proyección azimutal equivalente de Lambert

3,000   9,840
2,000   6,560
1,000   3,280
500   1,640
200   656

Málaga

Estrecho de Gibraltar   Ceuta

Melilla

— Frontera nacional
⊛ Capital
● Ciudad

ISLAS CANARIAS

La
Palma   Lanzarote
Tenerife   Fuerteventura
Gomera   Gran
Canaria
Hierro   28° N

OCÉANO ATLÁNTICO   0   50 mi

18° O   16° O   0   50 km

Guinea Ecuatorial (country panel)

Malabo ⊛

Isla
Bioko

Golfo de
Guinea

**GUINEA
ECUATORIAL**

0   50 Millas

0   50 Kilómetros

Proyección azimutal equivalente de Lambert

CAMERÚN

Isla
Bioko

**GUINEA
ECUATORIAL**

Ebebiyin

Bata

2° N

GABÓN

Río
Muni

Mbini

Isla
Annobón

PARQUE
NACIONAL
MONTE ALEN   **GABÓN**

OCÉANO
ATLÁNTICO

8° E   10° E   12° E

Guinea Ecuatorial

Capital: Malabo

Population: 668,225

Area: 10,831 sq mi / 28,051 sq km

Languages: Spanish and French (both official), Fang, Bubi, Ibo, pidgin English

Religions: Roman Catholic, traditional African religions, and other religions

Government: republic

Currency: *franco CFA*

Exports: oil, timber, cocoa, coffee

Playa, Guinea Ecuatorial

Estados Unidos

Estados Unidos

Capital: Washington, D.C.

Population: 313.2 million

Area: 3,717,813 sq mi / 9,631,418 sq km

Languages: English, Spanish, other Indo-European languages, Asian and Pacific Islander languages, other languages

Religions: Protestant, Roman Catholic, Jewish, Muslim, and other religions

Government: federal republic

Currency: U.S. dollar

Exports: motor vehicles, aircraft, medicines, telecommunications equipment, electronics, chemicals, soybeans, fruit, wheat, corn

Las grandes llanuras

Caras estadounidenses

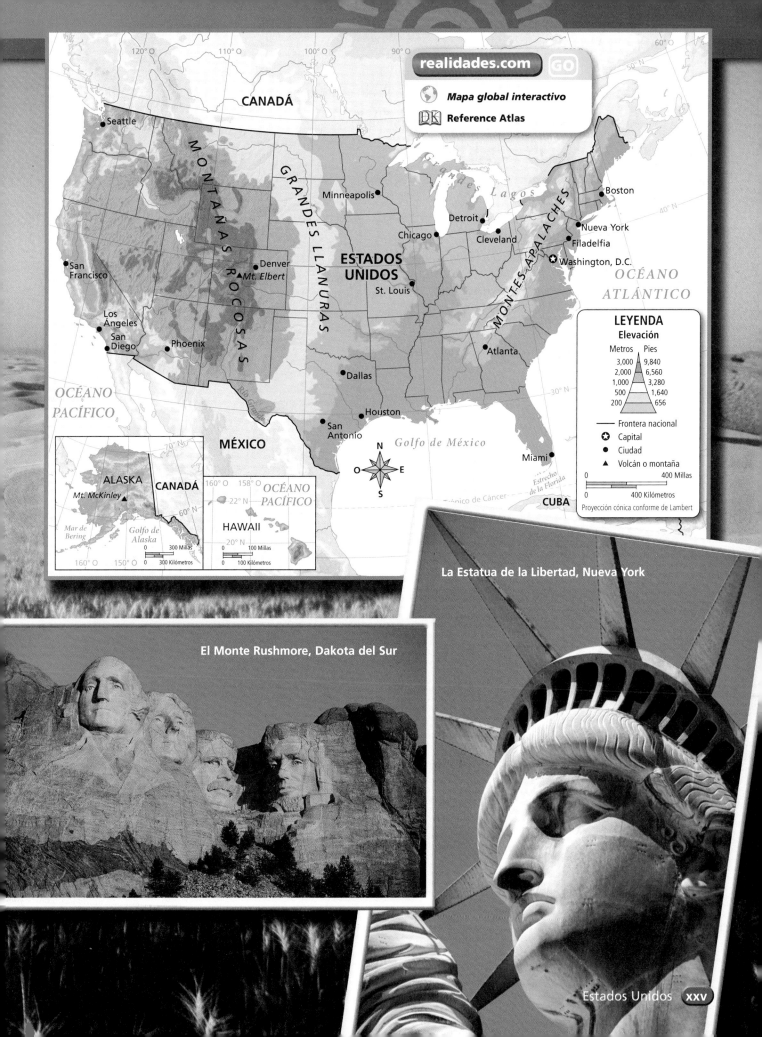

realidades.com GO

🌐 *Mapa global interactivo*

📖 Reference Atlas

CANADÁ

Seattle

MONTAÑAS ROCOSAS

GRANDES LLANURAS

Minneapolis

Grandes Lagos

Detroit

Boston

ESTADOS UNIDOS

Chicago

Cleveland

Nueva York

Filadelfia

MONTES APALACHES

☆ Washington, D.C.

Denver

▲ Mt. Elbert

St. Louis

San Francisco

OCÉANO ATLÁNTICO

Los Ángeles

San Diego

Phoenix

Dallas

Atlanta

OCÉANO PACÍFICO

Houston

San Antonio

Golfo de México

Miami

MÉXICO

N O E S

Estrecho de la Florida

Trópico de Cáncer

CUBA

LEYENDA
Elevación

Metros	Pies
3,000	9,840
2,000	6,560
1,000	3,280
500	1,640
200	656

—— Frontera nacional

☆ Capital

● Ciudad

▲ Volcán o montaña

0   400 Millas
0   400 Kilómetros

Proyección cónica conforme de Lambert

ALASKA

Mt. McKinley ▲

CANADÁ

OCÉANO PACÍFICO

Mar de Bering

Golfo de Alaska

0   300 Millas
0   300 Kilómetros

HAWAII

0   100 Millas
0   100 Kilómetros

La Estatua de la Libertad, Nueva York

El Monte Rushmore, Dakota del Sur

Para empezar

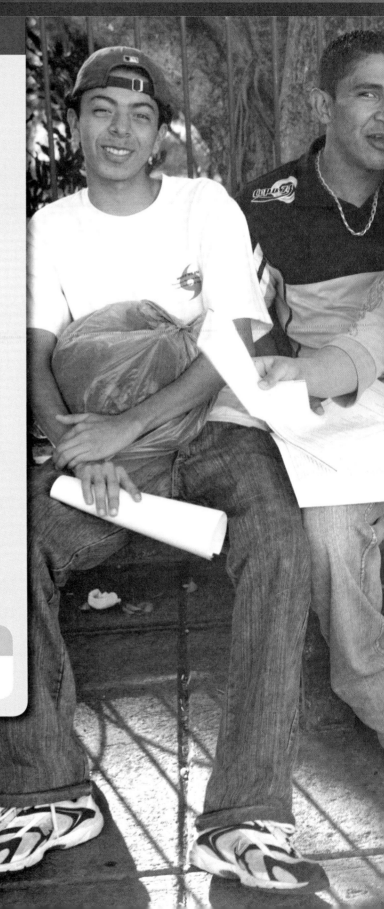

▼ **Chapter Objectives**

Communication

By the end of *Para empezar* you will be able to:

- Listen to greetings and announcements
- Read a description of the weather and a list of school supplies

You will demonstrate what you know and can do:

- Preparación para el examen, p. 23

You will also learn to:

1 En la escuela

- Greet people at different times of the day
- Introduce yourself to others
- Respond to classroom directions
- Begin using numbers
- Tell time
- Identify parts of the body

2 En la clase

- Talk about things in the classroom
- Ask questions about new words and phrases
- Use the Spanish alphabet to spell words
- Talk about things related to the calendar
- Learn about the Aztec calendar

3 El tiempo

- Describe weather conditions
- Identify the seasons
- Compare weather in the Northern and Southern Hemispheres

realidades.com GO

📖 **Reference Atlas**

🌎 **Mapa global interactivo**

Un grupo de amigos
en el Parque Darío,
Matagalpa, Nicaragua

Social relations are somewhat more formal
in Spanish-speaking countries than in the
United States, since new acquaintances usually
greet one another with a handshake. Friends,
however, greet each other with a hug or with
a kiss on the cheek.

- How does this compare with the way you
  greet people in the United States?

1 En la escuela

¡Hola! ¿Cómo te llamas?

▼ **Objectives**

▸ Greet people at different times of the day
▸ Introduce yourself to others
▸ Respond to classroom directions
▸ Begin using numbers
▸ Tell time
▸ Identify parts of the body

—**¡Buenos días, señor!**
—**¡Buenos días! ¿Cómo te llamas?**
—**Me llamo** Felipe.

—**¡Buenas tardes, señora!**
—**¡Buenas tardes! ¿Cómo te llamas?**
—Me llamo Beatriz.
—**Mucho gusto.**
—**Encantada.**

Nota
A woman or girl says *encantada*.
A man or boy says *encantado*.

—**¡Buenas noches! ¿Cómo te llamas?**
—**¡Hola!** Me llamo Graciela. **¿Y tú?**
—Me llamo Lorenzo.
—Mucho gusto.
—**Igualmente.**

▼ Exploración del lenguaje

Señor, señora, señorita

The words *señor, señora,* and *señorita* mean "sir," "madam," and "miss" when used alone. When they are used with people's last names they mean "Mr.," "Mrs.," and "Miss," and are abbreviated *Sr., Sra.,* and *Srta.* Note that the abbreviations are capitalized.

In Spanish you should address adults as *señor, señora,* or *señorita* or use the titles *Sr., Sra.,* and *Srta.* with their last names.

▼1 | | Escuchar

Buenos días

Listen as people greet each other. Then point to the clock that indicates the time of day when the greetings are probably taking place.

a.
b.
c.

▼2 | | Hablar

¿Cómo te llamas?

Follow the model to ask the name of the classmate on your right. After you have introduced yourself, do the same with the person on your left.

▶ Modelo

A —*¡Hola! ¿Cómo te llamas?*
B —*Me llamo <u>David</u>. ¿Y tú?*
A —*Me llamo <u>Antonio</u>. Mucho gusto.*
B —*Igualmente.*
o:—*Encantado.*

> **¿Recuerdas?**
> If you are a girl, you say *encantada*.

▼3 | | Hablar

¡Hola!

Work with a partner. Choose a clock from Actividad 1 and greet each other appropriately for the time of day. Then find out your partner's name. Follow the model. Change partners and repeat.

▶ Modelo

A —*<u>Buenas tardes</u>.*
B —*<u>Buenas tardes</u>. ¿Cómo te llamas?*
A —*Me llamo <u>Paco</u>. ¿Y tú?*
B —*Me llamo <u>Lourdes</u>. Mucho gusto.*
A —*Igualmente.*

Más práctica   GO
realidades.com | print
Core WB p. 1   ✔ ✔

Los nombres

Chicas
Alicia
Ana
Beatriz
Carmen
Cristina
Dolores (Lola)
Elena
Gloria
Inés
Isabel (Isa)
Juana
Luisa
Luz María (Luzma)
Margarita
María
María Eugenia (Maru)
Marta
Teresa (Tere)

Chicos
Alejandro
Antonio (Toño)
Carlos (Chacho, Cacho)
Diego
Eduardo (Edu)
Federico (Kiko)
Francisco (Paco)
Guillermo (Guille)
Jorge
José (Pepe)
Juan
Manuel (Manolo)
Miguel
Pablo
Pedro
Ricardo
Roberto
Tomás

¡Hola! ¿Cómo estás? 🔊

—Buenos días, Adela.
¿Cómo estás?
—**Bien, gracias,** Sr. Ruiz.
¿Y usted?
—Bien, gracias.

—Buenas tardes, Sr. Ruiz.
¿Cómo está Ud.?
—**Muy** bien, gracias. ¿Y tú?
—Bien, gracias.

—Buenas noches, Miguel.
¿Qué tal?
—**Regular.** ¿Y tú, Carlos?
¿Qué pasa?
—**Nada.**

—**¡Adiós, Srta.** Moreno!
¡Hasta luego!
—**¡Hasta mañana!**

—¡Hasta luego, Juan!
—**¡Nos vemos!**

¿Recuerdas?

Señor, señora, and *señorita* are abbreviated to **Sr., Sra.,** and **Srta.** before a person's last name.

▼ Exploración del lenguaje

Tú vs. *usted*

For most Spanish speakers there are two ways to say "you": *tú* and *usted.* Use *tú* when speaking to friends, family, people your own age, children, and pets. *Usted* is formal. Use it to show respect and when talking to people you don't know well, older people, and people in positions of authority. In writing, *usted* is almost always abbreviated *Ud.,* with a capital *U.*

Would you say *tú* or *Ud.* when talking to the following people?

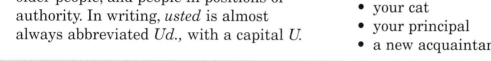

- your brother
- your teacher
- your best friend
- your friend's mother
- your cat
- your principal
- a new acquaintance who is your age

▼4 | 🔊 | Escuchar

¿Hola o adiós?

Make a chart on your paper with two columns. Label one *Greeting,* the other *Leaving.* Number your paper from 1–8. As you hear each greeting or leave-taking, place a check mark in the appropriate column next to the number.

	Greeting	Leaving
1.		
2.		
3.		

▼5 |  | Hablar

¡Hola! ¿Qué tal?

Work with a partner. Greet each other and ask how your partner is. Say good-bye. Then change partners and repeat.

 Modelo

A —*Hola, Luisa. ¿Qué tal?*
B —*Bien, Lupe. ¿Y tú?*
A —*Regular. ¡Hasta luego!*
B —*¡Adiós!*

▼6 Leer

Mucho gusto

Read the conversation on the right, then reply *sí* or *no* to these statements.

1. The people in the dialogue knew each other already.
2. The teacher is a man.
3. We know the last names of both people.
4. The student talks to the teacher in a formal tone.
5. Neither person is feeling well today.

Profesor:	Buenos días. Me llamo Rafael Guzmán. ¿Y tú?
Estudiante:	Me llamo María Rosa Hernández. Mucho gusto.
Profesor:	Igualmente. ¿Cómo estás, María Rosa?
Estudiante:	Bien, gracias. ¿Y Ud.?
Profesor:	Muy bien, gracias. Hasta luego.
Estudiante:	Adiós, señor.

Más práctica GO

realidades.com | print

Core WB p. 2 ✔ ✔
Comm. WB p. 1 ✔ ✔

¡Atención, por favor! 🔊

—¡Silencio, **por favor!** Abran el libro en la página diez.

—¡Atención! Cierren el libro.

—Repitan, por favor:
Buenos días.
—Buenos días.

—Levántense, por favor.

—Siéntense, por favor.

—Saquen una hoja de papel. Escriban los números.

—Entreguen sus hojas de papel.

▼7 | 🔊 | Escuchar

¡Siéntense!

You will hear some classroom commands. Listen carefully and act them out.

Los números

cero	uno	dos	tres	cuatro

cinco	seis	siete	ocho	nueve

10	diez		21	veintiuno, . . .
11	once		30	treinta
12	doce		31	treinta y uno, . . .
13	trece		40	cuarenta
14	catorce		50	cincuenta
15	quince		60	sesenta
16	dieciséis		70	setenta
17	diecisiete		80	ochenta
18	dieciocho		90	noventa
19	diecinueve		100	cien
20	veinte			

▼8 | Hablar

Las combinaciones

It is the first day of school, and you are helping some Spanish-speaking exchange students learn their locker combinations. Read the combinations that you see below.

1. 09-26-17
2. 16-07-30
3. 13-20-11
4. 22-19-29

5. 04-12-27
6. 15-01-28
7. 10-06-14
8. 18-21-25

▼9 | Pensar • Hablar

Los números

With a partner, provide the missing numbers in each sequence. Then say the number sequence aloud.

1. 1, 2, 3, . . . 10
2. 2, 4, 6, . . . 20
3. 1, 3, 5, . . . 19

4. 5, 10, 15, . . . 60
5. 3, 6, 9, . . . 39
6. 10, 20, 30, . . . 100

Más práctica GO

realidades.com | print

Core WB p. 3 ✔ ✔

▼10 | Hablar • Escuchar • Escribir

Números y más números

Tell your partner these numbers. He or she will write them using numerals, not words. Then check your partner's work.

1. the phone numbers used to dial for information and emergencies
2. the bar code number on the back of your Spanish book
3. the number of months until your next birthday
4. the number of students in your math class
5. the number of minutes it takes you to get from your home to school

Azulejo (tile) cerámico

¿Qué hora es? 🔊

In Spanish, to ask what time it is, you say *¿Qué hora es?* Here are some answers:

Es la una.

Son las dos.

Son las tres y cinco.

Son las cuatro y diez.

Son las cinco y cuarto.

Son las seis y media.

Son las siete menos veinte.

Son las ocho y cincuenta y dos.

▼11 | Hablar

¿Qué hora es?

Work with a partner to ask and answer questions about the time. Use these clocks.

📹 **Modelo**
A —¿Qué hora es?
B —*Son las diez.*

1.
2.
3.
4.

5.
6.

▼12 | 🔊 | Escuchar

La hora

Write the numbers 1–8 on a sheet of paper. Write the times you hear with numerals—1:00, 2:15, and so on.

Más práctica GO	realidades.com | print
Core WB p. 4	✔ ✔

"La persistencia de la memoria/The Persistence of Memory" (1931), Salvador Dalí

Oil on canvas, 9 1/2 x 13 in. (24.1 x 33 cm). Given anonymously. © 2004 Salvador Dalí, Gala-Salvador Dalí Foundation/Artists Rights Society (ARS), New York.† A.K.G., Berlin/Super Stock.

El cuerpo 🔊

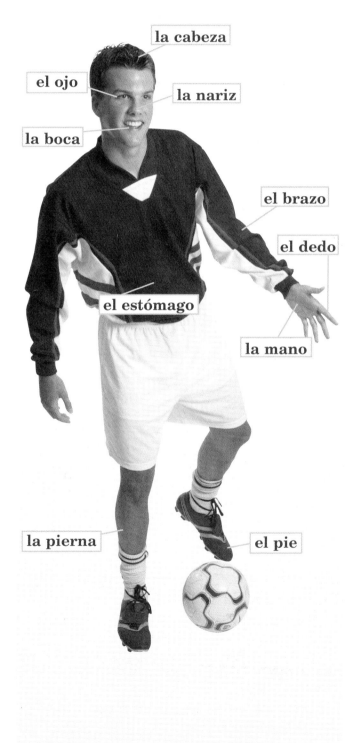

la cabeza

el ojo

la nariz

la boca

el brazo

el dedo

el estómago

la mano

la pierna

el pie

❝¡Ay! Me duele el pie**❞.**

▼13 | 🔊 | Escuchar

Señalen

You will hear some commands. Listen carefully and act out the commands. When you hear the word *señalen,* you should point to that body part.

▼14 Escuchar

Juego

Play the game *Simón dice . . .* (Simon Says). Listen and follow the leader's directions. Remember that if the leader does not say "*Simón dice,*" you should not do the action.

Más práctica GO		
	realidades.com	print
🔊 *Canción de hip hop*	✔	
Instant Check	✔	
Guided WB pp. 1–10	✔	✔
Core WB p. 5	✔	✔
Comm. WB pp. 1, 4	✔	✔
Hispanohablantes **WB** pp. 2–3		✔

2 En la clase

La sala de clases

▼ **Objectives**

▶ Talk about things in the classroom
▶ Ask questions about new words and phrases
▶ Use the Spanish alphabet to spell words
▶ Talk about things related to the calendar
▶ Learn about the Aztec calendar

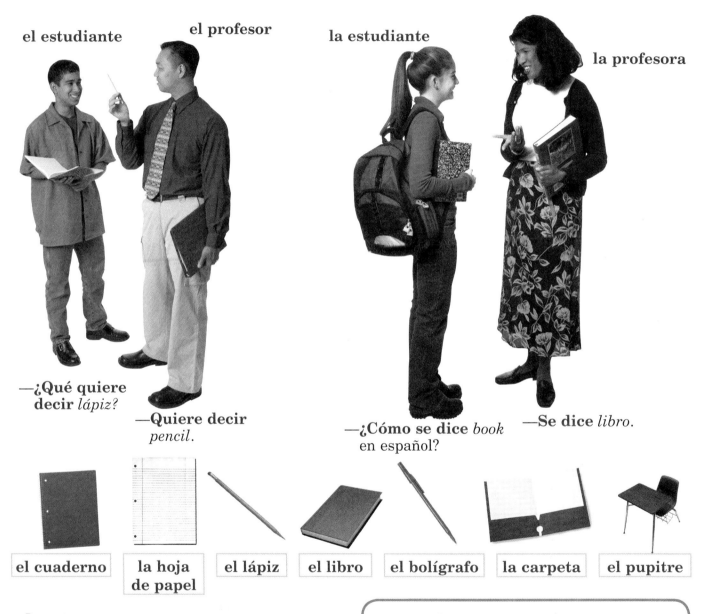

el estudiante · el profesor · la estudiante · la profesora

—¿Qué quiere decir *lápiz?*

—Quiere decir *pencil.*

—¿Cómo se dice *book* en español?

—Se dice *libro.*

| el cuaderno | la hoja de papel | el lápiz | el libro | el bolígrafo | la carpeta | el pupitre |

▼1 | ◀)) | Escuchar

El libro, el lápiz, . . .

You will hear the names of objects in your classroom. After you hear each word, hold up the object if you have it on your desk or point to it if it is somewhere in the classroom.

También se dice . . .

In many Spanish-speaking countries or regions, you will hear different words for the same thing. Words like these are highlighted in the *También se dice . . .* sections throughout your textbook.

For example, in Mexico and other countries, *pen* is **la pluma.**

▼2 |  | Hablar

¿Cómo se dice . . . ?

Discuss with a partner how you would say the following classroom objects in Spanish.

▶ **Modelo**

A —¿Cómo se dice <u>book</u> en español?
B —Se dice <u>libro</u>.

1.   2.   3.  4.   5.

Now ask each other what these Spanish words mean in English.

▶ **Modelo**

mano

A —¿Qué quiere decir <u>mano</u>?
B —Quiere decir <u>hand</u>.

6. estudiante   8. cabeza   10. brazo
7. pie   9. ojo

Gramática

Nouns

Nouns refer to people, animals, places, things, and ideas. In Spanish, nouns have gender. They are either masculine or feminine.

Most nouns that end in -o are masculine. Most nouns that end in -a are feminine.

Masculine	Feminine
el libro	la carpeta
el bolígrafo	la hoja de papel

The definite articles, *el* and *la,* also point out if a word is masculine or feminine. They both mean "the."

Spanish nouns that end in -e or a consonant must be learned as masculine or feminine. You should practice them with their definite articles, *el* or *la.*

Masculine	Feminine
el profesor	la noche
el lápiz	la conversación

▼3 Pensar • Escribir

¿Masculino o femenino?

Look at these words and decide whether each one is masculine or feminine. Rewrite each word and add the appropriate definite article *(el* or *la).*

1. pierna   5. pupitre
2. nariz   6. pie
3. cuaderno   7. profesora
4. carpeta   8. lápiz

Más práctica	GO

realidades.com | print

Core WB p. 6 ✔ ✔
Comm. WB p. 2 ✔ ✔

El alfabeto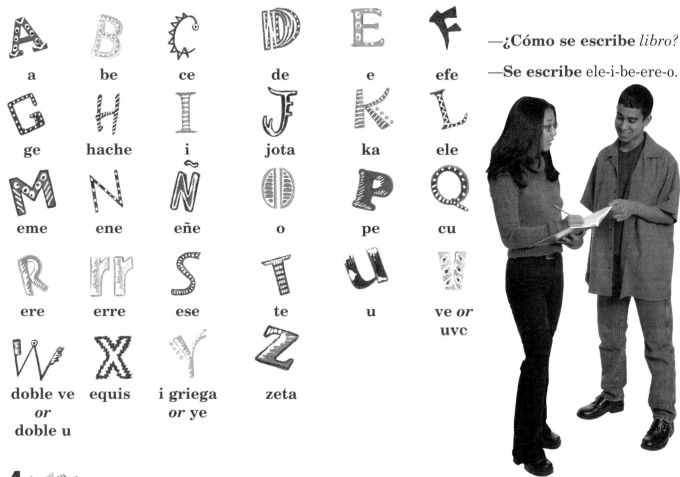

A	a
B	be
C	ce
D	de
E	e
F	efe
G	ge
H	hache
I	i
J	jota
K	ka
L	ele
M	eme
N	ene
Ñ	eñe
O	o
P	pe
Q	cu
R	ere
rr	erre
S	ese
T	te
U	u
V	ve *or* uvc
W	doble ve *or* doble u
X	equis
Y	i griega *or* ye
Z	zeta

—¿**Cómo se escribe** *libro?*

—**Se escribe** ele-i-be-ere-o.

▼**4** | 🔊 | **Escuchar • Escribir**

Escucha y escribe

On a sheet of paper, write the numbers 1–8. You will hear several words you know spelled aloud. Listen carefully and write the letters as you hear them.

▼**5** | 💬 | **Hablar • Escribir**

Pregunta y contesta

Work with a partner. Use the pictures to ask and answer according to the model. As Student B spells the words, Student A should write them out. When you are finished, check your spelling by looking at p. 10.

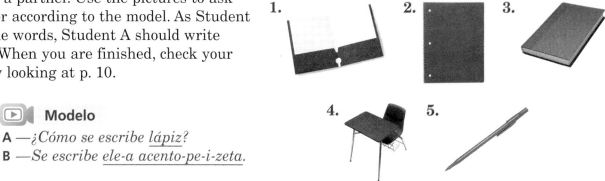

1. 2. 3.

4. 5.

▶️ **Modelo**

A —*¿Cómo se escribe* <u>*lápiz?*</u>

B —*Se escribe* <u>*ele-a acento-pe-i-zeta.*</u>

▼6 |  | Hablar

¿Cómo te llamas?

Work with a partner. Follow the model to find out each other's names and how they are spelled. Then change partners and repeat.

 **Modelo**

A —¿Cómo te llamas?
B —Me llamo María.
A —¿Cómo se escribe María?
B —Se escribe eme-a-ere-i acento-a.

🌎 Fondo Cultural | El mundo hispano

The Maya were among the early civilizations in the Western Hemisphere to develop a form of writing with symbols, known as hieroglyphics *(los jeroglíficos).* Each symbol, or glyph, represents a word or an idea.

• With what other hieroglyphic writing are you familiar?

Jeroglíficos mayas

▼ Exploración del lenguaje

Punctuation and accent marks

You have probably noticed that questions begin with an upside-down question mark *(¿)* and exclamations with an upside-down exclamation point *(¡)*. This lets you know at the beginning of a sentence what kind of sentence you are reading.

You probably also noticed the accent marks *(el acento)* on *días* and *estás.* When you write in Spanish, you must include these accent and punctuation marks.

Try it out! Rewrite these phrases and insert the correct punctuation and accent marks.

Como estas   Que tal   Hasta luego   Y tu

▼7 |  | Escuchar • Escribir • Hablar

Juego

① Play this game in pairs. Each player makes a list of five Spanish words that you have learned. Don't let your partner see your words.

② Spell your first word aloud in Spanish. Don't forget any accent marks. Your partner will write the word as you spell it. Then your partner will spell a word for you to write. Take turns until you have spelled all the words on your lists.

③ Check each other's papers. The winner is the player with the most words spelled correctly.

> **Strategy**
> **Sustaining a conversation**
> If you need your partner to spell a word again, say: *Repite, por favor.*

El calendario y la fecha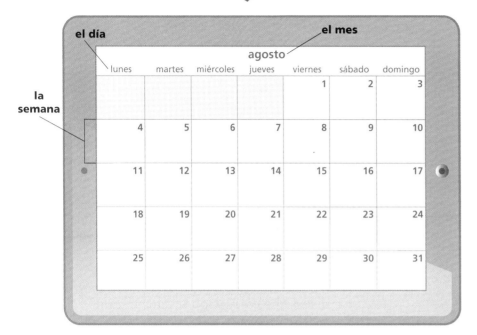

el día

el mes

agosto

lunes	martes	miércoles	jueves	viernes	sábado	domingo
				1	2	3
4	5	6	7	8	9	10
11	12	13	14	15	16	17
18	19	20	21	22	23	24
25	26	27	28	29	30	31

la semana

—¿Qué día es hoy?

—Hoy es lunes. **Mañana** es martes.

—¿**Cuántos** días hay en el mes de agosto?

— Hay treinta y un días.

Nota

Notice that the days of the week and the months of the year are not capitalized in Spanish, except at the beginning of sentences.

The first day of the week in a Spanish-language calendar is *lunes.*

Los meses del año

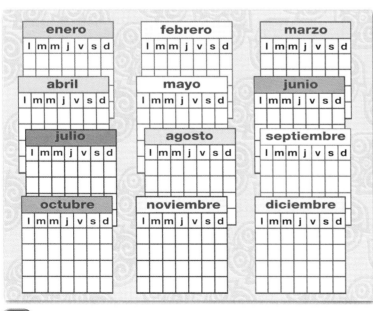

enero						
l	m	m	j	v	s	d

febrero						
l	m	m	j	v	s	d

marzo						
l	m	m	j	v	s	d

abril						
l	m	m	j	v	s	d

mayo						
l	m	m	j	v	s	d

junio						
l	m	m	j	v	s	d

julio						
l	m	m	j	v	s	d

agosto						
l	m	m	j	v	s	d

septiembre						
l	m	m	j	v	s	d

octubre						
l	m	m	j	v	s	d

noviembre						
l	m	m	j	v	s	d

diciembre						
l	m	m	j	v	s	d

—¿Cuál es la fecha?
—Es el 22 de agosto.

—¿Cuál es la fecha?
—Es **el primero** de agosto.

▼8 |  | **Hablar**

Hoy y mañana

Ask and answer according to the model.

▶ **Modelo**

lunes
A —*¿Qué día es hoy?*
B —*Hoy es lunes. Mañana es martes.*

1. martes
2. sábado
3. jueves
4. miércoles
5. viernes
6. domingo

El Cinco de Mayo es un día festivo en México.

▼**9** **Leer • Escribir**

Días de fiesta

Your friend never gets dates right. Correct the following sentences making the necessary changes.

1. El Día de San Patricio es el 14 de enero.
2. El Día de San Valentín es en junio.
3. Januká es en febrero.
4. La Navidad (*Christmas*) es el 25 de noviembre.
5. El Día de la Independencia de los Estados Unidos (*United States*) es el 4 de junio.
6. El Año Nuevo (*New Year's Day*) es en diciembre.
7. Hoy es el 3 de agosto.

▼10 Escribir

El calendario

Answer the questions based on the calendar page at the right.

hoy

1. ¿Cuál es la fecha de hoy?
2. ¿Qué día de la semana es?
3. ¿Qué día es mañana?
4. ¿Cuál es la fecha de mañana?
5. ¿Cuántos días hay en este (*this*) mes?
6. ¿Cuántos días hay en una semana?

			julio			
lunes	martes	miércoles	jueves	viernes	sábado	domingo
	1	2	3	4	5	6
7	8	9	10	11	12	13
14	15	16	17	18	19	20
21	22	23	24	25	26	27
28	29	30	31			

Fondo Cultural | España

Los sanfermines, or the "Running of the Bulls," is a popular two-week festival in Pamplona, Spain, named for the town's patron saint, San Fermín, who is commemorated on July 7 each year. The celebration includes daily bullfights, but before they begin the real excitement happens! As the bulls are released from their pens and run through the streets, many people run ahead or alongside them to the bullring.

• What festivals are you familiar with in which animals play a role?

La fiesta de San Fermín, en Pamplona, España

Más práctica	GO
	realidades.com | print
Instant Check	✔
Guided WB pp. 11–18	✔ ✔
Core WB pp. 7–8	✔ ✔
Comm. WB p. 5	✔ ✔
Hispanohablantes WB pp. 4–5	✔

▼11 Leer

El calendario azteca

The Aztecs were a nomadic tribe that finally settled in the valley of central Mexico in 1325. They established their capital, Tenochtitlán, on a swampy lake and built a mighty empire that dominated most of Mexico. The Aztec empire flourished until 1521, when it was defeated by the Spaniards, led by Hernán Cortés.

México

Conexiones | La historia

One of the most famous symbols of Mexico is the monolith, or huge stone, carved by the Aztecs in 1479. Known today as the Aztec calendar or the Sun Stone, the carving weighs almost 24 tons and is approximately 12 feet in diameter. The Aztecs dedicated it to the sun, represented by the face in the center. The calendar represents a 260-day year.

Representation of the sun, or Tonatiuh

One of the previous four world creations

This band shows the 20 days of the month.

▼12 Pensar

Los símbolos aztecas

Here are several glyphs representing days found on the Sun Stone. Match the glyph with the Spanish word. What do you think each of the glyphs represents? Why do you think the Aztecs included these symbols on their calendar?

1.

2.

3.

4.

5.

6.

a. Jaguar
b. Perro
c. Movimiento
d. Serpiente
e. Cráneo
f. Agua

▼ **Objectives**

▶ **Describe weather conditions**
▶ **Identify the seasons**
▶ **Compare weather in the Northern and Southern Hemispheres**

3 El tiempo

¿Qué tiempo hace?

Hace sol.

Hace calor.

Hace frío.

Hace viento.

Llueve.

Nieva.

Las estaciones

la primavera   **el verano**   **el otoño**   **el invierno**

▼1 | 🔊 | Escuchar

El tiempo

You will hear descriptions of different weather conditions. Write the numbers 1–6 on a sheet of paper. Then, next to each number, write the letter of the photo for which the weather is being described.

a.  b.  c.  d.

▼2 | 💬👥 | Hablar

¿Qué tiempo hace?

Work with a partner. Ask and answer the questions based on the city and weather information for each item.

Miami / julio /

▶ **Modelo**
A —*¿Qué tiempo hace en <u>Miami</u> en <u>julio</u>?*
B —*<u>Hace sol</u>.*

1. Denver / enero /

2. Chicago / octubre /

3. San Francisco / noviembre /

4. Washington, D.C. / junio /

5. Minneapolis / diciembre /

6. Dallas / agosto /

▼3 Hablar • Escribir

Las estaciones

Answer the questions based on where you live.

1. ¿Qué tiempo hace en la primavera?
2. ¿Qué tiempo hace en el otoño?
3. ¿En qué estación hace calor?
4. ¿En qué estación hace frío?
5. ¿En qué estación llueve mucho?
6. ¿En qué estación nieva?

Más práctica	GO	
realidades.com | print		
🔊 *Canción de hip hop*	✔	
Instant Check	✔	
Guided WB pp. 19–24	✔	✔
Core WB p. 9	✔	✔
Comm. WB p. 6	✔	✔
Hispanohablantes **WB** pp. 6–7		✔

Dos hemisferios

Read about the seasons in the Northern and Southern Hemispheres and then answer the questions.

 Conexiones | La geografía

Did you know that the seasons for the Northern and Southern Hemispheres are reversed? When it's winter in the Northern Hemisphere, it's summer in the Southern Hemisphere and vice versa. So if you want to ski all year round, go from the slopes of the Rockies in Colorado in December to those of the Andes in Bariloche, Argentina in July. Or for a December getaway to a warmer climate, go to one of the coastal resorts at Viña del Mar, Chile.

Colorado
(Estados Unidos)

enero

julio

norte

oeste — este

sur

enero

Chile

julio

1. En febrero, ¿qué tiempo hace en Chile?

2. En junio, ¿qué tiempo hace en Colorado?

3. En tu comunidad, ¿qué tiempo hace en diciembre? ¿Y en agosto?

ciudad	diciembre	julio
Asunción, Paraguay	85°F / 29°C	75°F / 24°C
Bogotá, Colombia	66°F / 19°C	64°F / 17°C
Buenos Aires, Argentina	78°F / 26°C	50°F / 10°C
Caracas, Venezuela	80°F / 27°C	80°F / 27°C
Chicago	36°F / 2°C	75°F / 24°C
Ciudad de México, México	70°F / 21°C	74°F / 23°C
Guatemala, Guatemala	72°F / 22°C	74°F / 23°C
La Habana, Cuba	76°F / 24°C	82°F / 28°C
La Paz, Bolivia	58°F / 15°C	55°F / 13°C
Lima, Perú	76°F / 24°C	76°F / 24°C
Los Ángeles	67°F / 19°C	88°F / 31°C
Miami	76°F / 24°C	97°F / 36°C
Nueva York	41°F / 5°C	74°F / 23°C
Quito, Ecuador	65°F / 18°C	67°F / 19°C
San José, Costa Rica	78°F / 26°C	78°F / 26°C
San Juan, Puerto Rico	74°F / 23°C	80°F / 27°C
Santiago, Chile	82°F / 28°C	50°F / 10°C
Seattle	41°F / 5°C	66°F / 19°C
St. Louis	36°F / 2°C	81°F / 27°C
Tegucigalpa, Honduras	70°F / 21°C	81°F / 27°C

Los Ángeles

Tegucigalpa, Honduras   Asunción, Paraguay

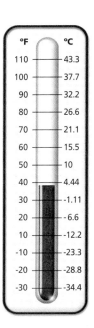

°F	°C
110	43.3
100	37.7
90	32.2
80	26.6
70	21.1
60	15.5
50	10
40	4.44
30	-1.11
20	-6.6
10	-12.2
-10	-23.3
-20	-28.8
-30	-34.4

▼5 | | Hablar

¿Hace calor o hace frío?

Work with a partner. Discuss the weather in six cities listed in the chart above.

 Modelo

A —¿Qué tiempo hace en *Chicago* en *diciembre*?
B —*Hace frío*.

▼6 | | Hablar

La temperatura es . . .

Working with a partner, ask about the temperature in six different places on the chart.

 Modelo

A —¿Cuál es la temperatura en *Quito* en *diciembre*?
B —*Sesenta y cinco* grados.
o: *Dieciocho* grados.

Nota

In most parts of the world, people express temperatures in Celsius. A simple way to convert from Celsius to Fahrenheit is to multiply the temperature by $\frac{9}{5}$, then add 32.

$$30°C = \underline{\;?\;} F$$
$$30 \times \tfrac{9}{5} = 54 + 32$$
$$30°C = 86°F$$

Para decir más . . .

la temperatura	temperature
grados	degrees

Repaso del capítulo

Vocabulario y gramática

En la escuela

to greet someone

Buenos días.	Good morning.
Buenas noches.	Good evening.
Buenas tardes.	Good afternoon.
¡Hola!	Hello!
¿Cómo te llamas?	What is your name?
Me llamo . . .	My name is . . .
Encantado, -a.	Delighted.
Igualmente.	Likewise.
Mucho gusto.	Pleased to meet you.
señor (Sr.)	sir, Mr.
señora (Sra.)	madam, Mrs.
señorita (Srta.)	miss, Miss

to ask and tell how someone is

¿Cómo está Ud.? *(formal)*	How are you?
¿Cómo estás? *(familiar)*	How are you?
¿Qué pasa?	What's happening?
¿Qué tal?	How are you?
¿Y tú? / ¿Y usted (Ud.)?	And you?
(muy) bien	(very) well
nada	nothing
regular	okay, so-so
gracias	thank you

to say good-bye

¡Adiós!	Good-bye!
Hasta luego.	See you later.
Hasta mañana.	See you tomorrow.
¡Nos vemos!	See you!

to tell time

¿Qué hora es?	What time is it?
Es la una.	It is one o'clock.
Son las . . . y/ menos . . .	It is . . . *(time)*.
y cuarto/menos cuarto	quarter past / quarter to
y media	thirty, half-past

to count up to 100 (Turn to p. 7.)

to talk about the body (Turn to p. 9.)

En la clase

to talk about the classroom

el bolígrafo	pen
la carpeta	folder
el cuaderno	notebook
el estudiante, la estudiante	student
la hoja de papel	sheet of paper
el lápiz	pencil
el libro	book
el profesor, la profesora	teacher
el pupitre	(student) desk
la sala de clases	classroom

to say the date

el año	year
el día	day
el mes	month
la semana	week
¿Qué día es hoy?	What day is today?
¿Cuál es la fecha?	What is the date?
Es el *(number)* de *(month)*.	It is the . . . of . . .
Es el primero de *(month)*.	It is the first of . . .
hoy	today
mañana	tomorrow

to say the days of the week and the months of the year (Turn to p. 14.)

to ask for help

¿Cómo se dice . . . ?	How do you say . . . ?
Se dice . . .	You say . . .
¿Cómo se escribe . . . ?	How is . . . spelled?
Se escribe . . .	It's spelled . . .
¿Qué quiere decir . . . ?	What does . . . mean?
Quiere decir . . .	It means . . .

other useful words

¿cuántos, -as?	how many?
en	in
hay	there is, there are
por favor	please

Más repaso (GO)   realidades.com | print

Instant Check   ✔
Puzzles   ✔
Core WB pp. 10–12   ✔
Comm. WB p. 114   ✔   ✔

El tiempo

to talk about the weather

¿Qué tiempo hace?	What's the weather like?
Hace calor.	It's hot.
Hace frío.	It's cold.
Hace sol.	It's sunny.
Hace viento.	It's windy.
Llueve.	It's raining.
Nieva.	It's snowing.

to talk about the seasons

la estación, *pl.* las estaciones	season
el invierno	winter
el otoño	fall, autumn
la primavera	spring
el verano	summer

Preparación para el examen

 1 Escuchar On the exam you will be asked to listen to and understand people as they greet each other and introduce themselves. To practice, listen to some students greet people in the school halls. Answer these questions about each greeting: What is the time of day? Was the greeting directed to an adult? How did that person respond?

To review, see pp. 2–5 and Actividades 1, 4.

2 Escuchar You will be asked to listen to and understand someone announcing the current date and time. To practice, listen to the message and answer the questions: What is the time of day? What is the date?

To review, see pp. 7–8 and Actividad 11; pp. 14–16 and Actividad 10.

3 Leer You will be asked to read and understand a description of the weather for a given day. To practice, read the weather forecast to the right. Answer the questions: What is the date? What are the high and low temperatures? What is the weather like?

To review, see pp. 18–21 and Actividades 2–6.

Dos de septiembre
Hoy en San Antonio hace sol.
La temperatura máxima es
75 grados y la mínima es 54.
No llueve.

 4 Leer You will be asked to read a list of school supplies and identify them. To practice, copy the school supply list below onto a sheet of paper. Please note: *un, una* mean "a" or "an." Then look to see whether you have any of the items on your desk right now. Make a check mark next to each item you have.

un cuaderno	un lápiz	una hoja de papel
un bolígrafo	una carpeta	un libro

To review, see p. 10.

1A ¿Qué te gusta hacer?

▼ Chapter Objectives

Communication

By the end of this chapter you will be able to:

- Listen to and read about activities people like and don't like to do
- Talk and write about what you and others like and don't like to do
- Describe your favorite activities and ask others about theirs

Culture

You will also be able to:

- Describe dances and music from the Spanish-speaking world and compare them to dances you know
- Compare favorite activities of Spanish-speaking teens to those of teens in the United States

You will demonstrate what you know and can do:

- Presentación oral, p. 49
- Preparación para el examen, p. 53

You will use:

Vocabulary
- Activities
- Expressing likes and dislikes

Grammar
- Infinitives
- Negatives
- Expressing agreement or disagreement

Exploración del mundo hispano

Country Connection
Favorite Activities

- España
- Estados Unidos
- República Dominicana
- México
- Puerto Rico
- Costa Rica
- Colombia
- Guinea Ecuatorial
- Argentina

realidades.com (GO)

 Reference Atlas

 Videocultura y actividad

 Mapa global interactivo

Patinando en línea, Barcelona, España

Arte y cultura | España

Pablo Picasso (1881–1973), one of the best-known Spanish artists of the twentieth century, had a long, productive career creating art in a wide range of styles and forms. He showed remarkable artistic talent as a child and had his first exhibition when he was 13 years old. "Three Musicians" is an example of Picasso's cubist painting style.

• Study the painting and list some characteristics that show why this style is known as "cubism."

"Musiciens aux masques / Three Musicians" (1921), Pablo Picasso ▶

Oil on canvas, 6' 7" x 7' 3 3/4". Mrs. Simon Guggenheim Fund. (55.1949). Digital Image © The Museum of Modern Art / Licensed by SCALA/ Art Resource, NY. Museum of Modern Art, New York, N.Y., U.S.A. © 2004 Estate of Pablo Picasso/Artists Rights Society ARS, New York.

Vocabulario en contexto

bailar

escuchar música

practicar deportes

nadar

correr

esquiar

—¡Me gusta mucho bailar!

—A mí también. Y también me gusta escuchar música.

—¡Hola, Beatriz! ¿Qué te gusta hacer? ¿Te gusta practicar deportes?

¡Sí! Me gusta mucho practicar deportes. Me gusta correr, nadar y esquiar. ¿Y a ti? ¿Qué te gusta hacer?

escribir cuentos

montar en monopatín

ver la tele

usar la computadora

dibujar

cantar

montar en bicicleta

jugar videojuegos

—¿Qué te gusta **más,** ver la tele
o montar en bicicleta?

—A mí me gusta mucho escribir cuentos
y dibujar. **¡No me gusta nada** cantar!

—¡Uy! **A mí tampoco.**

—**Pues,** no me gusta **ni** ver la
tele **ni** montar en bicicleta.
Me gusta usar la computadora
y jugar videojuegos. Y a ti,
¿qué te gusta más?

▼**1** | 🔊 | **Escuchar**

¿Te gusta o no te gusta?

You will hear Rosa say what she likes to do
and doesn't like to do. Give a "thumbs-up"
sign when you hear her say what she likes to
do, and a "thumbs-down" sign when she says
what she doesn't like to do.

▼**2** | 🔊 | **Escuchar**

Me gusta . . .

Listen to what some people like to do. Point
to the picture of the activity each describes.

Más práctica	GO	
realidades.com	print	
Instant Check	✔	
Guided WB pp. 25–28	✔	✔
Core WB pp. 13–14	✔	✔
Comm. WB p. 14	✔	✔
Hispanohablantes WB p. 12		✔

¿Qué te gusta hacer?

You're going to meet eight students from around the Spanish-speaking world and find out what they like and don't like to do. You'll be able to figure out where they live by looking at the globes on the page.

Saludos desde Madrid

Strategy

Using visuals
Look at the pictures with each postcard to help you understand the meaning of the new words.

• Can you predict what each student likes to do?

❝Soy Ignacio.
Me gusta mucho
tocar la guitarra❞.

❝Y yo me llamo Ana.
A mí me gusta **hablar por teléfono❞**.

Ciudad de México

66¡Hola! Me llamo Claudia y me gusta usar la computadora y **pasar tiempo con mis amigos**99.

66Yo soy Teresa. También me gusta usar la computadora, pero **me gusta más** jugar videojuegos**99**.

Recuerdos de San Antonio

66Yo soy Esteban. A mí me gusta **patinar**99.

66¡Hola, amigos! Me llamo Angélica y me gusta mucho montar en bicicleta**99**.

Saludos desde Costa Rica

❝Yo me llamo Raúl. Me gusta ir a la escuela . . . más o menos . . . , pero me gusta más **leer revistas**❞.

❝¿Qué tal, amigos? Soy Gloria. A mí me gusta **ir a la escuela**, y también me gusta **trabajar**❞.

▼3 Leer

Actividades favoritas

The students you saw in the video are doing their favorite activities. Number your paper from 1–6 and match the picture to the activity each student likes to do.

1.

2.

3.

a. patinar

b. montar en bicicleta

c. hablar por teléfono

d. tocar la guitarra

e. ir a la escuela

f. leer revistas

4.

5.

6.

▼4 Leer

¿Comprendes?

On a sheet of paper, write the numbers 1–6. Read the following statements by the characters in the *Videohistoria* and write *C (cierto)* if the statement is true, or *F (falso)* if it is false.

1. **Angélica:** No me gusta montar en bicicleta.
2. **Raúl:** Me gusta mucho leer revistas.
3. **Esteban:** Me gusta patinar.
4. **Claudia:** Me gusta pasar tiempo con mis amigos.
5. **Teresa:** No me gusta usar la computadora.
6. **Gloria:** Me gusta trabajar.

▼5 | (Talk!) 👥 | Escribir • Hablar

Y tú, ¿qué dices?

Choose the activity that you prefer to do on the following days of the week and write it on a separate sheet of paper. Share your answers with a classmate.

1. Hoy es sábado. Me gusta más ___ .
   a. trabajar
   b. leer revistas
   c. ver la tele

2. Hoy es lunes. Me gusta más ___ .
   a. usar la computadora
   b. patinar
   c. ir a la escuela

3. Hoy es miércoles. Me gusta más ___ .
   a. jugar videojuegos
   b. tocar la guitarra
   c. bailar

4. Hoy es domingo. Me gusta más ___ .
   a. pasar tiempo con amigos
   b. jugar al fútbol
   c. hablar por teléfono

Más práctica (GO)	realidades.com | print
Instant Check	✔
Guided WB pp. 29–32	✔ ✔
Core WB pp. 15–16	✔ ✔
Comm. WB pp. 7–9, 10	✔ ✔
Hispanohablantes **WB** p. 13	✔

Vocabulario en uso

▼**6** Escribir

Actividades populares

Use the word bank to match the vocabulary word with the appropriate picture.

dibujar	usar la computadora
correr	cantar
practicar deportes	ver la tele
bailar	montar en bicicleta
nadar	

Modelo

Me gusta <u>practicar deportes</u>.

1. Me gusta ___.

2. Me gusta ___.

3. Me gusta ___.

4. Me gusta ___.

5. Me gusta ___.

6. Me gusta ___.

▼**7** Escribir

Mi lista personal

Copy this chart on a separate sheet of paper. Using the activities from pp. 26–30, write four things that you like to do and four things that you don't like to do under the correct columns.

Modelo

Me gusta	No me gusta
correr	cantar

▼**8** Escribir

¿Te gusta o no te gusta?

Using the chart you made in Actividad 7, complete each of the following sentences with a different activity.

Modelo
Me gusta pasar tiempo con mis amigos.

1. Me gusta ___.
2. Me gusta mucho ___.
3. Y también me gusta ___.
4. No me gusta ___.
5. No me gusta nada ___ ___.
6. No me gusta ni ___ ni ___.

▼**9** | | **Hablar**

¡A mí también!

Using the information from Actividad 7, tell your partner three activities you like to do. Your partner will agree or disagree with you. Follow the model. Then switch roles and repeat the activity.

 Modelo
A —*Me gusta correr.*
B —*¡A mí también!*
o: *¡A mí no me gusta!*

Fondo Cultural | El mundo hispano

Outdoor cafés are popular throughout the Spanish-speaking world. Friends go there to enjoy a snack, something to drink, or a light meal. A café is a place where young people can sit and talk with one another and watch people go by.

• Are there outdoor cafés in your area that are similar to this one in Salamanca's *Plaza Mayor*? What kinds of places do you go to for a snack with your friends? Compare the places where you like to meet with the Spanish cafés in the photo.

En el verano, me gusta pasar tiempo con mis amigos en la Plaza Mayor de Salamanca.

¿Qué te gusta hacer?

Ask your partner whether he or she likes doing the activities below. Your partner will answer using one of the two responses shown. Then switch roles and answer your partner's questions.

▶ **Modelo**

A —¿Te gusta <u>montar en monopatín</u>?

B —Sí, me gusta mucho.

o: No, no me gusta nada.

Estudiante A
¿Te gusta . . . ?

Estudiante B

¡Respuesta personal!

▼11 | Leer • Hablar

¿Calor o frío?

With a partner, look at the following vacation brochures. Ask your partner if he or she likes to do the different activities offered at the two hotels. Then, using that information, decide which vacation destination would be best for him or her.

▼ Pronunciación |

The vowels *a*, *e*, and *i*

The vowel sounds in Spanish are different from those in English. In Spanish, each vowel has just one sound. Spanish vowels are also quicker and shorter than those in English.

The letter *a* is similar to the vowel sound in the English word *pop*. Listen to and say these words:

andar	cantar	trabajar
hablar	nadar	pasar

The letter *e* is similar to the vowel sound in the English word *met*. Listen to and say these words:

tele	me	es	Elena	deportes

The letter *i* is similar to the vowel sound in the English word *see*. As you have already seen, the letter *y* sometimes has the same sound as *i*. Listen to and say these words:

sí	escribir	patinar
lápiz	ti	mí

Try it out! Listen to and say this rhyme:

A-E-I El perro canta para ti.
A-E-I El tigre baila para mí.

Try it again, substituting *el gato* for *el perro* and *la cebra* for *el tigre*.

Gramática

▼ Objectives

▶ Write about and discuss activities
▶ Listen to descriptions of what someone likes to do
▶ Read about, listen to, and write about different types of Latin music

Infinitives

Verbs are words that are most often used to name actions. Verbs in English have different forms depending on who is doing the action or when the action is occurring:

I **walk**, she **walks**, we walk**ed**, etc.

The most basic form of a verb is called the infinitive. In English, you can spot infinitives because they usually have the word "to" in front of them:

to swim, **to** read, **to** write

Infinitives in Spanish, though, don't have a separate word like "to" in front of them. Spanish infinitives are only one word, and they always end in *-ar*, *-er*, or *-ir*:

na**dar**, le**er**, escri**bir**

Más ayuda	realidades.com

▶ **GramActiva Video**
Tutorial: Conjugation & Infinitive
Animated Verbs

◀)) **Canción de hip hop:** *Mambo*

✎ **GramActiva Activity**

▼12 Escribir

¿Cuál es?

On a sheet of paper, make a chart with three columns for the headings *-ar*, *-er*, and *-ir*. Then look at these pictures of activities. Write the infinitive for each activity under the corresponding head. Save your chart to use in Actividad 14.

Modelo

-ar	-er	-ir
nadar		

▼**13** | 🔊 | Escuchar • GramActiva

Tres papeles

Tear a sheet of paper into three equal parts. Write *-ar* on one piece, *-er* on another piece, and *-ir* on the third piece. You will hear several infinitives. Listen carefully to the endings. Hold up the paper with the ending that you hear.

▼**14** Escribir

El verbo es . . .

Here are some verbs in English. Look them up in the English-Spanish glossary at the back of the book and write down the infinitive form on the chart you made in Actividad 12.

1. to walk   2. to see   3. to eat   4. to study
5. to talk   6. to write   7. to share   8. to play

> **Strategy**
>
> **Using a dictionary or glossary**
> When you need to look up a verb, always look for the infinitive form.

▼**15** Escribir

El diccionario en uso

It's easy to talk about the things you like to do once you know the infinitive, because you just add the infinitive to *Me gusta.* Using the glossary at the back of the book, try writing six sentences about what you like to do.

Modelo
I like to play soccer.
Me gusta jugar al fútbol.

16 | Escribir • Hablar

Encuesta: ¿Qué te gusta hacer?

Ask four classmates to tell you two things they like to do (*¿Qué te gusta hacer?*) and two things they don't like to do (*¿Qué no te gusta hacer?*). Record their names and responses on a chart like this one.

Modelo

Nombre	Me gusta	No me gusta
Beto	nadar ir a la escuela	patinar cantar

17 | Escribir • Hablar

Encuesta: Los resultados

Working in a group, create a chart like the one to the right using the results of the interviews you did in Actividad 16. Use your chart to find the most popular and least popular activities among your group. Finally, share your findings with the class, using the two sentences below.

1. Las actividades más (*most*) populares:

2. Las actividades menos (*least*) populares:

Actividad	Me gusta	No me gusta
tocar la guitarra	|||		
cantar			||||
trabajar	||	┼┼┼┼

18 | Escuchar • Escribir

Escucha y escribe

Write the numbers 1–7 on a sheet of paper. You will hear Raúl say seven things that he likes to do. Write them down as he says them. Spelling counts!

¿Recuerdas?

Remember to include any accent marks when you spell a word.

¿Te gusta hablar por teléfono?

1. _____
2. _____
3. _____
4. _____
5. _____
6. _____
7. _____

▼**19** | (Talk!) | **Hablar • GramActiva**

Juego

Get together in groups and make a list of at least four things that you like to do. When everyone in the group knows how to say what they like to do in Spanish, you're ready to play.

1 The first person will start the game by saying one thing that he or she likes to do.

First Person:

Me gusta escuchar música.

2 The second person will repeat that information and add another activity.

Second Person:

Me gusta escuchar música y también esquiar.

3 The next person will repeat both activities and add a new one, and so on. See how long your group's sentence gets before someone leaves out an activity.

Next Person:

Me gusta escuchar música, esquiar y también escribir cuentos.

Más práctica GO	realidades.com | print	
Instant Check	✔	
Guided WB p. 33	✔	✔
Core WB p. 17	✔	✔
Comm. WB pp. 12, 15	✔	✔
Hispanohablantes **WB** pp. 14–17		✔

▼ Exploración del lenguaje

Cognates

Words that look alike and have similar meanings in English and Spanish are called **cognates** *(cognados)*. Here are examples from this chapter:

Spanish	English
popular	popular
usar	to use
guitarra	guitar
computadora	computer

> **Strategy**
>
> **Recognizing cognates**
> Identifying cognates will help you understand what you read and will increase your vocabulary.

Try it out! Look at pp. 26–30 and make a list of seven cognates from the vocabulary on those pages.

▼ Fondo Cultural | República Dominicana

Jaime Antonio González Colson (1901–1975) was an artist from the Dominican Republic. His works usually focused on the people and culture of his homeland.

The *merengue,* the dance shown in this painting, originated in the Dominican Republic in the nineteenth century. One of the instruments used to accompany it is the *güiro* (shown at the top right of the painting), made from a gourd and played by scraping it with a stick.

• What instruments set the rhythms in the music that you listen to?

"Merengue" (1937), Jaime Antonio González Colson
Courtesy of Museo Bellapart, Dominican Republic.

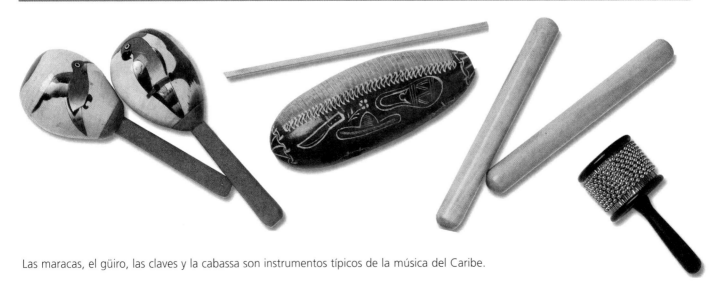

Las maracas, el güiro, las claves y la cabassa son instrumentos típicos de la música del Caribe.

▼**20** | 🔊 | Leer • Escuchar • Escribir

El baile y la música del mundo hispano

Each country in the Spanish-speaking world has distinct musical styles and traditions. Many of the unique rhythms and dances of Spanish-speaking countries are now popular in the United States. This music features instruments such as guitars, violins, accordions, and various types of percussion such as *güiros,* sticks, cymbals, cowbells, and drums. As you read the captions, see how many words you can understand due to their similarity with English words. After you read, your teacher will play examples of each type of music. Listen for the different instruments used.

Conexiones | La música

En Argentina, el tango es muy popular. Es un baile romántico.

El flamenco es un baile típico de España. El instrumento más importante en el flamenco es la guitarra.

En Puerto Rico, la salsa es el baile preferido. El ritmo de la salsa es popular en la música de los Estados Unidos también.

En la República Dominicana, el baile tradicional es el merengue. El merengue tiene muchos ritmos africanos.

La cumbia es el baile más famoso de Colombia.

- Reread each of the captions and make a list of seven cognates.

- Make a list of instruments you heard in the different pieces of music. You might need to listen to the music again.

Gramática

Negatives

To make a sentence negative in Spanish, you usually put *no* in front of the verb or expression. In English you usually use the word "not."

No me gusta cantar.	*I do **not** like to sing.*

To answer a question negatively in Spanish you often use *no* twice. The first *no* answers the question. The second *no* says, "I do *not . . . (don't)*." This is similar to the way you answer a question in English.

¿Te gusta escribir cuentos?	*Do you like to write stories?*
No, no me gusta.	***No, I don't.***

In Spanish, you might use one or more negatives after answering *"no."*

¿Te gusta cantar?	*Do you like to sing?*
No, no me gusta nada.	***No, I don't** like **it at all.***

If you want to say that you do not like either of two choices, use *ni . . . ni:*

No me gusta **ni** nadar **ni** dibujar.	*I **don't** like **either** swimming **or** drawing.*
	or: *I like **neither** swimming **nor** drawing.*

> **¿Recuerdas?**
> Did you remember that *nada* has another meaning?
> • ¿Qué pasa? **Nada.**
> In this case, *nada* means "nothing."

> **Más ayuda**   **realidades.com**
>
> ▶ *GramActiva* **Video**
> **Tutorials:** Affirmative and Negative, Making a Sentence Negative, Formation of Negative Sentences
> ✎ *GramActiva* **Activity**

▼**21** **Leer • Escribir**

Una persona muy negativa

Tomás is a new student in the class who is very negative. Number your paper from 1–5. Complete his conversation with Ana by writing one of these negative expressions: *no, nada, ni . . . ni*.

Ana: Hola, Tomás. ¿Te gusta escuchar música?

Tomás: No, _1._ me gusta.

Ana: Pues, ¿qué te gusta más, jugar videojuegos o usar la computadora?

Tomás: No me gusta _2._ jugar videojuegos _3._ usar la computadora.

Ana: ¿Te gusta practicar deportes?

Tomás: No, no me gusta _4._ practicar deportes.

Ana: Pues, Tomás, _5._ me gusta pasar tiempo con personas negativas.

Tomás: ¡A mí tampoco! *(Me neither!)*

▼22 | Hablar

¡No, no me gusta!

Today you feel as negative as Tomás. With a partner, respond to each question saying that you don't like to do any of these activities.

▶ Modelo

A —¿Te gusta *ver la tele?*
B —No, no me gusta *ver la tele.*

Estudiante A
¿Te gusta . . . ?

Estudiante B

No, no me gusta . . .

También se dice . . .
no me gusta nada = no me gusta para nada
(muchos países)

▼23 | Hablar

¿Qué te gusta más?

Find out what your partner likes more. Then switch roles.

▶ Modelo

A —¿Qué te gusta más, *nadar* o *esquiar?*
B —Pues, me gusta más *nadar.*
o:—Pues, no me gusta ni *nadar* ni *esquiar.*

1.

2.

3.

4.

Más práctica GO	realidades.com | print
Instant Check	✔
Guided WB pp. 34–35	✔ ✔
Core WB p. 18	✔ ✔
Comm. WB pp. 13, 16, 115	✔ ✔
Hispanohablantes WB pp. 18–19	✔

▼ **Objectives**
▶ Express agreement and disagreement about what you and others like to do
▶ Read and write opinions about activities

Gramática

Expressing agreement or disagreement

To agree with what a person likes, you use *a mí también*. It's like saying "me too" in English.

Me gusta pasar tiempo con amigos.	*I like to spend time with friends.*
A mí también.	**Me too.**

también

tampoco

If someone tells you that he or she dislikes something, you can agree by saying *a mí tampoco*. It's like saying "me neither" or "neither do I" in English.

No me gusta nada cantar.	*I don't like to sing at all.*
A mí tampoco.	**Me neither.**

▼**24** Escribir

Un buen amigo

You have the same likes and dislikes as Miguel, the new Spanish exchange student. Read his statements below and using either *a mí también* or *a mí tampoco,* write a sentence saying that you agree.

Modelo
Me gusta montar en monopatín.
A mí también. Me gusta mucho montar en monopatín.
No me gusta correr.
A mí tampoco. No me gusta nada correr.

1. Me gusta jugar videojuegos.
2. No me gusta ir a la escuela.
3. No me gusta escribir cuentos.
4. Me gusta pasar tiempo con mis amigos.
5. No me gusta usar la computadora.
6. Me gusta mucho patinar.
7. No me gusta tocar la guitarra.
8. No me gusta trabajar.

▼**25**  | Escribir • Hablar

¿También o tampoco?

Write a list of three things that you like to do and three things that you don't like to do. Tell your partner the activities on your list. Your partner will agree or disagree based upon his or her personal preferences. Follow the model.

▶ **Modelo**
A —*Me gusta mucho bailar.*
B —*A mí también.*
o: —*Pues, a mí no me gusta nada bailar.*
A —*No me gusta nada cantar.*
B —*A mí tampoco.*
o: —*Pues, a mí me gusta cantar.*

▼**26** Leer • Escribir

¿Comprendes?

Read the opinions of three students on videogames and answer the questions.

1. Who thinks that videogames are neither good nor bad? How often does he or she play videogames?

2. Who likes videogames a lot? With whom does this person play them?

3. Who doesn't like videogames? Why not?

4. ¿A ti te gusta jugar videojuegos?

Jugar videojuegos: ¿bueno o malo[1]?

Ni lo uno ni lo otro
"Jugar videojuegos no es ni bueno ni malo. Me gusta jugar a veces[2]."
Alicia

¡Es fabuloso!
"A mí también me gusta jugar videojuegos. Es fabuloso jugar con mis amigos."
Enrique

¡Es terrible!
"Jugar videojuegos es malo para los ojos[3]. ¡No me gusta nada!"
Sandra

[1] bad   [2] sometimes   [3] eyes

Más práctica GO	realidades.com | print
Instant Check	✔
Guided WB p. 36	✔ ✔
Core WB p. 19	✔ ✔
Comm. WB p. 13	
Hispanohablantes **WB** pp. 19–21	✔

El español en la comunidad

Hispanics in the United States make up approximately 16 percent of the total population and are the fastest-growing minority group. By the year 2050, the Hispanic population is expected to be almost 29 percent of the total U.S. population. Because of this, there are an increasing number of Spanish-language electronic and print media sources—Internet, television, radio, magazines, and newspapers—available throughout the country.

• Make a list of Spanish-language media sources in your community. Try to find local, regional, national, or even international sources, as well as both electronic and print media. If possible, bring in examples. How much can you understand?

These sources will help you improve your Spanish, and you'll learn about Spanish-speaking cultures as well.

Lectura

¿Qué te gusta hacer?

Here are some notes that four students have written to a popular teen magazine. All four are looking for e-pals. As you read their notes, think about how their likes and interests compare to yours.

> **Strategy**
>
> **Using cognates**
> Use what you already know about cognates to figure out what new words mean.

Puerto Rico
Marisol, 14 años

"¿Te gusta practicar deportes y escuchar música? ¡A mí me gusta mucho! También me gusta jugar al básquetbol. ¡Hasta luego!"

Colombia
Daniel, 13 años

"Me gusta mucho ver la tele y escuchar música clásica. También me gusta tocar el piano y pasar tiempo con amigos en un café o en una fiesta. ¿Y a ti?"

España
Silvia, 17 años

"Me gusta leer revistas, bailar y cantar. Soy fanática de la música alternativa. También me gusta hablar por teléfono con amigos. ¿Y a ti? ¿Qué te gusta hacer?"

Guinea Ecuatorial
Pablo, 15 años

"Me gusta mucho jugar al vóleibol y al tenis. Me gusta escribir cuentos y también me gusta organizar fiestas con amigos. No me gusta ni jugar videojuegos ni ver la tele. ¡Hasta pronto!"

¿Comprendes?

1. On a sheet of paper, draw a bar graph like the one below. Indicate on the graph how many of the four young people like each of these types of activities.

ver la tele				
escuchar música				
practicar deportes				
pasar tiempo con amigos				
	1	2	3	4

2. Of the four types of activities, which are the most popular with these four students?

3. Of the four students, with whom do you have the most in common?

4. Write a personal message similar to those in the magazine. Use one of them as a model.

Más práctica	GO
realidades.com	print	
Guided WB p. 37	✔ ✔
Comm. WB pp. 17, 116	✔ ✔
Hispanohablantes **WB** pp. 22–23	✔
Cultural Reading Activity	✔

España

The Spanish empire once included parts of Italy and the Netherlands, much of the Americas and the Caribbean, the Philippines, and colonies in Africa. Today, Spain is a country of rich regional and cultural traditions with a population of more than 40 million people.

Spain was one of the most important provinces of the ancient Roman empire. The Spanish language is very closely related to Latin, the language of that empire. Roman engineering also left its mark on the Spanish landscape, and some Roman bridges are still in use after almost 2,000 years! This photo shows the Roman aqueduct in Segovia, which was constructed entirely without mortar or clamps.

¿Sabes que . . . ?

Spain has four official languages: Spanish, Catalan, Basque, and Galician. Originally the language of Castile in central Spain, Spanish is the primary national language and is also spoken in most of Spain's former empire in what is today North, Central, and South America.

Para pensar

Spain has been influenced by many civilizations, including those of the ancient Greeks, Romans, and Moors. What civilizations have most affected the language, culture, and customs of the United States?

realidades.com GO

 Mapa global interactivo
 Reference Atlas

Originally a royal retreat, the Parque del Buen Retiro is now a favorite place for the traditional Sunday-afternoon *paseo* (stroll). Throngs of people come to enjoy the Retiro's lakes, gardens, and museums, or simply to spend time with friends or family. What are your favorite places to go walking with friends? Why? ▼

▲ Arabic-speaking Moors from North Africa ruled much of Spain for nearly 800 years. Córdoba in southern Spain became one of the most important cities in Islam, and its mosque, the Mezquita, was one of the largest in the world. The Alhambra in Granada (shown above) is a strongly fortified and beautiful complex of palaces and gardens. It was also the last stronghold of the Moors in Spain, falling to Spain's Catholic monarchs in 1492.

The Bilbao Guggenheim Museum opened in October 1997 and houses a collection of modern and contemporary art. The building's titanium-paneled curves and concrete blocks imitate the harbor of Bilbao, a principal seaport and former shipbuilding center in the heart of the Basque country in the north.

Repaso del capítulo

Vocabulario y gramática

to talk about activities

bailar	to dance
cantar	to sing
correr	to run
dibujar	to draw
escribir cuentos	to write stories
escuchar música	to listen to music
esquiar	to ski
hablar por teléfono	to talk on the phone
ir a la escuela	to go to school
jugar videojuegos	to play video games
leer revistas	to read magazines
montar en bicicleta	to ride a bicycle
montar en monopatín	to skateboard
nadar	to swim
pasar tiempo con amigos	to spend time with friends
patinar	to skate
practicar deportes	to play sports
tocar la guitarra	to play the guitar
trabajar	to work
usar la computadora	to use the computer
ver la tele	to watch television

to say what you like to do

(A mí) me gusta ___.	I like to ___.
(A mí) me gusta más ___.	I like to ___ better. (I prefer to ___.)
(A mí) me gusta mucho ___.	I like to ___ a lot.
A mí también.	Me too.

For *Vocabulario adicional,* see pp. 268–269.

to say what you don't like to do

(A mí) no me gusta ___.	I don't like to ___.
(A mí) no me gusta nada ___.	I don't like to ___ at all.
A mí tampoco.	Me neither.

to ask others what they like to do

¿Qué te gusta hacer?	What do you like to do?
¿Qué te gusta más?	What do you like better (prefer)?
¿Te gusta ___?	Do you like to ___?
¿Y a ti?	And you?

other useful words and expressions

más	more
ni . . . ni	neither . . . nor, not . . . or
o	or
pues	well . . .
sí	yes
también	also, too
y	and

Más repaso GO   realidades.com | print

Instant Check ✔
Puzzles ✔
Core WB pp. 20–21 ✔ ✔
Comm. WB pp. 117, 118–120 ✔ ✔

Preparación para el examen

On the exam you will be asked to . . .	Here are practice tasks similar to those you will find on the exam . . .	For review go to your print or digital online textbook . . .
1 Escuchar Listen to and understand a description of what someone likes to do	Listen to a voice mail from a student looking for a "match-up" to the homecoming dance. a) What are two things this person likes doing? b) What is one thing this person dislikes doing?	**pp. 26–31** *Vocabulario en contexto* **p. 27** Actividades 1–2 **p. 38** Actividad 18
2 Hablar Talk about yourself and what you like and don't like to do and ask the same of others	You agreed to host a student from the Dominican Republic for a week. What can you tell him or her about yourself in a taped message? Include a brief description of what you like to do. How would you ask the student to tell you something about himself or herself?	**p. 32** Actividad 7 **p. 33** Actividades 8–9 **p. 34** Actividad 10 **p. 38** Actividades 16–17 **p. 43** Actividades 22–23 **p. 49** *Presentación oral*
3 Leer Read and understand someone's description of himself or herself	Read this pen pal e-mail from a Spanish-language magazine. What does the person like to do? Does this person have anything in common with you? What is it? ¡Hola! A mí me gusta mucho usar la computadora y tocar la guitarra. No me gusta ni ir a la escuela ni leer. En el verano me gusta nadar y en el invierno me gusta esquiar. ¿Y a ti? ¿Qué te gusta hacer?	**pp. 26–31** *Vocabulario en contexto* **p. 31** Actividades 3–4 **p. 35** Actividad 11 **p. 42** Actividad 21 **p. 45** Actividad 26 **pp. 46–47** *Lectura*
4 Escribir Write about yourself with a description of things you like and don't like to do	A school in the Dominican Republic wants to exchange e-mails with your school. Tell your e-pal your name and what you like to do and don't like to do.	**p. 31** Actividad 5 **p. 32** Actividades 6–7 **p. 38** Actividades 16–17 **p. 44** Actividades 24–25 **p. 47** *¿Comprendes?*, No. 3
5 Pensar Demonstrate an understanding of cultural differences regarding dancing	How would you describe the Latin dances that have become popular in the United States? With what countries do you associate each dance? With what type of music or rhythms do you associate each dance?	**p. 41** Actividad 20 **p. 40** *Fondo cultural* **p. 48** *La cultura en vivo*

1B Y tú, ¿cómo eres?

▼ Chapter Objectives

Communication

By the end of this chapter you will be able to:

- Listen to and read descriptions of others
- Talk and write about your personality traits
- Describe your personality to others

Culture

You will also be able to:

- Compare cultural perspectives on friendship

You will demonstrate what you know and can do:

- Presentación escrita, p. 79
- Preparación para el examen, p. 83

You will use:

Vocabulary	Grammar
• Personality traits	• Adjectives
• Expressing likes and dislikes	• Definite and indefinite articles
	• Word order: Placement of adjectives

Exploración del mundo hispano

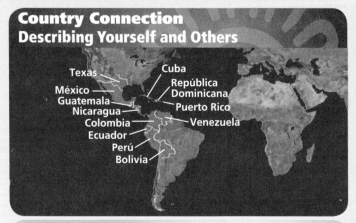

Country Connection
Describing Yourself and Others

Texas
Cuba
México
República Dominicana
Guatemala
Nicaragua
Puerto Rico
Colombia
Venezuela
Ecuador
Perú
Bolivia

realidades.com GO

 Reference Atlas

 Videocultura y actividad

Mapa global interactivo

Un grupo de amigos, San Juan del Sur, Nicaragua

Arte y cultura | México

Frida Kahlo (1907–1954) is one of the best-known Mexican painters. In spite of a childhood illness, a crippling traffic accident, and many hospital stays throughout her life, Kahlo was a successful painter and led a very active social life. She used her artwork as an outlet for her physical and emotional suffering.

• Frida Kahlo painted over fifty self-portraits. What is she saying about herself through this painting?

"Autorretrato con mono" (1938), Frida Kahlo ▶

Oil on Masonite, overall: 16" x 12" (40.64 x 30.48 cm). ©Banco de México Diego Rivera & Frida Kahlo Museums Trust. Av. Cinco de Mayo No. 2, Col. Centro, Del. Cuauhtemoc 06059, México, D.F. Reproduction authorized by the *Instituto Nacional de Bellas Artes y Literatura.* Courtesy of Albright-Knox Art Gallery, Buffalo, New York. Bequest of A. Conger Goodyear, 1966.

Read, listen to, and understand information about
▶ personality traits

Vocabulario en contexto

66¿El chico? **Es mi amigo. ¿Cómo se llama?** Se llama Marcos. **¿Cómo es?** Pues . . .

el chico

. . . **él** es **deportista. Le gusta** mucho practicar deportes.

Pero a veces es **impaciente** . . .

. . . también es **un** chico **desordenado**99.

66**Mi amiga** Sarita es **una buena** amiga. No es **muy** deportista . . .

la chica

. . . pero es una chica **artística** . . .

. . . y muy **ordenada.**

Es una chica muy **inteligente**99.

66 Hola, me llamo Luz. ¿Yo?
¿Cómo **soy**? Pues . . .

Más vocabulario

atrevido, -a	daring
paciente	patient
reservado, -a	shy
simpático, -a	nice, friendly
talentoso, -a	talented

. . . soy **estudiosa** . . .

. . . y **trabajadora** . . .

. . . y también **graciosa** . . .

. . . pero **según mi familia**
¡a veces soy **perezosa**! Y
tú, ¿cómo eres? **99**

▼1 | ◀)) | Escuchar

¿Marcos o Sarita?

Look at the pictures of Marcos and Sarita, and listen to the descriptions. If a word describes Marcos, point to his picture. If a word describes Sarita, point to her picture.

▼2 | ◀)) | Escuchar

¿Cierto o falso?

You will hear some statements about Luz. Give a "thumbs-up" sign if a statement is true, or a "thumbs-down" sign if it is false.

Más práctica GO

realidades.com | print

Instant Check	✔	
Guided WB pp. 39–42	✔	✔
Core WB pp. 22–23	✔	✔
Comm. WB p. 25	✔	✔
Hispanohablantes WB p. 32		✔

Amigos por Internet

See what happens when *Chica sociable* sends an e-mail message to Esteban.

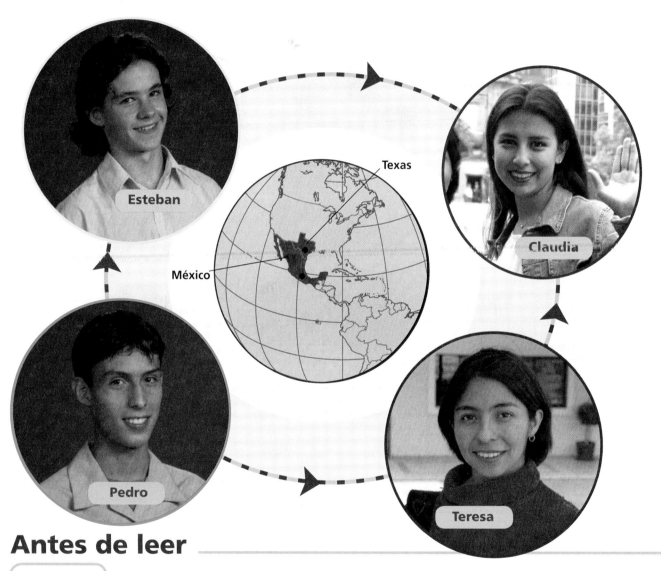

Antes de leer

Strategy | **Using cognates** You will see some unfamiliar words in this story. Many of these are cognates. Use their similarity to English words to determine their meaning.

- What does *sociable* mean? What does *ideal* mean?

1. Look at photo 1 on p. 59. What are the boys doing?
2. Look at photos 3 and 4 on p. 59. Are the students at different locations? Where are they? How do you think the students in the two photos might be connected?

Pedro: Esteban, escucha: "Hola, ¿cómo eres? ¿Qué te gusta hacer? Me gusta mucho hablar con mis amigos. Me llamo *Chica* **sociable**. Escríbeme".

Esteban: ¡Ja! *Chica sociable*. A responder. Escribe, Pedro . . .

Pedro: "Hola. Me llamo *Chico sociable.* ¡Qué coincidencia!".

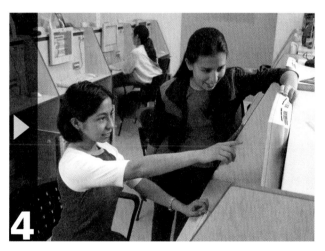

Pedro: "Me gusta pasar tiempo con mis amigos. **No soy** muy **serio.** Según mis amigos, soy gracioso".

Claudia: *¡Chica sociable!* ¡Ja!

Teresa: Yo soy *Chica sociable*.

Claudia: ¡No! ¿Tú **eres** *Chica sociable?* Mi buena amiga . . .

Teresa: "Soy muy desordenada. Me gusta hablar por teléfono. Y no me gusta ir a la escuela. Escríbeme. *Chica sociable"*.

Claudia: Un momento . . . uno más de mí. Escribe . . . "Yo soy *Chica misteriosa*. Soy amiga de *Chica sociable*. Soy muy simpática".

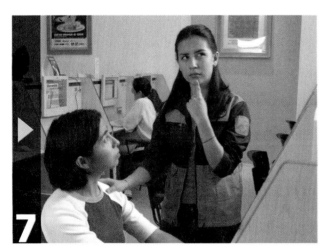

Claudia: "Y me gusta ir a la escuela. Soy estudiosa y trabajadora. Yo no soy tu chica ideal. *Chica misteriosa"*.

Esteban: Pues, Pedro. ¿*Chica sociable* o *Chica misteriosa*?

Pedro: *Chica misteriosa*. Me gusta la escuela y a ella le gusta la escuela también.

Esteban: Perfecto. A mí me gusta más *Chica sociable*.

▼**3** Escribir • Hablar

¿Comprendes?

Read each of the sentences below and indicate which character is being described: *Chica sociable* or *Chica misteriosa*.

1. Me gusta hablar por teléfono.

2. Me gusta ir a la escuela.

3. Soy simpática.

4. No soy muy ordenada.

5. Soy trabajadora.

Claudia

Teresa

▼**4** Leer • Pensar

¿Qué les gusta hacer?

Number your paper 1–8. Based on the *Videohistoria*, decide which characters you think would like to do the activities below. Write the names of all of the characters you have chosen beside each number.

1. trabajar
2. estudiar
3. bailar
4. leer

5. hablar
7. pasar tiempo con amigos
6. ir a la escuela
8. usar la computadora

Esteban

Pedro

Más práctica	GO
	realidades.com | print
Instant Check	✔
Guided WB pp. 43–46	✔ ✔
Core WB pp. 24–25	✔ ✔
Comm. WB pp. 18–20, 21	✔ ✔
Hispanohablantes WB p. 33	✔

Vocabulario en uso

▼5 Escribir

¿Cómo es el chico o la chica?

Number your paper 1–6. Choose the correct word to describe each of the people in the pictures and write the complete sentence on your paper.

Modelo
El chico es *(impaciente / estudioso)*.
El chico es <u>*impaciente*</u>.

1. La chica es *(reservada / artística)*.

2. El chico es *(desordenado / atrevido)*.

3. La chica es *(graciosa / perezosa)*.

4. La chica es *(artística / atrevida)*.

5. El chico es *(reservado / deportista)*.

6. El chico es *(estudioso / desordenado)*.

▼**6** Leer • Pensar

Nuevos amigos

Look at the profiles of the following students who are chatting online with you. Put them in pairs according to who you think would make good friends. Base your decision on personality traits and favorite activities.

1.

Catalina: Me gusta mucho correr. En general, soy deportista.

2.

Christian: Me gusta escribir cuentos. Soy estudioso.

3.

Flor: Soy reservada. No me gusta mucho hablar por teléfono.

4.

Alejandro: No me gusta nada nadar. Me gusta más jugar videojuegos.

5.

Liliana: Soy inteligente. Me gusta ir a la escuela y leer.

6.

Mayra: No soy muy sociable, pero a veces me gusta pasar tiempo con amigos.

7.

Alfonso: No soy deportista. Me gusta mucho usar la computadora.

8.

Guillermo: Me gusta practicar deportes. No soy muy artístico.

▼**7** Escribir

Mi amigo José

Maritza is talking about her friend José. Read the sentences, then choose the appropriate word to fill in each blank.

Modelo
No es un chico impaciente. Es muy paciente.

trabajador	deportista
paciente	estudioso
gracioso	desordenado
sociable	

1. Le gusta mucho practicar deportes. Es ___.
2. A veces no es serio. Es un chico ___.
3. Le gusta pasar tiempo con amigos. Es muy ___.
4. No es un chico ordenado. Es ___.
5. Le gusta ir a la escuela. Es ___.
6. No es perezoso. Es un chico muy ___.

▼ **Objectives**

► **Write about and discuss what you and others are like**
► **Describe your personality**
► **Read and write a self-descriptive poem**

Gramática

Adjectives

Words that describe people and things are called adjectives *(adjetivos)*.

Masculine	Feminine
ordenad**o**	ordenad**a**
trabajad**or**	trabajad**ora**
pacient**e**	pacient**e**
deportist**a**	deportist**a**

- In Spanish, most adjectives have both masculine and feminine forms. The masculine form usually ends in the letter *-o* and the feminine form usually ends in the letter *-a*.

- Masculine adjectives are used to describe masculine nouns.

  Marcos es ordenado   *Marcos is organized*
  y simpático.   *and nice.*

- Feminine adjectives are used to describe feminine nouns.

  Marta es ordenada   *Marta is organized*
  y simpática.   *and nice.*

- Adjectives that end in *-e* describe both masculine and feminine nouns.

  Anita es inteligente.   *Anita is smart.*
  Pedro es inteligente.   *Pedro is smart.*

- Adjectives whose masculine form ends in *-dor* have a feminine form that ends in *-dora*.

  Juan es trabajador.   *Juan is hardworking.*
  Luz es trabajadora.   *Luz is hardworking.*

- Some adjectives that end in *-a*, such as *deportista*, describe both masculine and feminine nouns. You will need to learn which adjectives follow this pattern.

  Tomás es deportista.   *Tomás is athletic.*
  Marta es deportista   *Marta is also*
  también.   *athletic.*

Más ayuda   **realidades.com**

 GramActiva Video
Tutorials: Adjectives, Adjective clauses

 Canción de hip hop: *¿Cómo soy yo?*

 GramActiva Activity

▼**8** Escribir

Roberto y Yolanda

Copy the Venn diagram on a sheet of paper. Which words from the list could only describe Roberto? Write them in the oval below his name. Which words could only describe Yolanda? Write them in the oval below her name. Which words could describe either Roberto or Yolanda? Write them in the overlapping area.

Modelo

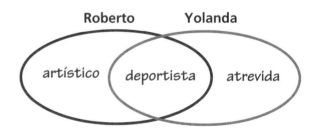

Roberto   Yolanda

artístico   deportista   atrevida

artístico	graciosa	ordenada	serio
atrevida	impaciente	paciente	sociable
deportista	simpático	perezosa	talentosa
estudiosa	inteligente	reservado	trabajador

▼**9** | | **Hablar**

¿Cómo es Paloma?

Work with a partner to ask and answer questions about the people shown below.

Paloma

Modelo

A —¿Cómo es Paloma?
B —Paloma es trabajadora.

1. Elena

2. Marisol

3. Felipe

4. Juan

5. Lola

6. Gloria

▼**10** | | **Hablar • GramActiva**

Juego

Choose an adjective to act out for a small group. The other students in the group will take turns asking you questions to guess which word you are demonstrating. The first student to guess the correct adjective, in the correct form, gets to perform the next charade.

Modelo

A —¿Eres ordenada?
B —¡Claro que sí! Soy ordenada.
o: ¡Claro que no! No soy ordenada.

Para decir más . . .

¡Claro que sí!   Of course!
¡Claro que no!   Of course not!
¿De veras?   Really?

11 Escribir

Yo soy . . .

Make a chart like the one on the right. Write at least three adjectives in each column to say what you are like and are not like. Include *muy* and *a veces* when they are appropriate. Save your chart to use in later activities.

Modelo

Soy	No soy
estudiosa	perezosa
muy trabajadora	impaciente
deportista	

12 | Hablar • Escribir

¿Cómo eres?

Working with a partner, use the chart that you made in Actividad 11 to talk about your personality traits. Take notes on what your partner tells you. You will be asked to use this information in the next Actividad.

Modelo

A —¿*Cómo eres?*
B —*Soy estudiosa y muy trabajadora. También soy deportista. ¿Y tú?*
A —*Soy artístico. Según mis amigos, soy talentoso. No soy perezoso.*

13 Escribir • Hablar

Mi amigo(a)

Use the information from Actividades 11 and 12 to write a short description of yourself and your partner. Follow the model, and be prepared to report back to the class.

Modelo

Me llamo Luisa. Soy estudiosa y trabajadora. Y soy artística. Mi amiga se llama Susana. Ella es simpática. También es artística y trabajadora.

▼14 | 👥 | ♻ | Hablar

¿Qué te gusta hacer?

Working with a partner, ask each other if you like to do the following activities and answer according to the model.

▶ Modelo

A —¿*Te gusta correr?*

B —*Sí, soy deportista.*

o: *No, no soy deportista.*

o: *Sí, pero no soy muy deportista.*

Estudiante A

Estudiante B

trabajador, -a
sociable
artístico, -a
deportista
estudioso, -a
talentoso, -a

¡Respuesta personal!

▼15 Escribir

Una persona famosa

Who is your favorite celebrity? Copy the paragraph on a separate piece of paper, filling in the blanks with words that describe your favorite celebrity and what he or she likes to do.

La persona famosa que me gusta más se llama __1.__ . Es __2.__ y __3.__ .
Le gusta __4.__ pero no le gusta __5.__ .
No es ni __6.__ ni __7.__ .

Simón Bolívar (1783–1830) liberated the territory that is now Venezuela, Colombia, Ecuador, Peru, and Bolivia. Bolívar helped these areas gain their independence from Spain. Simón Bolívar is remembered as a brave and daring leader and is known throughout South America as *El Libertador* (The Liberator).

• Name three leaders who had a similar influence on events of their time.

"Simón Bolívar" (siglo XIX), Anónimo
Chromolitho. Artist Unknown (pre 20th century).
Private Collection / Archives Charmet /
Bridgeman Art Library.

▼16 Pensar • Escribir

¿Qué es un buen líder?

A good leader has to have certain qualities. Copy this chart onto your paper, and fill in the adjectives that, in your opinion, describe what a good leader is and is not.

Es . . .	No es . . .

▼ Exploración del lenguaje

Cognates that begin with *es* + consonant

Many words in Spanish that begin with *es* + consonant are easy to understand because they have the same meaning as English words. Knowing this pattern helps you recognize the meaning of new Spanish words and learn them quickly.

Try it out! Look at these words, then cover up the *e* at the beginning. Name English words that come from the same root word.

estudiante **es**tudioso **es**cuela **es**tómago

esquiar **es**pecial **es**tricto **es**cena

Es muy estudioso. Le encanta estudiar.

▼17 Leer • Escribir

El poema "Soy Elena"

The following poem is called a *poema en diamante.* Can you guess why?
After you've read the poem, answer the questions.

Conexiones | La literatura

Soy Elena
En general, soy
reservada y ordenada.
A veces, soy atrevida,
graciosa o impaciente.
No soy ni deportista
ni artística.
¡Yo soy yo!

1. Which activity would you invite Elena to do based on what she has told you about herself?

   dibujar   montar en monopatín   escuchar música

2. Rewrite the poem replacing *Soy Elena* with *Soy Tomás.*

▼18 Escribir

Un poema personal

Write *un poema en diamante* about yourself. Choose adjectives that best describe you. Look back at your chart from Actividad 11 for some ideas. Substitute your adjectives in the poem above. Be sure to write the poem in the form of a diamond. You might want to use calligraphy or an appropriate font on the computer and add pictures to illustrate your work.

Más práctica GO	realidades.com	print
Instant Check	✔	
Guided WB pp. 47–48	✔	✔
Core WB p. 26	✔	✔
Comm. WB pp. 23, 26, 121	✔	✔
Hispanohablantes WB pp. 34–37		✔

Gramática

Definite and indefinite articles

El and *la* are called definite articles and are the equivalent of "the" in English. *El* is used with masculine nouns; *la* is used with feminine nouns. You've already seen words with definite articles:

el libro   ***the*** *book*   la carpeta   ***the*** *folder*

Un and *una* are called indefinite articles and are the equivalent of "a" and "an" in English. *Un* is used with masculine nouns; *una* is used with feminine nouns.

un libro   ***a*** *book*   una carpeta   ***a*** *folder*

el	*the*
la	*the*

un	*a, an*
una	*a, an*

Strategy

Learning by repetition
When you learn a new noun, say it aloud, along with its definite article. Eventually you will find that words just "sound right" with the correct definite article and you will know whether the nouns are masculine or feminine.

Más ayuda   **realidades.com**

GramActiva **Video**
Tutorial: Definite and Indefinite Articles

GramActiva **Activity**

▼19 | 🔊)) | Escuchar • GramActiva

¿El o la?

Write the word *el* in large letters on a sheet of paper or an index card. Write *la* in large letters on another sheet. You will hear eight words you already know. When you hear a masculine word, hold up the paper with *el*. When you hear a feminine word, hold up the paper with the word *la* on it.

▼20 Escribir

Buenos días, doctor

Julian is at the doctor's office for a check-up. As he examines Julian, the doctor follows a list to be thorough. Copy the list on your paper and help the doctor by adding the appropriate definite article for each body part.

☑ 1. ___ brazo
☑ 2. ___ cabeza
☑ 3. ___ nariz
☑ 4. ___ pierna
☑ 5. ___ estómago
☑ 6. ___ mano

▼**21** Escribir

La escuela de Diego

Diego is talking about people at his school. Copy the sentences on your paper and complete each one with *un* or *una*.

1. La Sra. Secada es ___ profesora simpática.

2. Alicia es ___ estudiante trabajadora.

3. Juan Carlos es ___ chico perezoso.

4. Víctor es ___ chico sociable.

5. El Sr. Guzmán es ___ profesor gracioso.

6. Adriana es ___ chica muy seria.

7. La Srta. Cifuentes es ___ profesora paciente.

8. Arturo es ___ estudiante talentoso.

▼**22** | 🗣 | ♻ | Hablar

¿Qué es?

Tell your partner the name of each object or body part pictured below.

 ▶ **Modelo**

A —*¿Qué es?*
B —*Es un brazo.*

1.

2.

3.

4.

5.

6.

7.

8.

▼ **Pronunciación** | 🔊 | 🗣

The vowels *o* and *u*

In Spanish, the pronunciation of the letter *o* is similar to the vowel sound in the English word *boat,* except that it is short. Listen then say these words, concentrating on making a short *o* sound:

bolígrafo	gracioso	cómo
teléfono	tampoco	otoño

In Spanish, the pronunciation of the letter *u* is similar to the vowel sound in the English word *zoo.* Listen to and say these words:

mucho	lunes	usted
octubre	estudioso	según

¡Ojo! Careful! Sometimes the words we mispronounce most are the ones that remind us of English words.

Try it out! Pronounce these words, concentrating on the Spanish vowel sounds:

agosto	regular	tropical	música
gusto	universidad	Uruguay	Cuba

El mundo

Más práctica GO	realidades.com	print

Instant Check	✔	
Guided WB p. 49	✔	✔
Core WB p. 27	✔	✔
Comm. WB pp. 23, 27	✔	✔
Hispanohablantes WB pp. 37–38		✔

▼ **Objectives**
▶ Write about and describe yourself and others
▶ Listen to and write a description of three teens
▶ Read and write an e-mail message

Gramática

Word order: Placement of adjectives

In Spanish, adjectives usually come after the noun they describe. Notice how *artística* follows *chica* in this Spanish sentence:

Margarita es una **chica artística**.   *Margarita is an **artistic girl***.

Did you notice in the English sentence that the adjective comes before the noun?

Here's a simple pattern you can follow when writing a sentence in Spanish:

Subject	Verb	Indefinite Article + Noun	Adjective
Margarita	es	una chica	muy artística
Pablo	es	un estudiante	inteligente
La señora Ortiz	es	una profesora	muy buena

¿Recuerdas?

To make a sentence negative, you place the word *no* before the verb.

- Eduardo no es un chico serio.
- No me gusta jugar videojuegos.

Más ayuda **realidades.com**

▶ **Tutorial:** Position of Adjectives

▼23 Escribir

Frases desordenadas

Create five sentences using the words in the following bubbles. Follow the "building blocks" pattern above and be sure to add a period at the end of each sentence.

una
Patricia
chica
deportista
es

Modelo
Patricia es una chica deportista.

1.
artística
es
una
Marina
chica

2.
Marcos
chico
es
reservado
un

3.
es
un
Tito
perezoso
chico

4.
chica
Teresa
es
inteligente
una

5.
Enrique
es
trabajador
un
chico

▼24 | 🔊 | Escuchar • Escribir

Escucha y escribe

You will hear a description of Arturo, Marta, and Belinda. Write what you hear.

▼25 Leer • Escribir

¿Cómo son los estudiantes?

Each of the following students is going to tell you what they like to do. Based on their statements, write a description of them. Be sure to use the correct word order.

Modelo
José: Me gusta nadar.
José es un chico deportista.

1. **Mariana:** Me gusta estudiar.
2. **Gustavo:** Me gusta mucho pasar tiempo con amigos.
3. **Luz:** Me gusta hablar por teléfono.
4. **Jorge:** Me gusta trabajar.
5. **Silvia:** Me gusta mucho bailar y cantar.
6. **Natalia:** Me gusta mucho el arte.
7. **Julian:** Me gusta usar la computadora.

El español en el mundo del trabajo

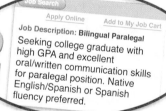

Job Search
Apply Online   Add to My Job Cart
Job Description: Bilingual Paralegal
Seeking college graduate with high GPA and excellent oral/written communication skills for paralegal position. Native English/Spanish or Spanish fluency preferred.

Paciente, inteligente, trabajador, ordenado . . .

These four qualities will make you a good candidate for any job. And if you add *bilingüe* to the list, your job qualifications will be enhanced.

- Make a list of careers where your knowledge of Spanish would be an asset. Which of these careers are of interest to you?

¿Cómo es . . .?

You are sitting in your school cafeteria with Marcos, a new exchange student from Costa Rica. Describe the other students based on their activities.

Modelo
Emilia es una chica talentosa.

▼**27** | (Talk!) | **Escribir • Hablar**

Y tú, ¿qué dices?

1. Según tu familia, ¿cómo eres?

2. Según tu mejor *(best)* amigo(a), ¿cómo eres?

3. Según tus profesores, ¿cómo eres?

▼28 Leer • Escribir

Un mensaje electrónico

You just received an e-mail message from another student in Panama City, but when you opened it up, some of the sentences were scrambled. Unscramble her message and then answer her questions by writing your own message.

¡Hola!

Me llamo Andreina:

una seria soy estudiante muy Yo. chica Yo artística soy una. ¿Eres inteligente? ¿Eres paciente? Mi mejor amiga es Claudia. **Claudia deportista chica una es. muy estudiante Claudia es trabajadora una.** ¿Cómo se llama tu mejor amigo? ¿Es deportista y talentoso?

Hola Andreina:

Me llamo ____.

Soy ____.

También, yo soy ____.

Mi mejor amigo(a) se llama ____.

Es ____.

También es ____.

Y a ti, ¿qué te gusta hacer?

¡Escríbeme pronto!

▼ Fondo Cultural | El mundo hispano

Cibercafés Many households in Spanish-speaking countries have computers and are online. However, *cibercafés,* places where people can access the Internet, are very popular. Some of the *cibercafés* are regular coffeehouses that serve snacks and drinks and have a few computers for customers to use, while others are equipped with dozens of computers. When people want to surf the Internet, play computer games, or e-mail friends, they can go to a *cibercafé* and get connected for a small fee.

• How much time do you spend on the computer? Would you spend money to go to a *cibercafé* if you didn't have a computer at home or at school? Why or why not?

Un cibercafé de la Ciudad de México

Más práctica	GO	
realidades.com | print		
Instant Check	✔	
Guided WB p. 50	✔	✔
Core WB p. 28	✔	✔
Comm. WB p. 24	✔	✔
Hispanohablantes WB pp. 39–41		✔

Lectura

Un self-quiz

Is there a relationship between colors and personality? According to a self-quiz in the magazine *Amigos,* your favorite colors reveal perfectly what your personality is like.

Strategy

Using visual clues to get meaning
You have not yet learned the Spanish words for colors, but see if you can figure out what they are from the visual clues in the article.

¿Cómo eres tú?
¡Los colores revelan tu personalidad!

¿Eres una chica? ¿Te gusta el rojo? ¿Eres un chico? ¿Te gusta el rojo?	Eres muy apasionada. Eres atrevido.
¿Eres una chica? ¿Te gusta el verde? ¿Eres un chico? ¿Te gusta el verde?	Eres una chica natural. Eres muy generoso.
¿Eres una chica? ¿Te gusta el azul? ¿Eres un chico? ¿Te gusta el azul?	Eres muy talentosa. Eres un chico sociable.
¿Eres una chica? ¿Te gusta el anaranjado? ¿Eres un chico? ¿Te gusta el anaranjado?	Eres una chica artística. Eres gracioso.
¿Eres una chica? ¿Te gusta el violeta? ¿Eres un chico? ¿Te gusta el violeta?	Eres una chica muy independiente. Eres un chico romántico.
¿Eres una chica? ¿Te gusta el amarillo? ¿Eres un chico? ¿Te gusta el amarillo?	Eres una chica muy trabajadora. Eres muy serio.

¿Comprendes?

1. You probably were able to understand most of the words in the quiz. Write the English meaning for these Spanish cognates from the reading:
   - **a.** revelan
   - **b.** natural
   - **c.** independiente
   - **d.** generoso
   - **e.** apasionada
   - **f.** romántico

2. According to the self-quiz, what should be the favorite colors of these teenagers?
   - **a.** A Beto le gusta estar con amigos.
   - **b.** A Margarita le gusta dibujar.
   - **c.** A Lorenzo le gusta el trabajo voluntario *(volunteer work)*.
   - **d.** A Lupe le gusta estudiar. Es muy seria.
   - **e.** A Isabel le gusta estar con amigos, pero también le gusta estar sola *(alone)*.

3. Which of the colors in this reading is your favorite? Do you agree with the description? Why or why not?

   Modelo
   amarillo
   ¡Sí! Soy una chica trabajadora. Me gusta la escuela.
   o: *¡No! Soy una chica perezosa. Me gusta ver la tele.*

▼ Fondo Cultural | Guatemala | México

Huipil is the word for the colorful, hand-woven blouse worn by female descendents of the Maya. The color, design, and style of weaving are unique to each *huipil* and identify the background and specific village of the weaver. Hundreds of designs and styles of weaving have been identified in the Mayan regions, principally Guatemala and parts of Mexico.

- What do you wear that might help someone identify your background?

Una mujer de Guatemala con huipil

Más práctica   GO

realidades.com | print

Guided WB p. 51 ✔ ✔
Comm. WB pp. 28, 122 ✔ ✔
Hispanohablantes **WB** pp. 42–45 ✔
Cultural Reading Activity ✔

Perspectivas del mundo hispano

¿Qué es un amigo?

Marcos, a Costa Rican student on an exchange program in the United States, writes:

“When I arrived in the United States, I was amazed at all the friends my host brother and sister had. They knew a lot of people. These friends came to the house frequently, and we went out in groups. People were very open when meeting me. We'd spend some time together and get to know each other in a short amount of time. And once you got to know them, you ended up talking about everything!”

Brianna, a U.S. student on an exchange program in Colombia, writes:

“After I spent my year in Colombia, I learned that the concept of friendship is a little different than in the United States. My host brother and sisters spent a lot of time with their family. They knew people at school and from after-school activities, but they had just a few close friends and we'd do things with them. It was definitely a smaller group than I was used to. It seems that it took longer to become close friends with people too.”

Dos amigas estudiando

In Spanish, two expressions are used frequently to describe friendly relationships: *un amigo,* which means "friend," and *un conocido,* which means "acquaintance." You already know the word *amigo. Conocido* comes from the verb *conocer,* which means "to meet." Each expression implies a different type of relationship.

Check it out! In many Spanish-speaking countries you'll find lots of expressions for someone who is your friend: *hermano, cuate (México), amigote (España),* and *compinche (Uruguay, Argentina, España).* Make a list of the expressions for "a friend" that are popular in your community. How would you explain them to someone from a Spanish-speaking country?

Think about it! Compare how the United States perspective on friendship is different from that of a Spanish-speaking country. Use the terms *amigo* and *conocido* as you make the comparison.

Presentación escrita

Amigo por correspondencia

Task
Write an e-mail in which you introduce yourself to a prospective pen pal.

❶ Prewrite To think about and organize the information you want to give, answer these questions:

- ¿Cómo te llamas?
- ¿Cómo eres?
- ¿Qué te gusta hacer?
- ¿Qué no te gusta hacer?

❷ Draft Write a first draft of your e-mail answering the questions above. Begin by introducing yourself: *¡Hola! Me llamo . . . .* End with *Escríbeme pronto.* ("Write to me soon.")

Modelo

¡Hola! Me llamo Patti. Soy atrevida y muy deportista. Me gusta mucho nadar y correr, pero me gusta más esquiar. ¡No me gusta nada jugar videojuegos! Escríbeme pronto.

> **Strategy**
>
> **Using the writing process**
> To create your best work, follow each step in the writing process.

❸ Revise Revise your first draft and share it with a partner. Your partner should check the following:

- Is it well organized?
- Does it answer the Prewrite questions?
- Are the spelling and adjective forms correct?
- Did you include the opening and the closing?

Decide whether or not to use your partner's suggestions and rewrite your draft.

❹ Publish Type up your e-mail. You might send it to a pen pal or your teacher, or print it for a classmate to answer.

❺ Evaluation The following rubric will be used to grade your e-mail.

Rubric	Score 1	Score 3	Score 5
Completion of task	You provide some of the required information.	You provide most of the required information.	You provide all of the required information.
Following the writing process	You provide only the prewrite questions.	You provide the prewrite questions and rough draft.	You provide the prewrite, rough draft, and final product.
Using adjectives correctly	You use only one adjective with grammar errors.	You use two adjectives with some grammar errors.	You use more than two adjectives with very few grammar errors.

El Caribe

A chain of islands extending from the Bahamas in the north to Trinidad in the south, the Caribbean or West Indies is a region of extraordinary cultural and linguistic diversity. The Spanish-speaking countries are Cuba, Puerto Rico, and the Dominican Republic, which occupies the eastern portion of the island of Hispaniola.

Christopher Columbus first landed on the island of Hispaniola in 1492. He returned the following year with 1,000 colonists and founded Isabela, the first European colony in America, on the northern coast of Hispaniola.

¿Sabes que . . . ?

Most Cubans are descendants of people who originally came to the island from Spain and Africa. Although almost all Cubans speak Spanish as their first language, some also speak Lucumi, which is closely related to West African languages. Many people in other parts of the Caribbean speak creole languages, which combine elements of African and European tongues.

Para pensar

African traditions have inspired reggae, calypso, salsa, merengue, and many other musical styles in the Caribbean. What are some of the musical styles from the United States that have been influenced by African traditions?

Estados Unidos
Islas Bahamas
Cuba
República Dominicana
Haití
Puerto Rico
Mar Caribe
OCÉANO ATLÁNTICO

realidades.com GO

 Mapa global interactivo

 Reference Atlas

The Universidad Autónoma de Santo Domingo, located in the capital of the Dominican Republic, Santo Domingo, is the oldest university in the Americas. It was founded in 1538—almost 100 years before Harvard—and continues to be one of the most important in the Caribbean.

Opened in 1963, the Arecibo Observatory in Puerto Rico has the largest single-dish radio telescope in the world. Some 200 scientists from around the world conduct research at Arecibo every year. In the early 1990s astronomers at Arecibo discovered the first planets outside our solar system.

The Caribbean is famous for its diverse musical styles that fuse African and European influences. Some groups even combine salsa, rumba, cha-cha-cha, and other Caribbean musical styles with jazz, hip-hop, and rock and roll.

Repaso del capítulo
Vocabulario y gramática

to talk about what you and others are like

artístico, -a	artistic
atrevido, -a	daring
bueno, -a	good
deportista	athletic
desordenado, -a	messy
estudioso, -a	studious
gracioso, -a	funny
impaciente	impatient
inteligente	intelligent
ordenado, -a	neat
paciente	patient
perezoso, -a	lazy
reservado, -a	reserved, shy
serio, -a	serious
simpático, -a	nice, friendly
sociable	sociable
talentoso, -a	talented
trabajador, -ora	hardworking

to ask people about themselves or others

¿Cómo eres?	What are you like?
¿Cómo es?	What is he/she like?
¿Cómo se llama?	What's his/her name?
¿Eres . . . ?	Are you . . . ?

to talk about what someone likes or doesn't like

le gusta . . .	he/she likes . . .
no le gusta . . .	he/she doesn't like . . .

to describe someone

es	he/she is
soy	I am
no soy	I am not

For *Vocabulario adicional*, see pp. 268–269.

to tell whom you are talking about

el amigo	male friend
la amiga	female friend
el chico	boy
la chica	girl
él	he
ella	she
yo	I

other useful words

a veces	sometimes
muy	very
pero	but
según	according to
según mi familia	according to my family

adjectives

Masculine	Feminine
ordenado	ordenada
trabajador	trabajadora
paciente	paciente
deportista	deportista

definite articles

el	the
la	the

indefinite articles

un	a, an
una	a, an

Más repaso GO	realidades.com | print
Instant Check	✔
Puzzles	✔
Core WB pp. 29–30	✔
Comm. WB pp. 123, 124–126	✔ ✔

Preparación para el examen

On the exam you will be asked to . . .	Here are practice tasks similar to those you will find on the exam . . .	For review go to your print or digital textbook . . .
1 Escuchar Listen to and understand a description of a friend	Listen as a character in a Spanish soap opera describes his ex-girlfriend. What does he think her good qualities are? What does he think her shortcomings are? Can you understand why he broke up with her?	**pp. 56–61** *Vocabulario en contexto* **p. 62** Actividad 5 **p. 63** Actividades 6–7 **p. 64** Actividad 8 **p. 65** Actividad 10
2 Hablar Talk about yourself in terms of how you see yourself	While you're talking to your Spanish teacher, you realize that she doesn't know the "real you." Tell her some things about yourself that would help her understand you.	**p. 66** Actividades 11–13 **p. 69** Actividad 18 **p. 74** Actividad 27
3 Leer Read and understand a description of someone	In a popular Spanish magazine, you see an interview with the actor who plays the part of a teenager, Carlos, in a TV show you have been watching. See if you can understand what he is saying about the character he plays: ¡No me gusta nada el chico! Él es muy inteligente, pero le gusta hablar y hablar de NADA. Es ridículo. Es muy impaciente y perezoso. Él no es ni simpático ni gracioso. Yo soy un actor . . . ¡no soy como Carlos!	**pp. 56–61** *Vocabulario en contexto* **p. 69** Actividad 17 **pp. 76–77** *Lectura*
4 Escribir Write a short paragraph describing yourself	The first issue of your school's online newspaper is called "Getting to Know You." Submit a brief profile of yourself. Mention what your family thinks of you and list some things you like to do. For example: Yo soy una chica deportista y muy sociable. Según mi familia, soy graciosa. Me gusta patinar y hablar por teléfono.	**p. 66** Actividades 11–13 **p. 69** Actividad 18 **p. 74** Actividad 27 **p. 75** Actividad 28 **p. 79** *Presentación escrita*
5 Pensar Demonstrate an understanding of cultural perspectives on friendship	Explain the differences between the terms *amigo* and *conocido* in Spanish-speaking cultures. How does this compare to words that we use in the United States?	**p. 78** *Perspectivas del mundo hispano*

2A Tu día en la escuela

▼ Chapter Objectives

Communication

By the end of this chapter you will be able to:

- Listen to and read descriptions of school subjects and schedules
- Talk and write about classes, school activities, and likes and dislikes
- Exchange information about classes and activities you and friends have in common

Culture

You will also be able to:

- Compare your school day with those of students in Spanish-speaking countries
- Compare sports and attitudes towards sports in the Spanish-speaking world and the United States

You will demonstrate what you know and can do:

- Presentación oral, p. 111
- Preparación para el examen, p. 115

You will use:

Vocabulary

- School subjects and schedules
- School supplies
- Class descriptions

Grammar

- Subject pronouns
- Present tense of *-ar* verbs

Exploración del mundo hispano

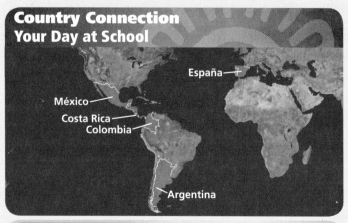

Country Connection
Your Day at School

España
México
Costa Rica
Colombia
Argentina

 realidades.com GO

 DK Reference Atlas

▶ *Videocultura y actividad*

Mapa global interactivo

Unos estudiantes, San Cristóbal de las Casas, México

Arte y cultura | Colombia

Colombian artist Fernando Botero (1932–) is among the best known and most respected Latin American artists. His works have been exhibited around the world in prestigious museums, galleries, and open-air places. Botero's style is unique and very recognizable. Pedrito Botero, shown in the painting, was the artist's son. He died in a car accident when he was four years old.

• Based upon the painting, how could you describe Botero's style?

"Pedrito" (1997), Fernando Botero ▶
Courtesy of the Marlborough Gallery, New York.

▼ **Objectives**

Read, listen to, and understand information about
▶ the school day
▶ subjects and classes
▶ school supplies

Vocabulario en contexto

El horario de Alicia

❝ Me gusta mucho mi **horario**. En la **primera hora**, tengo la **clase de** tecnología . . . ¡es mi clase **favorita**! Es **interesante** y **práctica**. Pero a veces es **difícil** ❞.

primera hora		tecnología
segunda hora		arte
tercera hora		ciencias sociales
cuarta hora		ciencias naturales
quinta hora		el almuerzo
sexta hora		español
séptima hora		matemáticas
octava hora		inglés
novena hora		educación física

Más vocabulario
décimo, -a   tenth

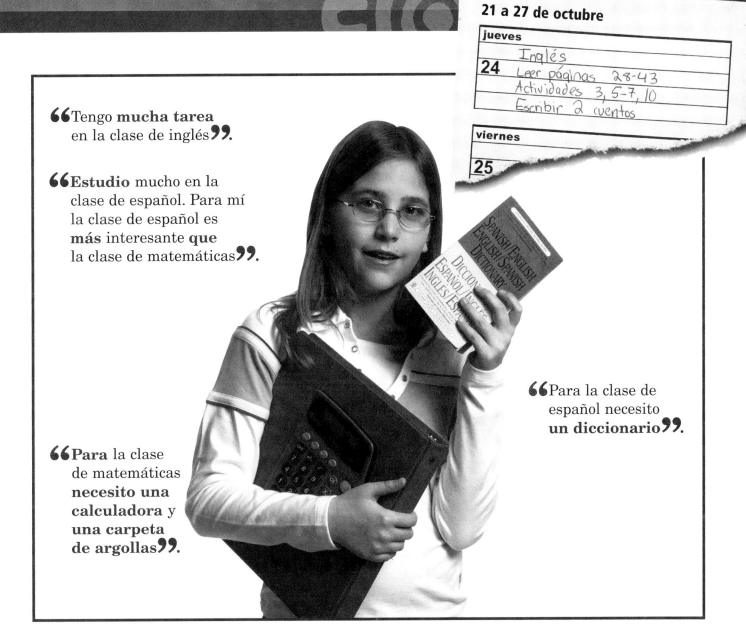

21 a 27 de octubre

jueves	
24	Inglés
	Leer páginas 28-43
	Actividades 3, 5-7, 10
	Escribir 2 cuentos

viernes	
25	

"Tengo **mucha tarea** en la clase de inglés".

"**Estudio** mucho en la clase de español. Para mí la clase de español es **más** interesante **que** la clase de matemáticas".

"Para la clase de español necesito **un diccionario**".

"**Para** la clase de matemáticas **necesito una calculadora** y **una carpeta de argollas**".

▼1 | Escuchar

¿Sí o no?

You will hear Alicia make several statements about her school day and schedule. Give a "thumbs-up" sign if what she says is true or a "thumbs-down" sign if what she says is false.

▼2 | Escuchar

El horario de Alicia

Listen to Alicia as she describes her class schedule. Touch the picture of each class as you hear it.

Más práctica	GO
realidades.com	print	
Instant Check	✔
Guided WB pp. 53–58	✔ ✔
Core WB pp. 31–32	✔ ✔
Comm. WB p. 35	✔ ✔
Hispanohablantes WB p. 52	✔

El primer día de clases

Es el primer día de clases en la Escuela Bilingüe de la Ciudad de México.

México

la Srta. Santoro

Teresa

Claudia

el Sr. Treviño

Antes de leer

Strategy

Using context clues You can often guess the meaning of new words by reading the words around them. Understanding what the rest of the sentence or paragraph is about is helpful in figuring out the meaning of individual words.

• Based on the words around it, what does *enseña* mean in panel 2?

1. What classes do you have every day? What classes do you expect the students in the *Videohistoria* to have?

2. Scan the text to find three classes that the students at the Escuela Bilingüe have. Do you have these classes?

3. Use the photos to see if you can guess what the problem is with Claudia's schedule. Then read the *Videohistoria* to find out whether your prediction was correct or not.

Claudia: Teresa, ¿qué clase **tienes** en la primera hora?

Teresa: Tengo la clase de inglés.

Claudia: ¿**Quién enseña** la clase de inglés?

Teresa: El señor Marín. Es un profesor muy **divertido.** ¿Y tú? ¿Qué clase tienes en la primera hora?

Claudia: Tengo la clase de matemáticas. Me gusta mucho. Para mí es muy **fácil.** Y, ¿qué tienes en la segunda hora?

Teresa: La clase de educación física.

Teresa: Y en la segunda hora, ¿qué clase tienes, Claudia?

Claudia: A ver . . . En la segunda hora, tengo la clase de matemáticas. ¡Y también tengo la clase de matemáticas en la tercera, en la cuarta, en la quinta y en la sexta hora!

Teresa: Necesitas hablar con el señor Treviño, en la oficina.

Claudia: Buena idea.

Claudia: Buenos días, señor Treviño. Necesito hablar con Ud. Tengo la clase de matemáticas . . .

Sr. Treviño: Sí, sí, Claudia, pero ahora no es posible. Mañana.

Srta. Santoro: Buenos días, estudiantes. Las matemáticas son muy interesantes y prácticas, ¿verdad?

Estudiantes: Sí, profesora.

Srta. Santoro: Y es muy importante **estudiar** y trabajar mucho . . .

Srta. Santoro: ¿Claudia?

Claudia: ¡Tengo seis clases de matemáticas hoy!

Srta. Santoro: ¡Seis! Es **aburrido**, ¿no? . . .

▼**3** Leer • Escribir

¿Comprendes?

Read each sentence. On your paper, write *sí* if the sentence is correct or *no* if it is incorrect.

1. Es el primer día de clases.
2. A Teresa le gusta la clase de inglés.
3. Para Claudia, la clase de matemáticas es difícil.
4. Claudia tiene la clase de educación física en la segunda hora.
5. Según la Srta. Santoro, la clase de matemáticas es muy práctica.
6. Tener seis clases de matemáticas es interesante.

▼**4** Pensar • Escribir

¿Dónde están?

Where are the students and faculty of the Escuela Bilingüe? Write the numbers 1–5 on your paper, and then beside each number write the name of the character who belongs in the room. Base your answers on the *Videohistoria*.

Claudia
Teresa
~~el Sr. Marín~~
la Srta. Santoro
~~el Sr. Treviño~~

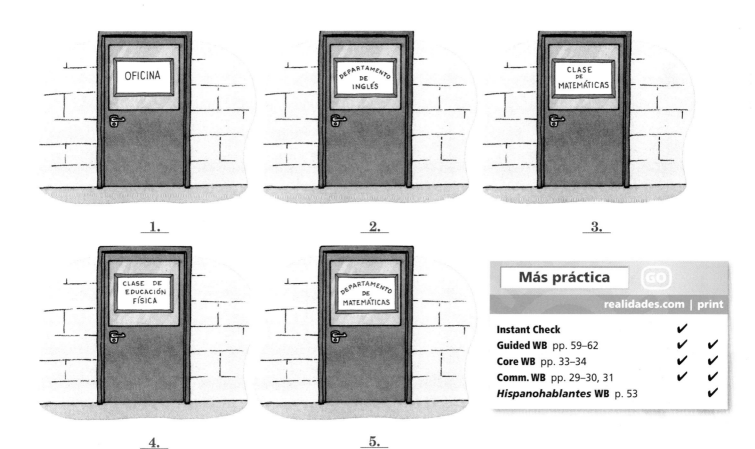

1.   2.   3.

4.   5.

Más práctica GO		
realidades.com | print		
Instant Check	✔	
Guided WB pp. 59–62	✔	✔
Core WB pp. 33–34	✔	✔
Comm. WB pp. 29–30, 31	✔	✔
Hispanohablantes **WB** p. 53		✔

Vocabulario en uso

▼**5** Leer • Escribir

Un horario

Read the list of classes offered at a school in Querétaro, Mexico, that specializes in the arts. On your paper, answer the questions about the schedule.

México

1. ¿Cuántas clases hay cada *(each)* semana?

2. ¿Cuántas horas de inglés hay?

3. ¿Cuántas clases de ciencias sociales hay?

4. ¿Cuántas clases de ciencias naturales hay?

5. Escribe los nombres de las diferentes clases de arte.

CENTRO DE EDUCACIÓN ARTÍSTICA

"IGNACIO MARIANO DE LAS CASAS"

PRIMER SEMESTRE

Español	5 h semanales
Matemáticas	5 h semanales
Historia universal	3 h semanales
Educación cívica y ética	3 h semanales
Biología	3 h semanales
Introducción a la física	3 h semanales
Inglés	3 h semanales
Danza	3 h semanales
Teatro	3 h semanales
Artes plásticas	3 h semanales
Música	3 h semanales

Total 37 h semanales

▼**6** Leer • Pensar

¿Qué les gusta?

Read the descriptions of the students below. Then, number your paper 1–6 and write the name of the class that you think each student would like.

1. A Juan le gusta mucho usar la computadora.

2. Sarita es muy deportista.

3. A Roberto le gusta leer.

4. A Miguel le gustan los números.

5. Gabriela es artística y le gusta pintar.

6. A Carolina le gusta hablar con amigos en México.

> inglés
> educación física
> matemáticas
> español
> arte
> tecnología

▼**7** | 👥 | **Leer · Hablar**

¿Estás de acuerdo?

Yolanda has interviewed her classmates for her school newspaper, *El Diario San Miguel,* to find out what they think about their classes.

❶ Number your paper 1–6. Read the article and based on your own classes, write *sí* if you agree with each statement or *no* if you disagree.

❷ Now tell your partner how you would change each statement that you disagree with in order to express your own opinion.

PUEBLA, MÉXICO   22 DE SEPTIEMBRE

EL DIARIO SAN MIGUEL

Periódico de la Escuela San Miguel   TERCERA EDICIÓN

LAS CLASES EN LA ESCUELA SAN MIGUEL

¿Te gustan tus clases? Las opiniones de los estudiantes de la Escuela San Miguel son muy diferentes.

Alejandro Zarzalejos, octavo año

"La clase de inglés no es muy difícil. Me gusta leer y escribir". **1.**

Ángel Suzuki, séptimo año

"La clase de matemáticas es divertida. La profesora es buena". **2.**

Laura Rodríguez, séptimo año

"Mi clase favorita es la educación física. Me gusta mucho el fútbol". **3.**

Pilar Soriano, octavo año

"La tecnología es muy aburrida. No me gusta nada jugar videojuegos". **4.**

Sara Martínez, octavo año

"El arte es interesante y la profesora es muy talentosa. Me gusta mucho dibujar". **5.**

Luis Soto, séptimo año

"La clase de español es fácil. Me gusta la tarea". **6.**

Mi horario

Write out your class schedule. Copy the chart on a separate sheet of paper and provide the information for each of your classes.

Modelo

Hora	Clase	Profesor(a)
la primera hora	la clase de inglés	la Sra. Sánchez

▼ Exploración del lenguaje

Connections between Latin, English, and Spanish

Many words in English and Spanish are based on Latin. Seeing the relationship between these words will help expand your English or Spanish vocabulary. Look at the list of Latin root forms for the numbers one through ten.

Try it out! For each Roman numeral listed, choose one of the root forms (if more than one is listed) and write down a Spanish and an English word you know that are based on that root.

Try it out! The Roman year used to begin with the month of March. Knowing that, can you explain why *septiembre, octubre, noviembre,* and *diciembre* use the Latin root forms for seven, eight, nine, and ten?

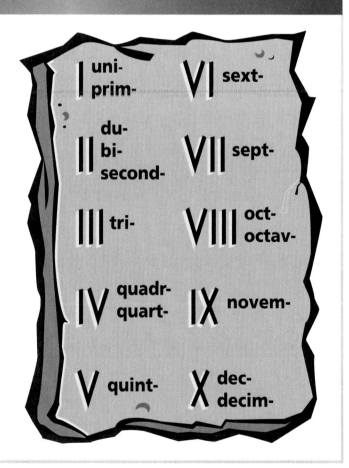

I uni- prim-
II du- bi- second-
III tri-
IV quadr- quart-
V quint-
VI sext-
VII sept-
VIII oct- octav-
IX novem-
X dec- decim-

Fondo Cultural | España

Many Spanish words are derived from Latin because Spain was once part of the Roman Empire. Rome occupied most of Spain from about 209 B.C. to 586 A.D. During that time, massive public structures, including aqueducts and theaters, were built. Some of these, such as the aqueduct that towers over the modern city of Segovia, are still standing. The Latin name for Spain was *Hispania*.

- Can you see the similarity between *Hispania* and the country's name in Spanish, *España*?

El Acueducto de Segovia

▼9 | 🗣👥 **| Hablar**

Mucha tarea

With a partner, ask and tell if you have homework in each class.

▶ **Modelo**

A —*¿Tienes mucha tarea en la clase de <u>matemáticas</u>?*

B —*Sí, tengo mucha tarea.*

o: —*No, no tengo mucha tarea.*

o: —*No estudio <u>matemáticas</u>.*

Estudiante A

Estudiante B

¡Respuesta personal!

▼10 Escribir

Me gusta más . . .

On your paper, write sentences stating which of the two classes you like better and why. Use the list of adjectives to help with your responses. Save your paper for Actividad 11.

aburrida	difícil
divertida	fácil
interesante	práctica

Modelo
Me gusta más la clase de español. Es divertida.
o: *Me gusta más la clase de inglés. No es aburrida.*
o: *No me gusta ni la clase de español ni la clase de inglés.*

1. MÚSICA / ESPAÑOL
2. ARTE / EDUCACIÓN FÍSICA
3. INGLÉS / MATEMÁTICAS
4. CIENCIAS SOCIALES / CIENCIAS NATURALES
5. TECNOLOGÍA / MÚSICA
6. CIENCIAS SOCIALES / MATEMÁTICAS

▼11 |  | Hablar

¿Qué te gusta más?

With a partner, ask and tell which classes from Actividad 10 you like best and why.

 Modelo
A —*¿Te gusta más la clase de <u>inglés</u> o la clase de <u>español</u>?*
B —*A ver . . . Para mí, la clase de <u>español</u> es más divertida que la clase de <u>inglés</u>.*

▼Fondo Cultural | El mundo hispano

Studying English While you're in Spanish class at your school, large numbers of Spanish-speaking students are studying to learn the most popular foreign language worldwide: English. Many children begin to study English in grade school and continue through high school. They often attend special language school for additional English classes. When visiting a Spanish-speaking country, you might easily find someone who is eager to practice his or her English skills with you in exchange for helping you improve your Spanish.

• Why do you think English is so popular in other countries? Are you studying Spanish for similar reasons?

Estudiantes mexicanos en una clase de inglés

El español en la comunidad

Do you know if there are any opportunities to learn Spanish outside of your school in your community? Use the Internet, look through college brochures, or look in the phone book to see if there are any Spanish classes or private lessons offered close to where you live.

• Why do you think people in your community would want to study Spanish?

▼12 | (Talk!) | Escribir • Hablar

Y tú, ¿qué dices?

1. ¿Qué clase te gusta más?
2. ¿Cómo es la clase?
3. ¿En qué hora tienes la clase?
4. ¿Quién enseña la clase?
5. ¿Tienes mucha tarea en la clase?

Me gusta más la clase de música.

Gramática

Subject pronouns

The subject of a sentence tells who is doing the action.
You often use people's names as the subject:

Gregorio escucha música.   *Gregory listens to music.*   **Ana** canta y baila.   *Ana sings and dances.*

You also use subject pronouns *(I, you, he, she, we, they)* to tell
who is doing an action. The subject pronouns replace people's names:

Él escucha música.   *He listens to music.*   **Ella** canta y baila.   *She sings and dances.*

Here are all the subject pronouns in Spanish:

yo	I	nosotros nosotras	we we
tú	you *(familiar)*	vosotros vosotras	you you
usted (Ud.)	you *(formal)*	ustedes (Uds.)	you *(formal)*
él ella	he she	ellos ellas	they they

Tú, usted, ustedes, and *vosotros(as)* all mean "you."

- Use *tú* with family, friends, people your age or younger, and anyone
  you call by his or her first name.

- Use *usted* with adults you address with a title, such as *señor, señora,
  profesor(a),* etc. *Usted* is usually written as *Ud.*

- In Latin America, use *ustedes* when speaking to two or more people,
  regardless of age. *Ustedes* is usually written as *Uds.*

- In Spain, use *vosotros(as)* when speaking to two or more people you
  call *tú* individually: *tú + tú = vosotros(as).* Use *ustedes* when talking
  to two or more people you call *usted* individually.

If a group is made up of males only, or of both males and females
together, use the masculine forms: *nosot**ros**, vosot**ros**, ell**os.***

If a group is all females, use the feminine forms:
*nosot**ras**, vosot**ras**, ell**as.***

You can combine a subject pronoun and a name
to form a subject.

Alejandro y yo = **nosotros**   Pepe y tú = **ustedes**

Carlos y ella = **ellos**   Lola y ella = **ellas**

Más ayuda   **realidades.com**

▶ **GramActiva** Video
Tutorials: Present indicative, Pronouns,
  Subject Pronouns, Subjects

✎ **GramActiva** Activity

▼13 | 👥 | Escuchar • Hablar • GramActiva

¡Señala!

Your teacher will name several subject pronouns. Point to people in the classroom who represent the pronoun you hear. After you have practiced with your teacher, practice with a partner.

▼14 Escribir

¿Es ella?

On your paper, write the subject pronouns you would use to talk about these people.

Modelo
Gloria
Ella.

1. Carlos
2. Felipe y yo
3. Pablo, Tomás y Anita
4. María y Sarita
5. el señor Treviño
6. tú y Esteban

▼15 Hablar

¿Tú, Ud. o Uds.?

Tell whether you would use *tú*, *Ud.*, or *Uds.* with these people.

1.
2.
3.
4.

5.
6.
7.
8.

Más práctica (GO)

realidades.com | print

Instant Check	✔	
Guided WB pp. 63–64	✔	✔
Core WB p. 35	✔	✔
Comm. WB pp. 32, 35–36, 127	✔	✔
Hispanohablantes **WB** pp. 54–57		✔

Gramática

Present tense of -ar verbs

You already know that the infinitive forms of Spanish verbs always end in *-ar, -er,* or *-ir.*

The largest group of verbs end in *-ar. Hablar* is one of these *-ar* verbs.

In order to express who is doing an action, you have to use verbs in ways other than in the infinitive form. To do this, you have to drop the *-ar* ending and make changes.

To create the forms of most *-ar* verbs, first drop the *-ar* from the infinitive, saving the stem:

hablar → habl-

Then add the verb endings *-o, -as, -a, -amos, -áis,* or *-an* to the stem.

Here are the forms of *hablar:*

(yo)	**hablo**	(nosotros) (nosotras)	**hablamos**
(tú)	**hablas**	(vosotros) (vosotras)	**habláis**
Ud. (él) (ella)	**habla**	Uds. (ellos) (ellas)	**hablan**

¿Recuerdas?

You already know many *-ar* verbs, such as *cantar* and *bailar.*

In Spanish, the present tense form of a verb can be translated into English in two ways:

Hablo español. *I speak Spanish.*
  I am speaking Spanish.

The verb endings always indicate who is doing the action. Because of this, you can often use the verb without a subject:

Hablo inglés.

¿Hablas español?

Subject pronouns are often used for emphasis or clarification.

Ella habla inglés pero **él** habla español.

Más ayuda   realidades.com

 GramActiva Video
Tutorials: Subject and verb agreement, Verbs, *-ar* verbs, Singular and Plural, Definite and Indefinite Articles
Animated Verbs

 Canción de hip hop: En la clase

 GramActiva Activity

▼**16** | 🔊 | Escuchar • Pensar • GramActiva

¿Una mano o dos?

You will hear eight *-ar* verbs. If the ending tells you one person is performing the action, raise one hand. If the ending tells you more than one person is doing something, raise both hands.

Strategy

Listening for information
Always listen carefully for the endings on verbs to know who is doing the action.

▼17 Pensar • Escribir

El detective

Number your paper 1–10. Play the detective and figure out what everyone is doing by matching the sentences with the correct names under the magnifying glass.

1. ___ estudia mucho en la clase.
2. ___ hablan con amigos.
3. ___ pasas mucho tiempo en la clase.
4. ___ usamos la computadora.
5. ___ dibujan muy bien.
6. ___ no montas en monopatín.
7. ___ hablamos español.
8. ___ escuchas música.
9. ___ baila con Carolina.
10. ___ patinan en el parque.

Tú
María y Graciela
Federico y yo
Carlos

▼18 Escribir • Hablar

¿Qué estudian?

Number your paper 1–6. Look at the pictures and tell what these people are studying.

Modelo
Tomás
Tomás estudia música.

1. Laura

2. Josefina, Elena y yo

3. tú

4. Catalina y José

5. Joaquín y tú

6. yo

▼19 | ♻ | Escribir

En la escuela

On your paper, use verbs from the box to complete the sentences about what different activities take place during school.

1. Lupe y Guillermo ____ mucho en la clase de arte.

2. Tú ____ la computadora en la clase de tecnología.

3. Yo ____ una calculadora y una carpeta para la clase de matemáticas.

4. Tomás y yo ____ deportes en la clase de educación física.

5. ¿Quién ____ la clase de ciencias naturales?

6. Marta ____ mucho en la clase de español.

Modelo

Yo estudio mucho en la clase de español.

necesitar	hablar	practicar	enseñar
dibujar	usar	patinar	bailar

▼20 | 👥 | Escuchar • Hablar • GramActiva

Juego

❶ Work with a partner and tear a sheet of paper into eight pieces of equal size. Write a different subject pronoun on each piece (*yo, tú, él, ella, Ud., nosotros, ellas, Uds.*). Place the subject pronouns face down in a pile.

❷ Your teacher will say an infinitive. One partner will select the top piece of paper from the pile, read the subject pronoun, and say the correct verb form. A correct answer earns one point. Place the "used" subject pronouns in a separate pile. Take turns selecting from the pile and answering.

❸ When your teacher calls time, shuffle the pieces of paper with subject pronouns and place them in a new pile face down. When the next verb is read aloud, continue play. The partner with the most correct answers is the winner.

En una escuela de México

Más práctica GO

realidades.com | print

Instant Check	✔	
Guided WB pp. 65–66	✔	✔
Core WB pp. 36–37	✔	✔
Comm. WB pp. 33–34, 37	✔	✔
Hispanohablantes **WB** pp. 58–61		✔

▼21 | 🔊 | Escuchar • Escribir

Escucha y escribe

Listen to a student describe this photo of himself and other students during their *recreo*. Write what you hear.

El recreo

▼ Fondo Cultural

El recreo In Spanish-speaking countries, students usually have *el recreo* (recess or break) in the school patio. Students take time to relax and spend time with friends, eat a snack, or participate in activities such as a quick game of basketball, soccer, or volleyball.

• How is this similar to your school? How is it different?

▼22 Leer • Escribir

Durante el recreo

During recess, Lola and the others at the Escuela Rubén Darío are always busy doing something. Based on their personality traits, match the students to the activity they would most likely be doing. After you have matched the person with the activity, write complete sentences on your paper describing what everyone does during *el recreo*.

1. yo *(deportista)*
2. Isabel y Carmen *(artísticas)*
3. Geraldo y yo *(estudiosos)*
4. tú *(sociable)*
5. el Sr. Campo *(trabajador)*

a. enseñar una clase de español
b. usar una calculadora para la tarea
c. dibujar en la cafetería
d. practicar deportes
e. hablar con amigos

Actividades y más actividades

1 Work with a partner. Look at the model for Step One below. Copy the Venn diagram on a sheet of paper. Label the oval on the left *Yo*. Label the oval on the right with the name of your partner. Label the overlapping area *Nosotros* or *Nosotras*.

2 From the word box, choose five activities you do a lot. Write your activities in the oval labeled *Yo*. Be sure to use the appropriate verb in the *Yo* form. Look at the model for Step Two below.

hablar por teléfono	dibujar
estudiar	cantar
hablar español	nadar
montar en bicicleta	bailar
pasar tiempo con amigos	trabajar
practicar deportes	escuchar música
usar la computadora	

Modelo
Step One

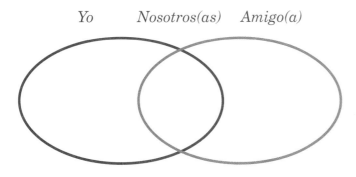

Yo   Nosotros(as)   Amigo(a)

Modelo
Step Two

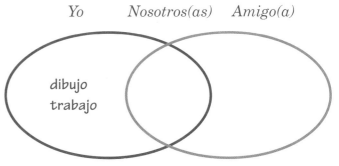

Yo   Nosotros(as)   Amigo(a)

dibujo
trabajo

3 Interview your partner. Ask questions to find out the five activities your partner wrote in the diagram. When you find an activity that your partner does, write it in the oval labeled with his or her name. Be sure to use the appropriate verb form. Look at the model for Step Three below.

4 Compare the two sides of your diagram. Write the activities that you and your partner both do in the center. Be sure to use the appropriate verb form. Look at the model for Step Four below. Then, use the completed diagram to write at least five complete sentences telling what you and/or your partner usually do.

 Modelo

A —¿Dibujas mucho?
B —A ver . . . No, no dibujo mucho.
A —Pues, ¿trabajas mucho?
B —Sí, trabajo mucho.

¿Recuerdas?

When you answer in the negative, you often use *no* twice. The first *no* answers the question. The second no goes before the verb and means "not."

Modelo
Step Three

Yo   Nosotros(as)   Amigo(a)

dibujo
trabajo   trabaja

Modelo
Step Four

Yo   Nosotros(as)   Amigo(a)

dibujo   trabajamos   trabaja
trabajo

▼24 Escribir

Los fines de semana

You are writing a letter to your friend Pablo who lives in Chile. Use the words that you have already learned to tell him what you and the people you know do on weekends (*los fines de semana*). Be sure to add words like *a veces* and *mucho*.

29 de septiembre

Querido Pablo: _____

¿Cómo estás? Aquí los fines de semana son muy divertidos y muy ocupados. El viernes yo __1.__ . El sábado mi amigo(a) y yo __2.__ . El domingo mis amigos __3.__ . El sábado el/la profesor(a) de español __4.__ . El viernes mi familia __5.__ . ¿Y tú? ¿Cómo pasas los fines de semana?

¡Escríbeme pronto!

▼25 Leer • Pensar

Los números mayas

Long before the Spaniards set foot in the Americas, many different civilizations already existed here. One of these, the Maya, lived in southern Mexico and Central America, where their descendants still make their home. One of the accomplishments of the ancient Maya was the development of a system of mathematics.

Conexiones | Las matemáticas

The Maya used three symbols to write numbers: a dot •, a bar ▬▬▬ , and a drawing of a shell. The dot equals 1, the bar equals 5, and the shell equals 0. Mayan numbers were written from bottom to top, not from left to right. Look at the Mayan numbers below.

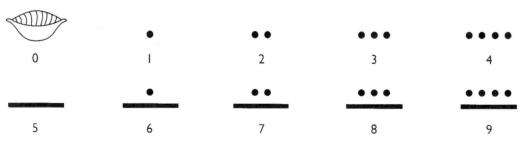

What would these Mayan numbers be in our numbering system?

1. ▬▬▬ 2. •••• ▬▬ 3. •• ▬▬▬▬

Now write these numbers in the Mayan system.

4. 13 5. 16 6. 19

Are you familiar with any other numbering systems that remind you of the Mayan system?

▼ Pronunciación | 🔊 | 💬

The letter c

In Spanish the pronunciation of the letter *c* depends on the letter that follows it.

When the letter *c* comes before *a, o, u,* or another consonant, it is pronounced like the *c* in *cat.* Listen to and say these words:

computadora	**ca**ntar	es**cu**ela
tampo**co**	**có**mo	to**car**
correr	practi**car**	**Car**los

When the letter *c* comes before *e* or *i*, most Spanish speakers pronounce it like the *s* in *Sally.* Listen to and say these words:

ve**ces**	so**ci**able	gra**ci**oso	gra**ci**as
ha**cer**	on**ce**	do**ce**	tre**ce**

Try it out! Listen to this rhyme. Listen particularly for the sound of the letter *c.* Then repeat the rhyme.

> **Cero más cuatro,**
> **o cuatro más cero,**
> **siempre¹ son cuatro.**
> **¿No es verdadero²?**
>
> ¹always   ²true

Say the rhyme again, first replacing *cuatro* with *doce,* then replacing *cuatro* with *trece.* Then say the rhyme quickly several times.

▼26 | 💬 | ♻ | Escribir • Hablar

Y tú, ¿qué dices?

1. En tu escuela, ¿quién enseña la clase de arte? ¿Quién enseña la clase de educación física?

2. En tu escuela, ¿quién canta muy bien *(well)*? ¿Quién dibuja muy bien?

3. ¿Escuchan tus amigos(as) mucha música? ¿Bailan bien tú y tus amigos(as)?

4. ¿Qué estudias en la primera hora?

5. ¿Qué clase tienes en la tercera hora?

Una estudiante en la clase de español

Lectura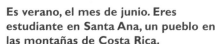

¡Estudiar español es divertido!

Consider what an immersion experience in Spanish would be like for you as you read this brochure from a Spanish language school in Costa Rica.

Strategy

Using photos
Look at the photos to help you understand the contents of a brochure or advertisement.

Costa Rica

La Escuela Español Vivo

¡Una experiencia fabulosa en Costa Rica!
¡Estudia español con nosotros en la Escuela Español Vivo!

Es verano, el mes de junio. Eres estudiante en Santa Ana, un pueblo en las montañas de Costa Rica.

¿Y cómo es una clase? Hay cinco estudiantes en tu clase. Uds. escuchan, hablan y practican el español todo el día. También usan la computadora.

En la escuela hay estudiantes de muchos países: Estados Unidos, Inglaterra, Francia, Brasil, Canadá, Japón, India, Sudáfrica y otros. ¡Todos estudian español!

Los sábados y los domingos hay actividades muy interesantes: visitar un volcán o un parque nacional, nadar en el océano Pacífico ... ¡y más!

sábados/domingos
- visitar un volcán
- visitar un parque nacional
- nadar en el océano Pacífico

El horario de clases en la escuela es:

hora	lunes a viernes
08:00–10:30	Clases de español
10:30–11:00	Recreo
11:00–13:00	Clases de español
13:00–14:00	Almuerzo
14:00–15:30	Conversaciones
15:30–16:30	Clase de música y baile

¿Por qué la Escuela Español Vivo?

- **La naturaleza de Costa Rica** en el pueblo de Santa Ana
- **Amigos de muchos países**
- **Mucha práctica y conversación en español**
- **Clases de música y baile**
- **Excursiones los sábados y domingos**

¿Comprendes?

1. When does the program take place?

2. Describe what a class is like.

3. What activities are offered on the weekends?

4. How many hours are spent on learning and using Spanish each week?

5. Would you like to study Spanish in Costa Rica? Why or why not?

Más práctica · GO

realidades.com | print

Guided WB p. 67	✔	✔
Comm. WB pp. 38, 128	✔	✔
Hispanohablantes WB pp. 62–63		✔
Cultural Reading Activity	✔	

▼ Fondo Cultural | El mundo hispano

La hora in Spanish-speaking countries is usually shown using the 24-hour clock on official schedules and timetables. Times in the morning are shown as 00:00 (midnight) through 11:59 (11:59 A.M.), 1:00 P.M. is shown as 13:00, 2:00 P.M. is 14:00, and so on.

- Look at the times in the *horario* from the brochure. What times are the conversation class and the music and dance classes?

En una estación de trenes de Madrid

La cultura en vivo

Aficionados al fútbol

El fútbol (soccer) is the favorite sport in most Spanish-speaking countries. In fact, it is the most popular sport in the entire world. It has grown in popularity in the United States over the past years. As with other sports you are familiar with, *fútbol* has loyal fans, cheers, team songs, and sometimes cheerleaders. If you attended a game in Venezuela at the Escuela Secundaria Bolívar you might hear the following chant:

Chiquitibúm a la bim bom bam
A la bío
A la bao
A la bim bom bam
¡Bolívar! ¡Bolívar!
¡Ra, ra, ra!

Jugando al fútbol, Rosario, Argentina

Except for the school name, the words of this chant do not have any meaning.

Here's another cheer:

¡Se ve! ¡Se siente!	**You see it, you feel it!**
¡Bolívar está presente!	**Bolívar is here!**
¡Que sí, que no!	**Oh, yes, oh, no!**
¡Bolívar ya ganó!	**Bolívar has already won!**
¡A la bío, a la bao!	**¡A la bío! ¡A la bao!**
¡El otro está cansao!	**The other team is tired!**

Try it out! In groups of five, select one of the chants and use it for a model to create a chant for one of your school teams. Present it to the class.

Think about it! How are these cheers and fan enthusiasm similar to or different from the cheers at your school?

Aficionados al fútbol, Bogotá, Colombia

Presentación oral

Mis clases

Task

Imagine that a student from Costa Rica has just arrived at your school. Tell the student about some of your classes.

1 Prepare Fill in a chart with information about three of your classes. Use this chart to think through what you may want to say about these classes.

Hora	Clase	Comentarios	Profesor(a)
primera	español	me gusta hablar español	la Sra. Salinas
cuarta	arte	difícil	el Sr. Highsmith
octava	ciencias naturales	divertida	la Sra. Huerta

> **Strategy**
>
> **Using graphic organizers**
> Simple charts can help you organize your thoughts for a presentation.

2 Practice Go through your presentation several times. You can use your notes in practice, but your teacher may not want you to use them when presenting. Try to:

• mention the information about your classes and teachers

• use complete sentences and speak clearly

Modelo

En la primera hora tengo la clase de español. Me gusta hablar español. La clase es muy divertida.
La Sra. Salinas es la profesora.

3 Present Describe the three classes you selected.

4 Evaluation The following rubric will be used to grade your presentation.

Rubric	Score 1	Score 3	Score 5
How complete your preparation is	You have information written down but without the use of the chart.	You used the chart, but only partially completed it.	You used the chart and provided all the information.
Amount of information you give	You describe three classes but only provide one piece of information about each class.	You describe three classes, but only provide two pieces of information about each class.	You describe five classes and include all requested information.
How easily you are understood	You are very difficult to understand, using only isolated words and phrases.	You are understandable, but have frequent errors in vocabulary and/or grammar.	You are easily understood. Your teacher does not have to "decode" what you are trying to say.

México

With a population of more than 100 million people, Mexico is the most populous Spanish-speaking country. It has been shaped by ancient indigenous civilizations, European colonialism, and immigration, as well as by its proximity to the United States.

The Mayan city of Tulum, situated on a cliff overlooking the Caribbean, was a major port from about 1200 until the Spaniards arrived in the early 1500s. The Mayan civilization dates from 750 B.C., and includes ancient cities throughout southern Mexico, including the Yucatan Peninsula, and parts of Central America. Today many people in these areas speak one of approximately 30 languages and dialects that developed from ancient Maya.

¿Sabes que . . . ?

The butterfly reserve at El Rosario, Michoacán, lies in the mountains not far from Mexico City. From November through February every year, millions of monarch butterflies migrate to this area from the north, covering the branches of the area's tall pine trees.

Para pensar

These two pages show a brief overview of Mexico. If you were asked to create a similar overview of the United States, what would you highlight? Select five photographs and write a brief caption for each one. Share your results with a small group or the whole class.

Estados Unidos

México

Golfo de México

OCÉANO PACÍFICO

Belice

Guatemala

El Salvador

realidades.com GO

 Mapa global interactivo

 Reference Atlas

Mexico's most famous dance company, el Ballet Folklórico de México, is a world-class troupe of more than 75 dancers and musicians. For more than five decades, this company has been touring the globe and performing traditional Mexican dances such as the *jarabe tapatío*, (better known in the United States as the Mexican hat dance), *la culebra*, and the *tilingo lingo*. ▶

Mexico's capital is one of the largest cities in the world. It is also one of the oldest, dating back to 1500 B.C. It was here that the Aztecs built their capital, Tenochtitlán, in the 1300s. When the Spaniards arrived in 1519, Tenochtitlán had a population of more than 100,000— making it larger than most European cities of that time.

▲ Many families in Mexico spend Sundays together. A popular spot for families in Mexico City is Xochimilco, where they can relax on colorful boats while enjoying a meal and music. The canals of Xochimilco are remnants of *chinampas*, the "floating gardens" that helped feed Tenochtitlán and other ancient cities in the valley of Mexico.

Repaso del capítulo

Vocabulario y gramática

to talk about your school day

el almuerzo	lunch
la clase	class
la clase de . . .	. . . class
arte	art
ciencias naturales	science
ciencias sociales	social studies
educación física	physical education
español	Spanish
inglés	English
matemáticas	mathematics
tecnología	technology / computers
el horario	schedule
en la . . . hora	in the . . . hour (class period)
la tarea	homework

to describe school activities

enseñar	to teach
estudiar	to study
hablar	to talk

to talk about the order of things

*primero, -a	first
segundo, -a	second
*tercero, -a	third
cuarto, -a	fourth
quinto, -a	fifth
sexto, -a	sixth
séptimo, -a	seventh
octavo, -a	eighth
noveno, -a	ninth
décimo, -a	tenth

*Changes to *primer, tercer* before a masculine singular noun.

to talk about things you need for school

la calculadora	calculator
la carpeta de argollas	three-ring binder
el diccionario	dictionary
necesitas	you need
necesito	I need

to describe your classes

aburrido, -a	boring
difícil	difficult
divertido, -a	amusing, fun
fácil	easy
favorito, -a	favorite
interesante	interesting
más . . . que	more . . . than
práctico, -a	practical

other useful words

a ver . . .	let's see . . .
mucho	a lot
para	for
¿Quién?	Who?
(yo) tengo	I have
(tu) tienes	you have

subject pronouns

yo	I	nosotros nosotras	we we
tú	you *(fam.)*	vosotros vosotras	you you
usted (Ud.)	you *(form.)*	ustedes (Uds.)	you *(form.)*
él ella	he she	ellos ellas	they they

hablar *to talk*

hablo	hablamos
hablas	habláis
habla	hablan

For *Vocabulario adicional*, see pp. 268–269.

Más repaso (GO)   realidades.com | print

Instant Check	✔	
Puzzles	✔	
Core WB pp. 38–39		✔
Comm. WB pp. 129, 130–132	✔	✔

Preparación para el examen

On the exam you will be asked to . . .	Here are practice tasks similar to those you will find on the exam . . .	For review go to your print or digital textbook . . .
1 Escuchar Listen and understand as people talk about their new schedules and what they think of their classes	Listen to two students who have just attended some of the classes on their new schedules. a) Which class does each one like? Why? b) Which class does each one dislike? Why?	**pp. 86–91** *Vocabulario en contexto* **p. 87** Actividades 1–2 **p. 93** Actividad 7 **p. 96** Actividades 10–11
2 Hablar Talk about activities you and your friends have in common	To get to know you, your homeroom advisor asks you to talk or write about what you and your friends have in common, such as school subjects that you all study, and music or activities that you all like. For example, *cantamos.* You might also tell how you and your friends are different. For example, *Yo toco la guitarra y ellos practican deportes.*	**p. 96** Actividad 11 **p. 103** Actividad 21 **pp. 104–105** Actividad 23 **p. 111** *Presentación oral*
3 Leer Read and understand someone's e-mail description of his classes	Read this e-mail that your friend received from his e-pal. What does the e-pal study in school? What does he think of his classes? Do you agree or disagree? Why? *¿Cómo son mis clases? A ver . . . Yo tengo ocho clases. Estudio ciencias naturales, inglés, español, educación física, geografía, matemáticas, tecnología y ciencias sociales. ¡Me gusta más la clase de inglés! Necesito hablar inglés aquí en Ecuador, pero es MUY difícil. Mi clase de geografía es muy aburrida y mi clase de educación física es muy divertida. Y, ¿cómo son tus clases?*	**pp. 86–91** *Vocabulario en contexto* **p. 92** Actividad 5 **pp. 108–109** *Lectura*
4 Escribir Write your schedule including hour, class, and teacher's name, and give opinions about the classes	Write a note to a counselor listing reasons why you want to drop two of the classes on your schedule. What might be some reasons for wanting to change classes? You might say that your first hour class is boring and that your second hour class is difficult for you.	**p. 94** Actividad 8 **p. 95** Actividad 9 **p. 96** Actividad 10 **p. 111** *Presentación oral*
5 Pensar Demonstrate an understanding of cultural practices concerning sports	Think about the sports at your school that attract the most fans. Are these the same sports that are most popular in Spanish-speaking countries? How do spectators show their enthusiasm? How is this similar to or different from the United States?	**p. 110** *La cultura en vivo*

2B Tu sala de clases

▼ Chapter Objectives

Communication

By the end of this chapter you will be able to:

- Listen to and read conversations and notes about school
- Talk and write about classes, classrooms, and where things are located
- Exchange information while describing someone's location

Culture

You will also be able to:

- Compare perspectives towards school and uniforms in the Spanish-speaking world and the United States

You will demonstrate what you know and can do:

- Presentación escrita, p. 141
- Preparación para el examen, p. 145

You will use:

Vocabulary

- Classroom items and furniture
- Computers
- Words to describe location and possession

Grammar

- The verb *estar*
- Plurals of nouns and articles

Exploración del mundo hispano

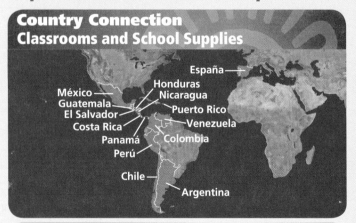

Country Connection
Classrooms and School Supplies

España
Honduras
Nicaragua
México
Guatemala
El Salvador
Puerto Rico
Costa Rica
Venezuela
Panamá
Colombia
Perú
Chile
Argentina

realidades.com **GO**

DK Reference Atlas

▶ *Videocultura y actividad*

🌐 *Mapa global interactivo*

Estudiantes mexicanos

Arte y cultura | México

Sor Juana Inés de la Cruz (1648–1695), born near Mexico City, was one of the greatest intellectuals of her time. She wrote poetry, essays, music, and plays. Sor Juana also defended a woman's right to an education at a time when few women had access to it. She entered a convent at the age of 19 and over the years built a library of several thousand books. Sor Juana's living quarters in the convent became a meeting place for other writers and intellectuals, who were drawn to her because of her intelligence and knowledge.

• How are various aspects of Sor Juana's life represented in this painting? If you were to pose for a portrait, what objects would represent you and your interests?

Retrato de Sor Juana Inés de la Cruz, siglo XVII ▶
Foto: Archivo Agencia El Universal

A primera vista | 🔊 | 📖

▼ Objectives

Read, listen to, and understand information about
▶ the classroom
▶ where objects are located

Vocabulario en contexto

la bandera

el reloj

el cartel

la puerta

las ventanas

el sacapuntas

la computadora

la papelera

el escritorio

la silla

> 66 ¡Hola! Me llamo Enrique. **Aquí está mi** sala de clases. Son las nueve y **los** estudiantes **están en** la clase de español. **Hay** muchos estudiantes en mi clase. ¿**Cuántos** estudiantes hay en **tu** clase? 99

la pantalla

el ratón

el teclado

la mesa

Para decir más ...
el disco compacto   compact disc
el DVD   DVD (disc)

—Elena, ¿es tu cuaderno?

—No, es el cuaderno **de** David.

La hoja de papel está **debajo del** bolígrafo.

El bolígrafo está **encima de la** hoja de papel.

El ratón está **al lado del** teclado.

La bandera está **detrás de** la computadora.

La silla está **delante de** la mesa.

▼1 | 🔊 | Escuchar

¿Qué hay en la sala de clases?

Look at Enrique's classroom. You will be asked if certain things are there. If you see the item mentioned, raise your hand and give a "thumbs-up" sign. If you don't see it, give a "thumbs-down" sign.

▼2 | 🔊 | Escuchar

En la sala de clases

Look at the picture of Enrique's classroom again. Listen to a description of various items in the room. As soon as you recognize an item, touch it.

Más práctica	GO	
realidades.com	print		
Instant Check	✔	
Guided WB pp. 69–72	✔	✔
Core WB pp. 40–41	✔	✔
Comm. WB p. 45	✔	✔
Hispanohablantes WB p. 72		✔

Un ratón en la clase

¿Qué pasa en la clase de ciencias sociales? Lee la historia.

México

Manolo

Teresa

Claudia

Carlos

Antes de leer

Strategy **Predicting outcomes** Look at the pictures before you read to help you predict what will happen.

• What is causing the disturbance in Teresa's class?

1. Find at least five cognates in the *Videohistoria*. How do these cognates help you understand the story?

2. Look at the photos in the *Videohistoria* and try to predict if Manolo will get away with his prank.

Claudia: ¿Qué es esto?

Teresa: Es mi hámster. Es para la clase de ciencias naturales.

Claudia: ¿Cómo se llama?

Teresa: Paquito.

Manolo: ¡Carlos! No tengo mi tarea.

Carlos: ¿Qué?

Manolo: Tengo una idea . . .

Carlos: ¡Un ratón! Profesora, ¡hay un ratón debajo de la silla!

Profesora: ¿Un ratón en la clase de ciencias sociales? **¿Dónde** está? ¿Dónde?

Estudiante: Ahora está debajo de la silla.

Manolo: Y ahora está al lado de la puerta. **Es un** ratón muy impaciente.

Teresa: ¡No es un ratón! Es mi hámster, y se llama Paquito.

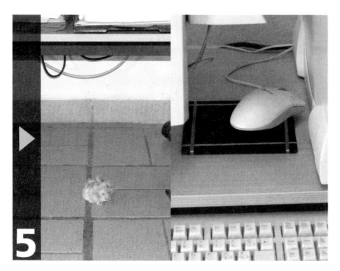

5

Claudia: ¡Está **allí,** delante de la mesa!

Teresa: ¡Ay, mi Paquito!

Manolo: Pues, ahora está detrás de la computadora.

Teresa: ¡Manolo! Es el ratón de la computadora. No es mi Paquito.

6

El director de la escuela, el Sr. Treviño, entra en la clase.

Carlos: ¡Ay! ¡Aquí está! Está en mi **mochila.**

Sr. Treviño: ¡Silencio, por favor!

7

Sr. Treviño: Teresa, hablamos en mi oficina.

Teresa: Sí, señor.

8

Profesora: Y ahora, Manolo, ¿tu tarea?

Manolo: Pues, profesora . . .

▼3 Leer

¿Comprendes?

Match each of the sentences with the *Videohistoria* character whom it describes.

el Sr. Treviño

Paquito

Claudia

Teresa

Manolo

1. No tiene la tarea.
2. Está debajo de la silla.
3. Tiene un hámster.
4. Es amiga de Teresa.
5. Es muy serio.

▼4 Leer • Escribir

Un hámster en la escuela

It's not a typical day at Claudia's school. Find out what is going on by putting the sentences below in the correct order. Rewrite the story on a separate sheet of paper.

a. El Sr. Treviño entra en la clase.

d. La profesora quiere *(wants)* la tarea de Manolo.

b. El hámster está debajo de la silla.

e. Teresa habla con *(with)* Claudia del ratón para la clase de ciencias naturales.

c. El Sr. Treviño y Teresa hablan en la oficina.

f. El hámster está en la mochila de Carlos.

Más práctica GO

realidades.com | print

Instant Check	✔	
Guided WB pp. 73–76	✔	✔
Core WB pp. 42–43	✔	✔
Comm. WB pp. 39–40, 41	✔	✔
Hispanohablantes WB p. 73		✔

Vocabulario en uso

▼5 Leer

¿Es lógico o no?

Juan Carlos is telling you about what he has in his backpack. Decide if what he is saying is logical or not. Number your paper from 1–6 and write *sí* if it is logical or *no* if it is not.

1. Un teclado está en mi mochila.
2. Hay un ratón en mi mochila.
3. Hay una mesa en mi mochila.
4. Un bolígrafo está en mi mochila.
5. Mi tarea está en mi mochila.
6. Hay una papelera en mi mochila.

▼6 Escribir

¿Qué hay?

Write the names of the things you see.

Modelo
Hay una bandera.

1.

2.

3.

4.

5.

6.

7.

8.

▼**7** **Leer • Escribir**

¿Dónde está?

Write the numbers from 1–9 on a sheet of paper. Complete the sentences to tell where the following items are located in Beto's bedroom. Choose from the words below and add the correct definite article.

al lado de
debajo de
delante de
detrás de
encima de

Modelo

El escritorio está debajo de la ventana.
La computadora está encima del escritorio.

1. El reloj está ___ mesa.
2. La papelera está ___ escritorio.
3. La silla está ___ escritorio.
4. El sacapuntas está ___ escritorio.
5. La computadora está ___ mesa.
6. El ratón está ___ teclado.
7. El cartel está ___ ventana.
8. La mochila está ___ silla.

Nota

When the preposition *de* is followed by the masculine definite article *el*, the contraction *del* must be used.

• La papelera está al lado **del** escritorio.

▼8 Escribir

¿Estás preparado(a) para la clase?

You want to make sure that you are prepared for class. Copy the checklist below onto your own paper. Place a check mark next to the items that you have and tell where they are.

el libro	✔	encima del escritorio
un cuaderno		
una carpeta		
la tarea		
un lápiz		
un bolígrafo		
un sacapuntas		
una mochila		
un diccionario		

▼9 | (Talk!) | ♻ | Hablar • Escribir

Juego

① Work with a partner. Your partner will face away from you and have a blank piece of paper and a pen or a pencil.

② Choose four classroom items and arrange them on your desk, putting objects on top of others, next to each other, and so forth.

③ Your partner will ask you questions about what is on your desk and how the items are positioned. Based on your answers, he or she will try to draw the arrangement on your desk.

④ When your teacher calls time, see how closely the picture matches the actual arrangement. Then switch roles.

▶ **Modelo**

A —¿Tienes un sacapuntas?
B —No, no tengo un sacapuntas.
A —¿Tienes una calculadora?
B —Sí, tengo una calculadora.
A —¿Dónde está?
B —Está encima de la carpeta.

Para decir más . . .

a la izquierda de   to the left of
a la derecha de   to the right of

▼ Exploración del lenguaje

Language through gestures

In Spanish, just as in English, nonverbal body language in the form of gestures, or *gestos,* is very important to communication.

You saw the expression *¡Ojo!* in the video *Un ratón en la clase.* The word literally means "eye," but it is used to mean "be careful" or "pay attention." It is usually accompanied by a gesture, and often people use the *¡Ojo!* gesture without saying the word.

¡Ojo!

Unas estudiantes en uniforme

▼ Fondo Cultural | El mundo hispano

School uniforms Many schools in Spanish-speaking countries require their students to wear uniforms. Often students wear a full uniform, like the ones you see in the photo. Sometimes the uniform consists of something more like a smock that is worn over a student's regular clothes and helps protect them from becoming dirty or torn during the school day.

• How are these uniforms similar to or different from those worn by students in the United States?

▼10 | (talk!) | Escribir • Hablar

Y tú, ¿qué dices?

Describe your classroom.

1. ¿Dónde está la puerta?
2. ¿Hay un reloj en tu clase? ¿Dónde está?
3. ¿Cuántos escritorios y sillas hay?
4. ¿Hay una bandera en tu clase? ¿Dónde está?
5. ¿Qué más *(What else)* hay en tu clase?

► Write about and discuss the location of people and things

► Listen to a description of the position of people in a photo

► Compare prices for backpacks in Spanish-speaking countries

Gramática

The verb *estar*

The -*ar* verbs you have used until now are called **regular verbs** because they follow a regular pattern. Verbs that do not follow a regular pattern are called **irregular verbs.**

Estar is irregular because the *yo* form doesn't follow a regular pattern and because the forms *estás, está,* and *están* require accent marks.

Use *estar* to tell how someone feels or where someone or something is located.

¿Recuerdas?

You have used the verb *estar* to ask how someone is.

• ¿Cómo **estás?**

• ¿Cómo **está** Ud.?

(yo)	estoy	(nosotros) (nosotras)	estamos
(tú)	estás	(vosotros) (vosotras)	estáis
Ud. (él) (ella)	está	Uds. (ellos) (ellas)	están

Más ayuda   **realidades.com**

▶ *GramActiva* Video
Tutorial: *Estar*
Animated Verbs

✎ *GramActiva* Activity

▼11 Leer

¿Están en clase hoy?

Your teacher asks you to take attendance. Find out who is present and who isn't by matching the people with the completion of the sentence.

1. Tú
2. Martina y Clarisa
3. Carmen y yo
4. Guillermo
5. Yo

a. está en clase hoy.
b. estoy en clase hoy.
c. no estás en clase hoy.
d. estamos en clase hoy.
e. no están en clase hoy.

▼12 Escribir

¡Hola! ¿Cómo estás?

Write the correct forms of *estar* on a separate sheet of paper.

Marcos: ¡Buenos días! ¿Cómo __1.__ Uds.?

Paula y Roberta: ¡Hola, Marcos! Nosotras __2.__ bien, gracias. ¿Y tú?

Marcos: __3.__ muy bien. ¿Dónde __4.__ Pedro y Juana?

Roberta: Pedro __5.__ en la sala de clases. Juana __6.__ en la oficina.

▼13 | (Talk!) | ♻ | Hablar

¿En qué clase están?

Following the model, take turns with a partner to give the correct forms of *estar*.

 ella

Modelo
Ella está en la clase de tecnología.

1. yo

2. los profesores

3.  la profesora

4. nosotros

5.  ella

6.  tú

▼14 | ♟♟ | Hablar

¿Están los amigos allí?

The following people are supposed to study together in the library, but nobody is there. Explain that they are not there and tell where they are by using the correct form of *estar* and any of the places listed below.

Modelo
Paco no está allí. Está en la clase de educación física.

1. Yo
2. María
3. Tú
4. Natalia y Roberto
5. Uds.
6. Timoteo

| estar |

en la clase de inglés
en la oficina del director
en la clase de matemáticas
en la sala de clases
en la clase de español
en la clase de arte

▼15 Hablar • Escribir

En mi clase

Look around your classroom. Tell where the following people and things are located in relationship to the word in parentheses. Use the verb *estar*, and follow the model.

Modelo
yo (mi silla)
Yo estoy en mi silla.

1. la papelera (el escritorio)
2. el teclado (la computadora)
3. los estudiantes (la sala de clases)
4. yo (mi escritorio)
5. mi mochila (la silla)
6. los estudiantes (el/la profesor(a))

▼16 | | Escuchar

¿Cierto o falso?

Write the numbers 1–6 on a sheet of paper. Listen to the statements about Javier's Spanish club photo and write *cierto* or *falso* based on the information provided as you view the photograph from *your* perspective.

▼17 |  | Hablar

¿Y dónde están todos?

Work with a partner. Using the club picture above, find out where the various students are located from *Javier's* perspective.

1. Julián y Mateo
2. Rosa
3. Sara
4. yo
5. el Sr. Salas
6. Lucita y José
7. Benito
8. Sara y yo

 Modelo
A —¿Y dónde está <u>Lucita</u>?
B —*Lucita está <u>encima del escritorio</u>.*

▼18 |  | Escribir • Hablar

Juego

Work with a partner. Write down the name of someone in the classroom. Your partner can only ask *sí* or *no* questions to find out the name. When your partner has guessed the mystery student's identity, switch roles.

 Modelo
A —¿Está al lado de Tomás?
B —No.
A —¿Está detrás de mí?
B —Sí.
A —¿Es Patricia?
B —Sí.

Para decir más ...	
a la izquierda to the left	detrás de mí behind me
a la derecha to the right	detrás de ti behind you

▼19 Leer • Pensar

Los precios de las mochilas en el mundo hispano

Conexiones | Las matemáticas

Most countries have their own currencies. In Mexico, people pay in *pesos*, in Peru they use *nuevos soles*, and so on. The value of each currency can go up or down daily in relation to other countries' currencies. For example, a dollar might be worth 10 Mexican pesos one day and 11 *pesos* the following day. Read the prices for *una mochila* in six different countries.

España 24 euros

México 425 pesos

Perú 80 nuevos soles

Venezuela 100 bolívares fuertes

Puerto Rico 25 dólares

Guatemala 200 quetzales

1. How much does a typical *mochila* cost in your community?
2. Convert the prices for *una mochila* into dollars. You can find a currency converter on the Internet.
3. How do these prices compare to those in your community? Why might the same item have different values in different countries?

▼20 Pensar • Escribir

De vacaciones

The following people are spending their vacations in various Spanish-speaking countries. Based on the currency they are using, say where they are. Use the information in Actividad 19 to help you.

Modelo
Clara usa quetzales.
Clara está en Guatemala.

1. Yo uso euros.
2. Ellos usan pesos.
3. Tú usas nuevos soles.
4. Ustedes usan quetzales.
5. Federico usa bolívares.

Más práctica	GO	
	realidades.com	print
Instant Check	✔	
Guided WB pp. 77–78	✔	✔
Core WB p. 44	✔	✔
Comm. WB pp. 42, 46	✔	✔
Hispanohablantes WB pp. 74–77		✔

Gramática

| ▼ **Objectives**
▶ **Identify and describe the location of objects around school**
▶ **Exchange information about the location of things in a classroom**

The plurals of nouns and articles

In Spanish, to make nouns plural you usually add *-s* to words ending in a vowel and *-es* to words ending in a consonant.

silla → sillas   teclado → teclados   cartel → carteles

Singular nouns that end in *z* change the *z* to *c* in the plural.

el lápiz → los lápices

The plural definite articles are *los* and *las*. Like *el* and *la*, they both mean "the."

las sillas   *the chairs*

The plural indefinite articles are *unos* and *unas*. They both mean "some" or "a few."

unos carteles   *some posters*

Singular	Plural
el reloj	los relojes
la ventana	las ventanas
un escritorio	unos escritorios
una mesa	unas mesas

¿Recuerdas?

You have used the definite and indefinite articles in the singular form.

el, la *the*

un, una *a (an)*

Más ayuda   realidades.com

GramActiva Video
Tutorials: Noun-adjective agreement, Singular-plural formation

Canción de hip hop: ¿Qué hay?

GramActiva Activity

▼21 | Leer • Hablar

¡A estudiar!

Marta and Berta are getting ready for school. Read the dialogue with a partner, completing the sentences with the correct definite articles.

Marta: ¿Dónde están __1.__ lápices?

Berta: Aquí están, en __2.__ mochila.

Marta: ¿Y tienes __3.__ bolígrafos y __4.__ libros?

Berta: No. Están allí, encima de __5.__ mesa, y debajo de __6.__ ventanas.

Marta: Ah, sí. ¿Y __7.__ cuadernos y __8.__ carpetas? ¿Dónde están?

Berta: Están encima de __9.__ mesa, y detrás de __10.__ computadoras.

▼22 |  | Escuchar • Hablar

Las palabras plurales

You will hear eight words. Say the plural form of the words as you hear them.

Modelo
You will hear: *el libro*
You will say: *los libros*

▼23 | | Escribir

Más plurales

On a sheet of paper, write the plural forms of the articles and nouns below.

1. el cuaderno
2. una clase
3. la bandera
4. una mochila
5. la papelera
6. un escritorio
7. el profesor
8. un pupitre

▼24 | (Talk?) | Hablar

Una mesa desordenada

Sometimes your classmates are disorganized and they leave their things all over the table. With a partner, look at the drawing and take turns asking and telling where different things are located.

▶ **Modelo**
A —*¿Dónde están las carpetas?*
B —*Las carpetas están debajo de los ratones.*

In some countries such as Mexico, Colombia, Costa Rica, and Chile, students attending public schools generally do not have lockers in which to store their things before each class. Most students carry the books and school supplies they need for the day in book bags. In some countries, such as Mexico, students will wear their gym clothes instead of their required school uniforms on the days they have physical education.

• If you didn't have a locker at school, what books and school supplies would you bring every day and which ones would you leave at home?

Estudiantes durante el descanso *(break)*, Santa Clara, Cuba

▼**25** | ♻ | Escribir

El armario de Ramón

You are looking at Ramón's messy locker. Write five sentences about what you see. Be sure to use the indefinite articles.

Modelo

Hay unos cuadernos.

▼26 | ♻ | Escribir

Necesito mucho

You need some of the things that the following people have. Look at the photos and write eight sentences following the model.

Modelo
Necesito <u>los cuadernos de Flor</u>.

Flor

Nota

In Spanish, you can express possession by using *de* and the name of the owner of the item.

• el escritorio **de** la profesora
the teacher's desk

1.

Ricardo

2.

el profesor

3.

Carmen

4.

el director

5.

Milagros

6.

Rosa

7.

Enrique

8.

Juan

▼27 | 🗨 | Hablar

Es el cuaderno de . . .

Work in a group of four. Each of you should choose a classroom object you have brought to class. Show your group what you have chosen. Your teacher will collect all the items, then place them in view in different parts of the classroom. Ask your group where your object is.

▶ **Modelo**
A —*¿Dónde está mi calculadora?*
B —*Tu calculadora está debajo de la silla de Margarita.*

Una clase de inglés

Look at this picture of an English class in Chile and write five sentences about what you see.

Modelo

El libro de Claudia está encima del escritorio.

En el dibujo hay . . .

Write at least three questions about the picture in Actividad 28, and then ask your partner those questions. Use some of the phrases in the box below.

¿Qué es esto?	¿Quién está . . . ?
¿Cuántos(as) . . . hay?	¿Hay . . . ?
¿Dónde está(n) . . . ?	¿Qué hay . . . ?

Modelo

A —*¿Cuántos estudiantes hay en la clase?*
B —*Hay cuatro estudiantes.*
A —*¿Dónde está la profesora?*
B —*Está al lado de la bandera.*

El español en el mundo del trabajo

School districts in the United States have many positions in which employees need to speak Spanish. For example, school counselors work with new students and parents from Spanish-speaking countries. Counselors help them set up schedules, talk about school policies, and answer questions. Both the parents and the new students feel much more comfortable when the counselor can communicate with them in Spanish.

- Does your district need employees who speak Spanish? In what other jobs within a school system would speaking Spanish be helpful?

▼30 | (Talk!) | Escribir

Y tú, ¿qué dices?

Look around your classroom and write at least five sentences describing objects and people that you see. Be sure to tell where they are located.

Más práctica GO		
	realidades.com | print	
Instant Check	✔	
Guided WB pp. 79–80	✔	✔
Core WB pp. 45–46	✔	✔
Comm. WB pp. 43–44, 46–47	✔	✔
Hispanohablantes **WB** pp. 79–81		✔

▼ Pronunciación | 🔊 | (Talk!)

The letter *g*

In Spanish, the letter *g* sounds like *g* in *go* when it is followed by *a*, *o*, or *u*, although it often has a slightly softer sound than in English. Listen to and say the following words:

Gustavo	domin**go**	ten**go**
a**go**sto	pre**gu**nta	lue**go**
ami**go**	ar**go**llas	**ga**to

In Spanish, the letter *g* sounds like the letter *h* in *hot* when it is followed by *e* or *i*. Listen to and say the following words. Some of these words you have not yet heard or seen. Can you guess the meanings of these cognates?

inteli**ge**nte	**ge**neroso	**ge**neral
gimnasio	tecnolo**gí**a	biolo**gí**a

Try it out! See if you can guess how to pronounce the following Spanish first names. Say each name in Spanish, keeping in mind the pronunciation rules for the *g* sound.

Gabriela	Ángela	Gerardo
Gilberto	Gustavo	Rodrigo
Olga	Rogelio	Gregorio

Lectura

Lee este artículo sobre el UNICEF.

Strategy

Predicting outcomes
Think about what you would consider to be basic rights for children around the world. Jot down four of them on a piece of paper. As you read the article, see if your ideas are included.

El UNICEF y una convención para los niños[1]

¿Sabes que es un privilegio estar en una escuela, tener una mochila con libros, unos lápices, una calculadora, unas hojas de papel y un profesor bueno? En ciertas[2] naciones, ir a la escuela es difícil o no es posible.

El UNICEF es la organización internacional de las Naciones Unidas que trabaja para los niños. UNICEF es una sigla[3] inglesa que significa "Fondo Internacional de Emergencia de las Naciones Unidas para los Niños". Tiene siete oficinas regionales en diversas naciones y un Centro de Investigaciones en Italia.

El 20 de noviembre de 1989, la Organización de las Naciones Unidas escribió[4] "una convención para los niños" en inglés, árabe, chino, ruso y francés.

[1]children [2]certain [3]acronym [4]wrote

Esta convención dice que[5] los niños de todas[6] las naciones necesitan:

- dignidad
- una casa
- protección
- una buena dieta
- la práctica de deportes
- atención especial para los niños con problemas físicos
- amor y la comprensión de la familia
- expresar sus opiniones
- una comunidad sin[7] violencia
- ir a la escuela para ser inteligentes y sociables

[5]says that [6]all [7]without

¿Comprendes?

1. It is easy for students of every nation to attend school and own a backpack. True or false?

2. How many offices in different nations does UNICEF have?

3. What do the letters UNICEF stand for?

4. Where is the *Centro de Investigaciones?*

5. The convention is for children of all nations. True or false?

6. According to the convention, what are four things that children need?

Más práctica	GO
	realidades.com | print
Guided WB p. 81	✔ ✔
Comm. WB pp. 48, 133–134	✔ ✔
Hispanohablantes **WB** pp. 82–83	✔
Cultural Reading Activity	✔

Perspectivas del mundo hispano

¿Cómo es la escuela?

Did you know that students in many Spanish-speaking countries spend more time in school than you do? The graph to the right shows the length of the school year in various countries.

Here are some other facts you may not know:

- In many schools, when a teacher enters the classroom, the students stand.
- The teacher may call the students by their last name.
- The students, on the other hand, are more likely to address their teacher simply as *maestro(a), profesor(a),* or just *profe,* without a last name.
- Class time is generally spent with the teacher lecturing rather than with class discussion.
- Many public and private schools require uniforms.

Días de escuela

País	Días
Chile	235
Colombia	210
México	205
España	200
Argentina	185
Estados Unidos	180

País

Check it out! How are other schools in your area similar to or different from yours? How are they similar to or different from those in Spanish-speaking countries? Make a list of schools in your area and describe these similarities and differences. Are some schools more formal? Do students take classes that are different from the ones you take?

Think about it! Based on the information above, what might you assume are the attitudes toward school in Spanish-speaking cultures? How are these the same or different from attitudes in your community? List five suggestions that might help an exchange student from Mexico City adjust to your school's system.

Presentación escrita

Tu sala de clases

Task

Your pen pal from Mexico is coming to visit your school. Write him or her a note describing your Spanish classroom.

1 Prewrite Sketch your classroom, showing and labeling the items you intend to describe.

2 Draft Write the first draft of your note. Use your sketch to remember which items you want to describe and where they are. Use the model to organize your draft.

Modelo

En mi sala de clases hay cuatro ventanas. Mi pupitre está delante del escritorio de la profesora. La bandera está al lado de la puerta. Las computadoras están encima de la mesa.

3 Revise Check your note for correct spelling, as well as for the categories under Evaluation. Share your note with a partner, who will check for the following:

• Is your note easy to understand?
• Could you add other information?
• Are there any errors?

Rewrite your note, making any necessary changes.

4 Publish Make a final copy of your note for display in the classroom or for your portfolio.

5 Evaluation The following rubric will be used to grade your note.

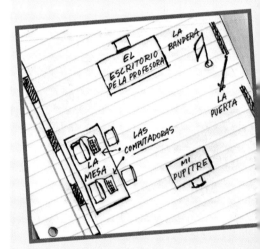

Strategy

Creating visuals
Creating a sketch or a drawing can help you remember the things you want to write about in a description.

Rubric	Score 1	Score 3	Score 5
Use of newly acquired vocabulary	You use very little variation of vocabulary with frequent usage errors.	You use limited vocabulary with some usage errors.	You use an extended variety of vocabulary with very few usage errors.
Correct use of the verb estar	You use many repetitions of incorrect verb forms.	You use frequent repetitions of incorrect verb forms.	You use very few incorrect verb forms.
Amount of information	You provide information about two or fewer items in the classroom.	You provide information about three or fewer items in the classroom.	You provide information about four or more items in the classroom.

América Central

Central America is made up of seven countries: Belize, Guatemala, El Salvador, Honduras, Nicaragua, Costa Rica, and Panama. Spanish is the official language in all of these countries except Belize, which was colonized by the British.

Costa Rica has set aside large tracts of land for conservation, helping to preserve fragile ecosystems. The oldest park in Costa Rica, Santa Rosa, protects endangered sea turtle nesting sites and the last dry tropical forest in Central America.

¿Sabes que . . . ?

Carlos V of Spain first proposed a canal across the Isthmus of Panama in 1524. In the 1880s, French efforts to build a canal across the isthmus were hindered in large part by diseases. Panama won its independence from Colombia in 1903. That same year, a treaty was signed with the United States granting rights to the Canal Zone. The United States completed the canal in 1914, and it was turned over to Panama in 1999.

Para pensar

In the early nineteenth century some people imagined that the United States would extend south to Panama. How do you think the United States would be different today if their predictions had come true? How do you think Mexico and Central America would be different?

México
Belice
Guatemala
Honduras
El Salvador
Nicaragua
Mar Caribe
Costa Rica
Panamá
OCÉANO PACÍFICO

realidades.com GO

 Mapa global interactivo

DK **Reference Atlas**

Founded by the Spanish in 1524, the Nicaraguan city of Granada became an important trading center. The town enjoys easy access to the Caribbean, yet is located less than 100 miles from the Pacific. In the nineteenth and twentieth centuries Nicaragua was proposed as an alternate site for a canal linking the Atlantic and Pacific oceans.

Much of Guatemala's large indigenous population is of Mayan descent. These women are wearing the traditional hand-woven *huipil*, which is a very "communicative" part of their clothing. The *huipil* identifies the wearer's village, her marital status, her religious beliefs, wealth, and personality. A well-woven *huipil* may last between 20 to 30 years.

From the 1500s to the end of the 1700s, the coasts of Spanish America were plagued by pirates. Panamanian ports were perfect targets, since the silver and gold mined in Peru were loaded on Panama's Pacific coast and carried overland to the Atlantic, where they were put on ships bound for Spain. Fuerte San Lorenzo, on Panama's Atlantic coast, was part of a network of forts that were meant to protect ships and their precious cargo.

▸ Review the vocabulary and grammar
▸ Demonstrate you can perform the tasks on p. 145

Repaso del capítulo
Vocabulario y gramática

to talk about classroom items

la bandera	flag
el cartel	poster
la computadora	computer
la mochila	bookbag, backpack
la pantalla	(computer) screen
la papelera	wastepaper basket
el ratón	(computer) mouse
el reloj	clock
el sacapuntas	pencil sharpener
el teclado	(computer) keyboard

to talk about classroom furniture

el escritorio	desk
la mesa	table
la silla	chair

to talk about parts of a classroom

la puerta	door
la ventana	window

to indicate location

al lado de la / del	next to, beside
allí	there
aquí	here
debajo de la/del	underneath
delante de la/del	in front of
detrás de la/del	behind
¿Dónde?	Where?
en	in, on
encima de la/del	on top of

to indicate possession

de	of
mi	my
tu	your

to identify (description, quantity)

¿Cuántos, -as?	How many?
Es un(a) . . .	It's a (an) . . .
Hay	There is, There are
¿Qué es esto?	What is this?

to identify gender and quantity of nouns

los, las	the
unos, unas	some

estar *to be*

estoy	estamos
estás	estáis
está	están

For *Vocabulario adicional,* see pp. 268–269.

Repaso

Más repaso GO realidades.com | print

Instant Check ✔
Puzzles ✔
Core WB pp. 47–48 ✔ ✔
Comm. WB pp. 135, 136–138 ✔ ✔

Preparación para el examen

On the exam you will be asked to...	Here are practice tasks similar to those you will find on the exam...	For review go to your print or digital textbook...
1 Escuchar Listen to and identify classrooms and locations	Listen as a student frantically asks some of his friends where he left his homework. Can you identify all the classrooms and places they suggest that he look?	pp. 118–123 *Vocabulario en contexto* p. 124 Actividades 5–6 p. 135 Actividad 27
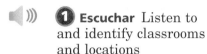 **2 Hablar** Talk about where someone is located by describing where that person is in relation to objects in the classroom	You are trying to find out the name of someone in your class. You ask the person next to you, but he doesn't understand whom you are talking about. Give at least three statements that would help him identify the person. You might include where he or she is in relation to the teacher's desk, the window, someone else's desk, and so on.	pp. 118–123 *A primera vista* p. 125 Actividad 7 p. 126 Actividad 9 p. 130 Actividades 16–17 p. 133 Actividad 24 p. 135 Actividad 27 p. 136 Actividad 29
3 Leer Read and understand a letter that contains questions and concerns about school issues	The school counselor has asked you to help him read a note written by a new Spanish-speaking student at school. After reading it, tell the counselor what questions the student has about her classes. *Necesito una clase para la primera hora. ¿Cómo es la clase de tecnología, fácil o difícil? ¿Qué necesito para la clase? ¿Cuántos estudiantes hay en la clase? ¿Hay mucha tarea?*	pp. 118–123 *Vocabulario en contexto* p. 128 Actividad 11 pp. 138–139 *Lectura*
4 Escribir Write an e-mail to a friend about one of her classes	You have just moved to a new town and are sending an e-mail to a friend from your old school. You have lots of questions for your friend about her classes. Write at least three questions about one of her classes: whether she likes it, how many students are in it, where her desk is in the room, what else is in the room, etc.	pp. 118–123 *Vocabulario en contexto* p. 124 Actividad 6 p. 125 Actividad 7 p. 136 Actividad 28 p. 137 Actividad 30
5 Pensar Demonstrate an understanding of cultural differences in schools	Think about how students and teachers interact within a typical classroom in a Spanish-speaking country. What are at least four things that you might find different from most schools in the United States?	p. 127 *Fondo cultural* p. 134 *Fondo cultural* p. 140 *Perspectivas del mundo hispano*

¿Desayuno o almuerzo?

▼ Chapter Objectives

Communication

By the end of this chapter you will be able to:

- Listen to and read descriptions of meals and menus
- Talk and write about foods you and others like and dislike
- Exchange information about food preferences

Culture

You will also be able to:

- Prepare a snack from the Spanish-speaking world and compare it to snacks you enjoy
- Trace the history of some foods originally native to the Americas and Europe

You will demonstrate what you know and can do:

- Presentación oral, p. 171
- Preparación para el examen, p. 175

You will use:

Vocabulary	Grammar
• Foods and beverages for breakfast and lunch	• Present tense of *-er* and *-ir* verbs
• Expressions of frequency	• *Me gustan, me encantan*

Exploración del mundo hispano

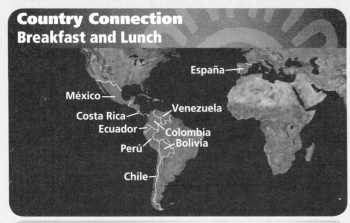

Country Connection
Breakfast and Lunch

España
México
Costa Rica
Ecuador
Venezuela
Colombia
Bolivia
Perú
Chile

realidades.com GO

 Reference Atlas

 Videocultura y actividad

 Mapa global interactivo

Un almuerzo con toda la familia

🌐 Arte y cultura | España

Bartolomé Murillo (1617–1682) was the first Spanish painter to become famous throughout Europe. Several of his early paintings featured children from his native Sevilla. Murillo used color, light, and a natural portrayal of his subjects to create memorable masterpieces.

• Study the painting and come up with three adjectives that describe it. Would you say the impression Murillo gives of the boys is positive or negative? Why?

"Niños comiendo fruta" (ca. 1650), Bartolomé Murillo ▶
© ARS, NY. Copyright Scala/Art Resource, NY. Alte Pinakothek, Munich, Germany.

Vocabulario en contexto

El Supermercado de la Plaza

¡Abierto las 24 horas!

¡Ofertas de hoy!

¡Toda la comida que necesitas!

$2.29 — las salchichas

$2.45 — el tocino

$2.35 — el jamón

el cereal $3.59 — SALVADO CON PASAS

$3.25 — el queso

$.79 — el yogur de fresa

$1.29 — los huevos

los plátanos $.69

$1.80 — el jugo de manzana

$2.50 — el jugo de naranja

$1.39 — la limonada

la leche $1.75

$2.40 — el té

$1.89 — el pan

$2.29 — las galletas

el agua* $1.09

*Note that *agua* is a feminine noun. However, you use the masculine article *el* to make it easier to say.

❝ **El desayuno** es mi **comida** favorita. **En el desayuno,** yo **como** cereal **con** leche, tocino y **pan tostado. Todos los días bebo** jugo de naranja. **Nunca** bebo té **sin** leche. Y tú, ¿qué **comes** en el desayuno? ❞

❝Me encanta el Restaurante de la Plaza La comida es muy buena. **En el almuerzo,** como una ensalada de frutas o un sándwich de jamón y queso. **Siempre** bebo agua. Es importante **beber** mucha agua, ¿verdad?❞

El Restaurante de la Plaza

¡Para un almuerzo **rápido!**

la ensalada de frutas — $3.25

el sándwich de jamón y queso — $3.50

la pizza — $1.75

la hamburguesa — $3.75

el café — $1.00

el perrito caliente — $1.50

los refrescos — $1.00

las papas fritas — $1.25

los jugos — $1.35

la sopa de verduras — $1.80

el té helado — $1.00

▼**1** | 🔊 | **Escuchar**

¿Beber o comer?

Listen to the names of ten foods or beverages. If an item is a food, pantomime eating. If it's a beverage, pantomime drinking.

▼**2** | 🔊 | **Escuchar**

¿El desayuno o el almuerzo?

Listen as different people tell what they are eating. Hold up one hand if the meal is *el desayuno* and hold up both hands if it is *el almuerzo.*

Más práctica	GO
	realidades.com | **print**
Instant Check	✔
Guided WB pp. 83–85	✔ ✔
Core WB pp. 49–50	✔ ✔
Comm. WB p. 56	✔ ✔
Hispanohablantes WB p. 92	✔

El desayuno

Tomás es de los Estados Unidos. Está en Costa Rica para estudiar.
¿Qué come el primer día? Lee la historia.

Costa Rica

Papá

Mamá

Tomás

Raúl

Gloria

Antes de leer

Strategy

Using prior experience You can use experiences that you have already had to help you understand what you read. Think about eating breakfast. Do you like a big breakfast? A small one? No breakfast at all?

• What do you think Tomás and Raúl have for breakfast?

1. Look at photo 2. Can you figure out from the picture what *¡Qué asco!* means?

2. Look at the photos and describe the problem Tomás is having at breakfast.

Mamá: A ver . . . tocino, salchichas, huevos . . .

Papá: ¡Uy! Es mucha comida. No **comprendo.** Tú nunca comes el desayuno.

Mamá: No es mi desayuno. Es para Tomás, **por supuesto.** Los americanos comen mucho en el desayuno.

Raúl: No comes mucho en el desayuno, ¿verdad?

Tomás: ¡No! ¡Qué asco!

Tomás: No me gusta nada el desayuno. A veces bebo jugo de naranja y como pan tostado.

Raúl: Yo tampoco como mucho.

Mamá: Buenos días, Tomás. Aquí tienes tu desayuno. Huevos, tocino, salchichas, pan tostado, cereal con leche . . .

Tomás: Gracias. Es un desayuno muy bueno. **Me encantan** los huevos y el tocino.

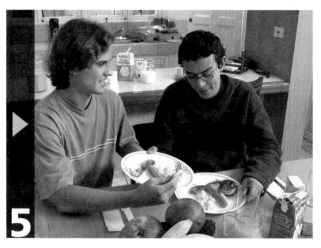

Tomás: Comparto los huevos, el tocino y las salchichas.

Raúl: ¿Compartes tu desayuno? Muchas gracias, Tomás.

Raúl: ¿Y qué **bebes?**

Tomás: Jugo de naranja, por favor.

Mamá: Te gusta la leche, ¿no?

Tomás: Más o menos.

Raúl: Papá, ¿unos huevos?

Papá: No, gracias. ¡La comida es para Uds.!

Mamá: ¿Cuál es tu almuerzo favorito, Tomás?

Tomás: Me gustan las hamburguesas, la pizza, **la ensalada . . .**

Mamá: Bueno . . . ¡pizza, hamburguesas y ensalada en el almuerzo!

▼3 Escribir

La lista

Copy Raúl's mother's shopping list on a separate sheet of paper. Then scan the *Videohistoria* and place a check mark next to the items that she uses to make breakfast for Raúl and Tomás.

Lista para el supermercado

yogur	tocino
queso	jugo de naranja
salchichas	huevos
jamón	pan
galletas	cereal
plátanos	leche

▼4 Leer • Hablar

Los gustos de Tomás

Read the following sentences and tell how Tomás would react, according to the *Videohistoria*. If he would like what is mentioned, say "*¡Me encanta!*" If he wouldn't like it, say "*¡Qué asco!*"

1. En el desayuno hay pan tostado.
2. En el desayuno hay jugo de naranja.
3. En el almuerzo hay pizza.
4. Hoy hay un desayuno muy grande.
5. Hoy hay ensalada en el almuerzo.

▼5 Leer

¿Comprendes?

Read the following sentences. Write the numbers 1–6 on your paper and write *C (cierto)* if a sentence is true, or *F (falso)* if it is false.

1. Tomás está en Costa Rica.
2. La mamá de Raúl siempre come mucho en el desayuno.
3. A Tomás le gusta comer mucho en el desayuno.
4. Hoy Tomás no come mucho en el desayuno.
5. Tomás comparte el desayuno con Raúl.
6. A Tomás le gustan las hamburguesas y la pizza.

Más práctica	GO	
realidades.com	print	
Instant Check	✔	
Guided WB pp. 89–92	✔	✔
Core WB pp. 51–52	✔	✔
Comm. WB pp. 49–50, 51	✔	✔
Hispanohablantes WB p. 93		✔

Vocabulario en uso

▼**6** Pensar • Escribir

Las diferencias

The two kitchens below look identical, but there are several differences. Make a list of as many differences between *la cocina de Ana* and *la cocina de Lola* as you can find.

Modelo

No hay papas fritas en la cocina de Lola.

la cocina de Ana

la cocina de Lola

▼7 Pensar • Escribir

El desayuno y el almuerzo

Think about what people usually eat for breakfast and lunch. Copy the Venn diagram on a sheet of paper. Which foods pictured in Actividad 6 would usually be eaten for breakfast or lunch? Write the Spanish words in the appropriate oval for *el desayuno* or *el almuerzo*. Which items could be eaten for either breakfast or lunch? Write them in the overlapping area.

Modelo

el desayuno   los dos   el almuerzo

el cereal   la hamburguesa

▼8 | ♻ | ◀)) | Escuchar • Escribir

¿Dónde están?

You will hear eight descriptions of the drawing of *la cocina de Ana* in Actividad 6. Write the numbers 1–8 on your paper and write the correct food or beverage.

▼9 Escribir

¿Qué bebes?

① On a sheet of paper, make three columns with these headings: *Todos los días, A veces, Nunca.* Under each heading, write the names of the beverages pictured below based on how often you drink them.

1.

2.

3.

4.

5.

6.

7.

② Write complete sentences telling how often you drink these beverages.

Modelo
Bebo limonada todos los días.

10 | (Talk!) 👥 | Hablar

¿Qué comes?

Working with a partner, discuss the things
that you eat and don't eat.

▶️ Modelo

A —*¿Comes cereal?*
B —*Sí, como cereal todos los días.*
o: —*No, nunca como cereal.*

Estudiante A

1.
2.
3.
4.
5.
6.
7.

Estudiante B

Sí, todos los días . . .
Sí, a veces . . .
Sí, siempre . . .
No, nunca . . .
No, ¡qué asco!

▼ Exploración del lenguaje

Using a noun to modify another noun

In English, we often use one noun to describe another noun: *vegetable soup, strawberry yogurt*. Notice that the noun that is being described comes second.

In Spanish, however, the noun that is being described comes first and is followed by *de* + the describing noun: *sopa* **de** *verduras, yogur* **de** *fresa*. Notice that you don't use a definite article in front of the second noun.

The form of the noun following *de* does not change even when the first noun becomes plural.

   el sándwich de **jamón**
   los sándwiches de **jamón**

Try it out! Name five or more examples of foods or beverages from this chapter that follow this pattern.

• Now that you know the pattern, say what the food or beverage would be in Spanish using the words paired with the pictures below.

el tomate   la lechuga

la piña   el pollo

▼11 | Hablar

¿Qué preparas?

You are preparing a meal for your friend. Use *de* and any of the words in the box below to come up with something special. (Some of your combinations may be a bit strange!) Tell your partner what you are making and he or she will respond with *¡Qué asco!* or *¡Me encanta(n)!*

▶ **Modelo**
un sándwich
A —*Preparo un sándwich de manzanas y huevos.*
B —*¡Qué asco!*
o:—*¡Me encanta!*

También se dice . . .
la naranja = la china *(el Caribe)*
el sándwich = el bocadillo *(España);* la torta *(México)*
el plátano = la banana, el guineo *(el Caribe)*
las papas = las patatas *(España)*
el jugo = el zumo *(España)*
beber = tomar *(México)*

1. un sándwich
2. una sopa
3. un jugo
4. una ensalada
5. un yogur

verduras	salchichas	plátanos	frutas
fresas	jamón	tocino	perritos calientes
manzanas	queso	huevos	

▼12 | Hablar

Mis comidas favoritas

With a partner, talk about the foods you like and don't like.

▶ **Modelo**
A —*Te gustan los plátanos, ¿verdad?*
B —*Sí, ¡por supuesto! Me encantan.*

Estudiante A

1. 2. 3. 4.

5. 6. 7.

Estudiante B

Sí, ¡por supuesto! Me encantan.
Sí, más o menos.
No, no me gustan.
No, ¡qué asco!

¡Respuesta personal!

Juego

1 Copy this blank Bingo card on a separate piece of paper. You will need to make it big enough to write a vocabulary word and a person's name in each square.

2 After you have made your Bingo card, write the name of a food or drink from the *Repaso del capítulo* on p. 174 in any order that you want. Be sure to leave enough space at the bottom of each square to write a person's name.

3 Now that you have made your game card, you are ready to interview your classmates. Ask a classmate if he or she drinks a beverage or eats a food item that you have on your card. If the answer is *no,* you will need to ask someone else the same question. If the answer is *sí,* write the classmate's name at the bottom of that square. You can only have a classmate's name on your card once, so after you have found a classmate who says *"sí,"* look for a different person for each of the remaining items on your card. The first person to say *"¡Bingo!"* after completing a horizontal or vertical row wins.

📹 **Modelo**

A —*Marco, ¿bebes limonada?*
B —*No, ¡qué asco!*
A —*Sarita, ¿bebes limonada?*
C —*Sí. Me encanta.*

You write: *Sarita*

▼**14** Leer • Pensar

El intercambio entre dos mundos

Conexiones | La historia

Think about how your meals would be different without chicken, pork, beef, milk, cheese, sugar, grapes, and food made from the grains wheat and barley. Europeans brought all these foods to the Americas.

Both sides of the Atlantic Ocean benefited from a product exchange. Starting in the fifteenth century, Columbus took back to Europe a wide range of foods from the Americas that Europeans had never seen before. These foods included corn, beans, squash, tomatoes, limes, avocados, chiles, peanuts, cashews, turkey, pineapples, yams, potatoes, vanilla, and chocolate. Today these foods are found in dishes in many countries.

• What is your favorite meal? Do the ingredients originally come from the Americas, Europe, or elsewhere?

▼**15** Leer • Escribir

Enchiladas de pollo

Read the list of ingredients for a traditional Mexican dish of *enchiladas*. Based upon the information you just read and saw on the map, write which ingredients had their origins in the Americas and which came from Europe.

Enchiladas
de pollo¹ con salsa de tomate

Ingredientes

12 tortillas do maíz²
1 taza³ de pollo
1 taza de queso fresco⁴
6 tomates grandes⁵
2 cebollas⁶ no muy grandes
crema
aceite⁷ de maíz

¹chicken   ²corn   ³cup   ⁴fresh   ⁵large   ⁶onions   ⁷oil

Gramática

Present tense of *-er* and *-ir* verbs

To create the present-tense forms of *-er* and *-ir* verbs, drop the endings from the infinitives, then add the verb endings *-o, -es, -e, -emos / -imos, -éis / -ís,* or *-en* to the stem.

Here are the present-tense forms of *-er* and *-ir* verbs using *comer* and *compartir:*

¿Recuerdas?

The pattern of present-tense *-ar* verbs is:

toco	tocamos
tocas	tocáis
toca	tocan

(yo)	**como**	(nosotros) (nosotras)	**comemos**
(tú)	**comes**	(vosotros) (vosotras)	**coméis**
Ud. (él) (ella)	**come**	Uds. (ellos) (ellas)	**comen**

(yo)	**comparto**	(nosotros) (nosotras)	**compartimos**
(tú)	**compartes**	(vosotros) (vosotras)	**compartís**
Ud. (él) (ella)	**comparte**	Uds. (ellos) (ellas)	**comparten**

- Regular *-er* verbs that you know are *beber, comer, comprender, correr,* and *leer.*

- Regular *-ir* verbs that you know are *compartir* and *escribir.*

- You also know the verb *ver.* It is regular except in the *yo* form, which is *veo.*

Más ayuda **realidades.com**

 GramActiva Video
Tutorial: *-er* verbs, *-ir* verbs, Regular verbs, Stem-endings
Animated Verbs

 Canción de hip hop: ¿Qué comes?

 GramActiva Activity

▼16 Escribir

¿Quiénes comparten el almuerzo?

On a separate sheet of paper, write complete sentences saying what each person is sharing and with whom.

Modelo

Elena / una manzana / Raúl
Elena comparte una manzana con Raúl.

1. Tomás / una pizza / María
2. tú / unos sándwiches / Ramón
3. nosotros / unas papas fritas / los estudiantes
4. Uds. / unas galletas / el profesor

Unos amigos comparten el almuerzo, Ciudad de México.

5. ellas / unos perritos calientes / nosotros
6. tú y yo / unos plátanos / Luis y Roberta
7. yo / ¿–? / mi amigo

▼17 Leer • Escribir

Una tarjeta postal

Read the following postcard from your friend Carolina in Venezuela.
Number your paper from 1–8 and write the correct form of the
appropriate verb in parentheses.

¡Hola!

Elena y yo estamos en Caracas. Nosotras __1.__
(comprender / correr) todos los días y __2.__
(comer / ver) muy bien.

Los estudiantes aquí __3.__ (comer / leer)
mucha pizza y __4.__ (ver / beber) mucho café.
Ellos __5.__ (leer / beber) muchos libros y
__6.__ (escribir / ver) mucho también para
las clases. Las clases son difíciles pero
me encantan.

En la clase de español nosotros __7.__
(correr / leer) revistas y cuentos en español.
Elena __8.__ (comprender / beber) muy bien
pero para mí es un poco difícil.

Tengo que estudiar. Hasta luego.

Tu amiga,
Carolina

▼18 Escribir

El desayuno con la familia Acevedo

You have been invited to Sunday breakfast at the Acevedo house.
Write five sentences to describe what everyone is doing. Be sure to
use a different subject and a different verb for each sentence.

Modelo
Nosotros vemos la tele.

el Sr. Acevedo
yo
Francisco y Marta
la Sra. Acevedo
nosotros

ver la tele
leer una revista
correr a la puerta
compartir un desayuno muy bueno
beber jugo de manzana
comer yogur de fresas
¡Respuesta personal!

▼19 | (Talk?) 👥 | Hablar

¿Qué beben y qué comen?

Work with a partner. Use the verbs *comer* and *beber* to ask questions. Then answer them, following the models.

Juan / desayuno

▶️ **Modelo**

A —*¿Qué come Juan en el desayuno?*
B —*Juan come pan tostado.*

Miguel y Carlos / almuerzo

▶️ **Modelo**

A —*¿Qué beben Miguel y Carlos en el almuerzo?*
B —*Miguel y Carlos beben limonada.*

> **Para decir más . . .**
>
> **la crema de cacahuates**   peanut butter
> **el pan dulce**   breakfast pastry
> **el panqueque**   pancake
> **el pollo**   chicken

1. Raúl y Gloria / desayuno

2. tú / almuerzo

3. Graciela y Carlos / desayuno

4. Carolina / almuerzo

5. tu familia y tú / desayuno

6. tú / almuerzo

¡Respuesta personal!

▼20 | 👥 | Hablar • Escribir

Los sábados y la comida

Talk about what you and your classmates eat and drink for breakfast and lunch on Saturdays. Make a chart like the one below on a sheet of paper and complete each box with information about yourself. Then survey two classmates to find out what their habits are. Record the information in the chart.

Modelo

Los sábados, ¿qué comes en el desayuno? ¿Qué bebes?
¿Qué comes en el almuerzo? ¿Qué bebes?

	¿Qué comes?	¿Qué bebes?
el desayuno	**yo:** huevos, pan tostado, tocino **Sandra:** cereal, plátanos	
el almuerzo		

▼21 Escribir • Hablar

Los hábitos de la clase

Use your completed chart from Actividad 20 to write summary statements based on your survey. Be prepared to read your sentences to the class.

Modelo

Sandra y yo comemos huevos y cereal en el desayuno.
Gregorio no bebe jugo de naranja en el desayuno y le gusta mucho la leche.
Sofía come cereal y bebe leche en el desayuno.

▼22 | |  | Escribir • Hablar

Y tú, ¿qué dices?

1. ¿Qué comen tú y tus amigos en el almuerzo?
2. ¿Compartes la comida con tus amigos? ¿Qué compartes?
3. ¿Qué bebes en el desayuno?
4. ¿Qué libros lees en tu clase de inglés?
5. ¿Quién corre rápido *(fast)* en tu clase de educación física?
6. ¿Ves la tele en tu clase de ciencias sociales? ¿Qué ves?

¿Recuerdas?

Since the verb endings indicate who is doing the action, you can often use the verb without the subject pronoun.

• **escribo** *I write*
• **escribimos** *we write*

▼ Fondo Cultural | El mundo hispano

El desayuno From the popular *churros* (fried dough rolled in sugar) and hot chocolate in Spain to the *pan dulce* served in many countries, a wide variety of foods can be found on the breakfast table in the Spanish-speaking world. Most often, people prefer a light breakfast of bread or a roll, coffee or tea, and possibly juice. Items such as cereal, milk, eggs, ham, or sausage are less common.

• In Spain you can ask for a *desayuno americano.* What do you think you would be served?

El pan dulce es un desayuno popular en México.

Más práctica GO   realidades.com | print

Instant Check	✔	
Guided WB pp. 93–94	✔	✔
Core WB p. 53	✔	✔
Comm. WB pp. 53, 57	✔	✔
Hispanohablantes WB pp. 94–97		✔

Gramática

Me gustan, me encantan

Use *me gusta* and *me encanta* to talk about a singular noun.

> Me gusta el té pero me encanta el té helado.

Use *me gustan* and *me encantan* to talk about plural nouns.

> Me encantan las fresas pero no me gustan mucho los plátanos.

When you use *me gusta(n)* and *me encanta(n)* to talk about a noun, include *el, la, los,* or *las.*

> Me encanta el jugo de naranja pero no me gusta la leche.

> ¿Qué te gustan más, las hamburguesas o los perritos calientes?

Más ayuda   realidades.com

▶ *GramActiva* Video
Tutorial: *-ar* verbs

▶ *GramActiva* Activity

▼23 | 🔊 | Escuchar • GramActiva

¿Gusta o gustan?

1 Tear a sheet of paper in thirds. On the first piece, write *No.* On the second piece write *me gusta.* On the third piece, write *n.*

2 You will hear eight food items. Indicate when you like or don't like the items by holding up one, two, or all three pieces of paper. Remember to use *me gustan* when the item you hear is plural.

▼24 Escribir

¿Qué te gusta?

Indicate how much you do or do not like the following foods.

Modelo
Me gustan las manzanas.
o: *No me gustan nada las manzanas.*
o: *Me encantan las manzanas.*

1.    2.   3.    4.   5.   6.

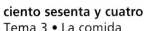

▼25 | | Leer • Escribir

Un *quiz* personal

A popular magazine has provided this survey to see how much you and a friend have in common. Read the survey. Then, for each item on the quiz, write a sentence describing which choice you like the most. Write your sentences on a sheet of paper.

Modelo
Me gusta más la comida italiana.

¿Qué te gusta más?

¿Tu amigo(a) y tú son muy similares o muy diferentes?

Completa este quiz y compara tus respuestas con las de un(a) amigo(a).

1. la comida mexicana o la comida italiana
2. el desayuno o el almuerzo
3. el cereal con fruta o el cereal sin fruta
4. las revistas o los libros
5. la música rock o la música rap
6. los amigos graciosos o los amigos serios
7. las hamburguesas con queso o las hamburguesas sin queso

Respuestas similares:

7–6	¡Uds. son gemelos!¹
5–4	Tienen mucho en común, ¿verdad?
3–2	¡Un poco similar y un poco diferente!
1–0	¿Los opuestos² se atraen?³ ¡Por supuesto!

¹twins ²opposites ³attract

▼26 | | | Hablar

¿Amigos similares o diferentes?

Working in pairs, take turns asking your partner about the survey items in Actividad 25. Keep track of your similarities and differences. See how the magazine rates you.

▶ **Modelo**
A —*¿Qué te gusta más, la comida mexicana o la comida italiana?*
B —*Me gusta más la comida italiana.*
o: *No me gusta ni la comida mexicana ni la comida italiana.*
A —*A mí me gusta la comida mexicana.*
o: *A mí también.*
o: *A mí tampoco.*

▼**27** | 🗨️👥 | **Leer • Hablar • Escribir**

Necesito mucho del supermercado

You and your friend are going food shopping in San Antonio, Texas. Look at the following advertisement and decide with your partner what items you should put on your shopping list. When you decide that you need an item, write it on your list.

▶️ **Modelo**

A —¿*Necesitamos huevos?*
B —*Sí, me encantan los huevos.*
o: —*No, ¡qué asco! No me gustan los huevos.*

El Supermercado Mendoza

$3.69 las galletas Chocolífico
$2.19 el tocino Rancho Tejano
$3.39 el cereal Salvado con pasas
$0.99 los plátanos centroamericanos
$2.25 las papas de Idaho
$2.85 la leche Vacarica 1/2 galón
$2.19 los huevos
$2.75 las fresas frescas
$1.89 los refrescos Mendoza
$1.49 las manzanas de Washington

El español en la comunidad

Foods from different Spanish-speaking countries have become very popular in the United States. Visit a local grocery store and make a list of different foods that come from Spanish-speaking countries.

• Which of these foods have you tried? How do they compare to foods that you normally eat?

▼ Pronunciación | 🔊 | 💬

The letters *h* and *j*

In Spanish, the letter *h* is never pronounced. Listen to and say these words:

hora	hablar	hasta	hola
hoy	hace	hacer	hotel

The letter *j* is pronounced like the letter *h* in *hat* but with more of a breathy sound. It is made far back in the mouth—almost in the throat. Listen to and say these words:

trabajar	dibujar	jugar	videojuegos
hoja	jueves	junio	julio

Try it out! Find and say five or more examples of foods or beverages from this chapter that have *h* or *j* in their spelling.

Try it out! Say this *trabalenguas* (tongue twister) three times, as fast as you can:

Debajo del puente de Guadalajara había un conejo debajo del agua.

▼28 Leer • Escribir

¿Qué comida hay en el Ciberc@fé @rrob@?

Menú del Ciberc@fé @rrob@

Desayunos

No. 1 Huevos: *(jamón, tocino, chorizo[1])* $27.00
Con cóctel de fruta $30.00

No. 2 Sincronizadas: *(tortilla de harina,[2]* $33.00
queso amarillo, jamón)
Con cóctel de fruta $36.00

No. 3 Cuernitos: *(jamón, queso, tomate* $30.00
y lechuga)
Con cóctel de fruta $33.00

No. 4 Chilaquiles: *verdes o rojos* $21.00
Con cóctel de fruta $24.00

No. 5 Omelet: *(con pollo, jamón, tomate,* $27.00
cebolla, champiñones[3] o queso)

No. 6 Crepas *(champiñones, jamón, pollo)* $19.00

Refrescos $7.50   Café $6.00   Jugos $11.50   Té o té helado $6.00

Tel.: 212 03 95

16 de septiembre #65
Col. Centro

Strategy

Skimming
Look quickly through the menu. What meal is featured? Find three dishes you recognize and two that are new to you.

❶ Read the menu and answer the questions on a separate sheet of paper.

1. Comes el desayuno No. 1 con té. ¿Cuál es el precio *(price)* del desayuno?

2. No te gustan nada los huevos. ¿Qué comes del menú?

3. Te encanta la fruta. ¿Qué bebes?

❷ Use the cyber café menu as a model menu to create a lunch menu using the vocabulary in this chapter.

Más práctica	GO

realidades.com | print

Instant Check	✔	
Guided WB pp. 95–96	✔	✔
Core WB pp. 54–55	✔	✔
Comm. WB pp. 53–55, 58, 251	✔	✔
Hispanohablantes WB pp. 98–101	✔	

[1]spicy sausage   [2]flour   [3]mushrooms

Lectura

Frutas y verduras de las Américas

Hay muchas frutas y verduras que son originalmente de las Américas que hoy se comen en todos los países. Las verduras más populares son la papa, el maíz, los frijoles y muchas variedades de chiles. También hay una gran variedad de frutas como la papaya, la piña y el aguacate. Estas frutas y verduras son muy nutritivas, se pueden preparar fácilmente y son muy sabrosas. La papaya y la piña son frutas que se comen en el desayuno o de postre. ¿Cuáles de estas frutas comes?

Strategy

Making guesses
When you find an unknown word, try to guess the meaning. Is it a cognate? What might it mean within the context of the reading and other words around it? Keep reading and the meaning may become clear.

la papaya

Es una fruta con mucha agua. Es perfecta para el verano. Tiene más vitamina C que la naranja.

el aguacate

La pulpa del aguacate es una fuente de energía, proteínas, vitaminas y minerales. Tiene vitaminas A y B.

el mango

Aunque[1] el mango es originalmente del Asia, se cultiva en las regiones tropicales de muchos países de las Américas. Tiene calcio y vitaminas A y C, como la naranja.

[1]Although

Licuado de plátano

El licuado es una bebida muy popular en los países tropicales. ¡Es delicioso y muy nutritivo!

Ingredientes:
- 1 plátano
- 2 vasos de leche
- 1 cucharadita de azúcar
- hielo

Preparación:
1. Cortar el plátano.
2. Colocar los ingredientes en la licuadora.
3. Licuar por unos 5 ó 10 segundos.

¿Comprendes?

1. ¿Qué vitaminas tienen las frutas en la página anterior?

2. De las frutas y verduras en el artículo, ¿cuáles (which ones) te gustan? ¿Cuáles no te gustan?

3. ¿Qué otras frutas te gustan? ¿Comes estas frutas en el desayuno o en el almuerzo?

4. ¿Qué fruta no es originalmente de las Américas?

Chile

Fondo Cultural | Chile

Frutas y verduras During winter, the United States imports a wide range of fruits from Chile such as cherries, peaches, and grapes. When you purchase grapes from a supermarket in January, look to see if they have a label that says *Producto de Chile* or *Importado de Chile*.

- What are some other fruits and vegetables in your local market that are products of other countries?

Uvas de Chile

Más práctica	GO

realidades.com | print

Guided WB p. 97	✔	✔
Comm. WB pp. 59, 140	✔	✔
***Hispanohablantes* WB** pp. 102–103		✔
Cultural Reading Activity		✔

La cultura en vivo

Churros y chocolate

In many Spanish-speaking countries, a popular snack is the combination of *churros y chocolate. Churros* are long, slender doughnut-like pastries fried in hot oil. Small restaurants called *churrerías* specialize in *churros* and cups of delicious hot chocolate. You can also find *churros* being sold in stands on the street.

Try it out! Here's the recipe to try. *Churros* are high in fat and calories, so you won't want to sample too many of them!

Churros

1 cup water	$\frac{1}{2}$ cup unsalted butter *(= 1 stick)*
$\frac{1}{4}$ teaspoon salt	1 cup all-purpose flour
4 large eggs	oil for deep-frying
1 cup sugar	

Chocolate y churros

Un molinillo

In a heavy saucepan, bring water, butter, and salt to a full boil. Remove from heat. Add the flour all at once, stirring briskly. Stir until the mixture pulls away from the side of the pan and forms a ball. Put the mixture in a bowl. With an electric mixer on medium speed, add one egg at a time. After adding the last egg, beat the mixture for one more minute.

With adult supervision, heat 2–3 inches of oil to 375° F in a deep, heavy pan. Fit a pastry bag or cookie press with a $\frac{1}{2}$-inch star tip. Pipe out 6-inch-long tubes of dough into the oil. ***Be extremely cautious adding dough to the oil, because the oil may spatter and burn you!*** Fry, turning a few times, for 3–5 minutes or until golden brown. Place the sugar on a plate. Drain the *churros* well on paper towels and then roll them in the sugar.

Chocolate caliente

To make hot chocolate in Mexico, cacao beans are ground to a powder. Cinnamon, powdered almonds, and sugar are then added, and hot milk is poured in. The mixture is whipped with a wooden whisk called *un molinillo* or *un batidor.* You can find Mexican-style chocolate for making *chocolate caliente* in many supermarkets.

Think about it! What kinds of food and drink do you and your friends like? Is chocolate among the popular choices? Can you think of combinations of food and drink that are popular with many people in the United States? Are these combinations popular elsewhere?

| Objectives

▶ Role-play an interview about classes, favorite activities, and favorite foods

▶ Use a list of questions to get the information you want

Presentación oral

¿Y qué te gusta comer?

Task
You and a partner will role-play a telephone conversation between an exchange student from the United States and a member of his or her host family in Uruguay.

❶ Prepare Be sure to prepare for both roles. Here's how:

Host student: List at least four questions for the exchange student. Find out what he or she likes to study, eat and drink for breakfast and lunch, and his or her favorite activities.

Exchange student: Write some possible answers to questions from the host student and be prepared to give information about yourself.

❷ Practice Work with a partner to practice different questions and different responses. Here's how you might start your conversation:

> **HOST STUDENT:** ¡Hola, Pablo! Soy Rosa.
>
> **EXCHANGE STUDENT:** ¡Hola, Rosa! ¿Cómo estás?
>
> **HOST STUDENT:** Bien, gracias. Pues Pablo, ¿te gusta . . . ?

Continue the conversation. Use your notes in practice, but not to present.

❸ Present You will be paired with another student, and your teacher will assign roles. The host student begins the conversation. Listen to your partner's questions and responses and keep the conversation going.

❹ Evaluation The following rubric will be used to grade your presentation.

> **Strategy**
> **Making lists**
> Making lists of questions can help you in conversations where you need to find out specific information.

Rubric	Score 1	Score 3	Score 5
Completion of task	You ask or answer two questions during the conversation.	You ask or answer three questions during the conversation.	You ask or answer four or more questions during the conversation.
How easily you are understood	You are extremely difficult to understand. Your teacher could only recognize isolated words and phrases.	You are understandable, but have frequent errors in vocabulary and/or grammar that hinder your comprehensibility.	You are easily understood. Your teacher does not have to "decode" what you are trying to say.
Your ability to keep the conversation going	You provide no conversational response or follow-up to what your partner says.	You provide frequent response or follow-up to what your partner says.	You always provide a response to your partner, listen, and ask follow-up questions or volunteer additional information.

ciento setenta y uno **171**
Capítulo 3A

América del Sur

Parte norte

Venezuela, Colombia, Ecuador, Peru, and Bolivia form a region of contrasts, with mountains and lowlands, rain forests and deserts, immense wealth and extreme poverty, remote villages and modern cities. A rugged geography, ancient indigenous civilizations, and abundant natural resources have made this one of the most culturally diverse regions in the world.

Constructed more than 500 years ago, the terraced fields in the highlands of Bolivia were a sophisticated system for conserving soil and water, and some remain in use today. In the 1980s archaeologists reconstructing ancient agricultural systems on the shore of Lake Titicaca (at 12,500 feet the highest navigable body of water in the world) found that these ancient systems worked better in this difficult environment than many modern agricultural techniques.

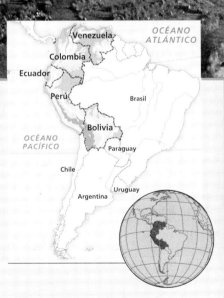

¿Sabes que . . . ?

The term *America* first appeared on a German map in 1507. The Americas are named for the Italian navigator Amerigo Vespucci, who produced the first European charts of mainland South America in 1497.

Para pensar

The countries of northern South America are lands of varied geography. Think about the North American continent. It is also a land of geographical contrasts. In what ways are both regions rich in natural resources, environmentally protected areas, and ancient civilizations?

realidades.com **GO**

 Mapa global interactivo

 Reference Atlas

"Rediscovered" in 1911, the mountaintop city of Machu Picchu in Peru was part of the Incan empire, which in the sixteenth century extended from present-day Ecuador to Chile. Machu Picchu's buildings were made of huge, precisely carved stone blocks that were hauled into place without wheels or heavy draft animals. ▶

Venezuela is one of the most important sources of oil consumed in the United States. Other important Latin American oil producers include Mexico, Colombia, and Ecuador, with new deposits being found every year. Latin America and Canada account for approximately 46 percent of oil imports to the United States. In contrast, the Middle East accounts for approximately 23 percent.

The Galápagos Islands, also called *las islas encantadas* (the enchanted islands), lie 600 miles off the coast of Ecuador. It is believed that the Incas may have traveled to the islands in large ocean-going rafts. In 1835, the naturalist Charles Darwin spent weeks here studying the islands' unique animal life. *Galápagos* are giant tortoises that are native to these islands, which are now a national park and wildlife sanctuary.

Repaso del capítulo
Vocabulario y gramática

to talk about breakfast

en el desayuno	for breakfast
el cereal	cereal
el desayuno	breakfast
los huevos	eggs
el pan	bread
el pan tostado	toast
el plátano	banana
la salchicha	sausage
el tocino	bacon
el yogur	yogurt

to talk about lunch

en el almuerzo	for lunch
la ensalada	salad
la ensalada de frutas	fruit salad
las fresas	strawberries
la galleta	cookie
la hamburguesa	hamburger
el jamón	ham
la manzana	apple
las papas fritas	French fries
el perrito caliente	hot dog
la pizza	pizza
el queso	cheese
el sándwich de jamón y queso	ham and cheese sandwich
la sopa de verduras	vegetable soup

to talk about beverages

el agua *f.*	water
el café	coffee
el jugo de manzana	apple juice
el jugo de naranja	orange juice

For *Vocabulario adicional,* see pp. 268–269.

la leche	milk
la limonada	lemonade
el refresco	soft drink
el té	tea
el té helado	iced tea

to talk about eating and drinking

beber	to drink
comer	to eat
la comida	food, meal
compartir	to share

to indicate how often

nunca	never
siempre	always
todos los días	every day

to say that you like / love something

Me / te encanta(n) ___.	I / you love ___.
Me / te gusta(n) ___.	I / you like ___.

other useful words

comprender	to understand
con	with
¿Cuál?	Which? What?
más o menos	more or less
por supuesto	of course
¡Qué asco!	How awful!
sin	without
¿Verdad?	Really?, Right?

present tense of -er verbs

como	comemos
comes	coméis
come	comen

present tense of -ir verbs

comparto	compartimos
compartes	compartís
comparte	comparten

Más repaso GO   realidades.com | print

Instant Check	✔
Puzzles	✔
Core WB pp. 56–57	✔
Comm. WB pp. 141, 142–144	✔ ✔

Preparación para el examen

On the exam you will be asked to . . .	Here are practice tasks similar to those you will find on the exam . . .	For review go to your print or digital textbook . . .
1 Escuchar Listen and understand as people describe what they eat and drink for lunch	Listen as three students describe what they typically eat and drink for lunch. Which is most like the kind of lunch you eat? Did they mention anything you could not buy in your school cafeteria?	**pp. 148–153** *Vocabulario en contexto* **p. 149** Actividades 1–2 **p. 155** Actividad 8
2 Hablar Tell someone what you typically eat for breakfast and ask the same of others	Your Spanish club is meeting for breakfast before school next week. Find out what other people in your class typically eat for breakfast. After you tell at least two people what you eat for breakfast, ask what they like to eat. Does everyone eat the same kind of breakfast or do you all like to eat different things?	**p. 156** Actividad 10 **p. 157** Actividad 12 **p. 162** Actividades 19–20 **p. 163** Actividad 21 **p. 171** *Presentación oral*
3 Leer Read and understand words that are typically found on menus	You are trying to help a child order from the lunch menu below, but he is very difficult to please. He doesn't like any white food. And he refuses to eat anything that grows on trees. Which items from the menu do you think he would refuse to eat or drink? **ALMUERZO** hamburguesa plátanos pizza manzana ensalada leche	**pp. 148–153** *Vocabulario en contexto* **p. 159** Actividad 15 **p. 167** Actividad 28 **pp. 168–169** *Lectura*
4 Escribir Write a list of foods that you like and others that you dislike	Your Spanish club is sponsoring a "Super Spanish Saturday." Your teacher wants to know what foods the class likes and dislikes so that the club can buy what most people like. Write the headings *Me gusta(n)* and *No me gusta(n)* in two columns. List at least four items that you like to eat and drink for breakfast and four items for lunch. Then list what you don't like to eat and drink for these same meals.	**p. 155** Actividades 7, 9 **p. 160** Actividad 16 **p. 163** Actividad 21 **p. 164** Actividad 24
5 Pensar Demonstrate an understanding of cultural differences regarding snacks	Think about food combinations in the United States. What combination in Spanish-speaking countries is similar to coffee and doughnuts? Where are you able to buy it?	**p. 170** *La cultura en vivo*

Para mantener la salud

Mercado de la Boquería,
Barcelona, España

▼ Chapter Objectives

Communication

By the end of this chapter you will be able to:

- Listen to and read descriptions of healthy and unhealthy lifestyles
- Talk and write about food, health, and exercise
- Exchange information while expressing your opinions about food choices and health

Culture

You will also be able to:

- Understand cultural perspectives on medicines and health care
- Compare traditional foods, markets, and festivals in the Spanish-speaking world with those in the United States

You will demonstrate what you know and can do:

- Presentación escrita, p. 201
- Preparación para el examen, p. 205

You will use:

Vocabulary	Grammar
• Food groups	• Plurals of adjectives
• Discussing health	• The verb *ser*
• Indicating preferences, agreement, and disagreement	
• Describing food	

Exploración del mundo hispano

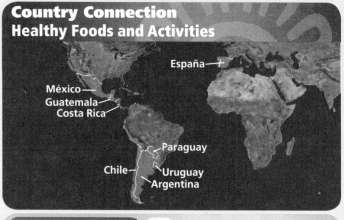

Country Connection
Healthy Foods and Activities

España

México
Guatemala
Costa Rica

Paraguay

Chile
Uruguay
Argentina

realidades.com GO

 Reference Atlas

▶ **Videocultura y actividad**

Mapa global interactivo

Arte y cultura | México

Diego Rivera This detail of a mural entitled "La Gran Tenochtitlán" by Mexican artist Diego Rivera (1886–1957) is located in the Palacio Nacional in Mexico City. It shows *el tianguis,* the bustling marketplace at Tenochtitlán, capital of the Aztec Empire. In the center right there are many kinds of food being traded, including tomatoes, squash, and different varieties of chile peppers. This mural is one of many by Rivera that focus on pre-Columbian life and civilizations.

• What impression do you think Rivera is giving about life in a pre-Columbian civilization?

Detalle de "La Gran Tenochtitlán" (1945), Diego Rivera ▶

Detail of mural. Patio Corridor, National Palace, Mexico City, D.F., Mexico. The Great City of Tenochtitlan, detail of a woman selling vegetables, 1945 (mural), Rivera, Diego (1886–1957)/Palacio Nacional, Mexico City, Mexico/Giraudon/The Bridgeman Art Library.

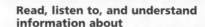
Vocabulario en contexto

Read, listen to, and understand information about
▶ food groups
▶ healthy activities
▶ ways to describe food

El plato nutritivo es la forma más práctica de indicar la comida que **debes** comer **cada día. Para mantener la salud,** es importante comer de **todos** los grupos.

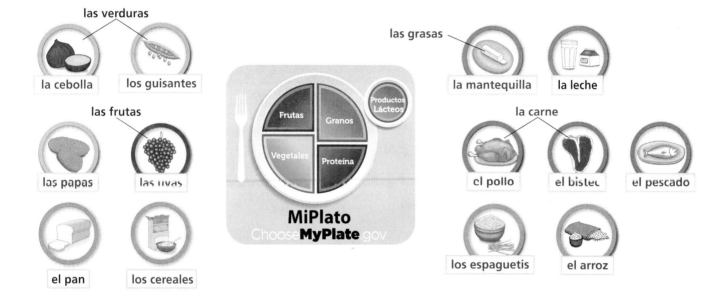

las verduras

la cebolla   los guisantes

las frutas

las papas   las uvas

el pan   los cereales

MiPlato
Choose **MyPlate**.gov

las grasas

la mantequilla   la leche

la carne

el pollo   el bistec   el pescado

los espaguetis   el arroz

66¡Me encantan las verduras! Como **muchas** ensaladas con lechuga y tomates**99**.

66 También me gustan las zanahorias y las judías verdes**99**.

las zanahorias

la lechuga

los tomates

las judías verdes

66¡Mi amiga Claudia no come comida buena **para la salud!** Come muchos pasteles y helado. **Son horribles99**.

el helado

los pasteles

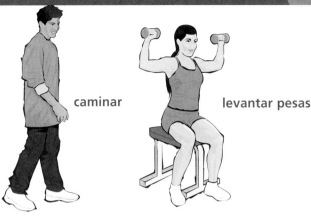

caminar   levantar pesas

—¿Qué **haces** para mantener la salud?

—Pues, cada día **hago ejercicio.** Camino, monto en bicicleta y practico deportes.

—¡Uf! **Tengo hambre. ¿Por qué** no comemos **algo** en el restaurante "A tu salud"? Los sándwiches son muy **sabrosos.**

—¡Por supuesto!

▼**1** | 🔊 | Escuchar

Debes comer . . .

Your teacher is giving a lecture on foods that you should eat from the Food Guide Pyramid. Touch each item as it is mentioned. You won't understand everything in the sentences, so listen carefully for the names of the foods.

▼**2** | 🔊 | Escuchar

Para mantener la salud

Listen to students talk about things they do. Give a "thumbs-up" sign if they are describing things that are healthy and a "thumbs-down" sign if the things are unhealthy.

Más práctica GO	realidades.com	print
Instant Check	✔	
Guided WB pp. 99–104	✔	✔
Core WB pp. 58–59	✔	✔
Comm. WB p. 66	✔	✔
Hispanohablantes **WB** p. 112		✔

Para mantener la salud

¿Qué hacen Raúl, Tomás y Gloria para mantener la salud?
Lee la historia.

Costa Rica

Raúl

Gloria

Tomás

Antes de leer

Strategy **Using visuals to make predictions** Use the pictures to try to predict what will happen before you read the story. As you read, predicting what will happen next will help you understand the story better.

• How did your predictions compare with what you read?

1. Look at photo 1. Does Tomás think that coffee is good for your health?
2. Look at photo 5. What does Tomás do for exercise?
3. Look at photo 6. How is Tomás feeling?

Tomás: Tengo sed . . .

Raúl: ¿Qué prefieres? ¿Te gusta el café? El café de Costa Rica es muy bueno.

Tomás: ¡Pero el café es malo para la salud! Prefiero una bebida como . . . un jugo de fruta.

Raúl: ¡Ah! Estoy de acuerdo, un refresco.

Tomás: Raúl, ¿por qué hablas de *refrescos?* A mí me gustan los jugos de fruta.

Gloria: Porque, Tomás, ¡un *refresco* en Costa Rica *es* un jugo de fruta!

Raúl: Dos refrescos de mango con leche.

Gloria: Y un refresco de mango con agua, por favor.

Tomás: ¡Es *muuuy* sabroso!

Gloria y Raúl: Sí, sí . . . ¡y todos los refrescos aquí son buenos para la salud!

Gloria: Tomás, ¿qué haces para mantener la salud?

5

Tomás: ¡Me gusta hacer algo cada día! Hago ejercicio, levanto pesas o camino todos los días.

6

Tomás: Tengo hambre.

Raúl: ¿Por qué no comemos en La soda?*

*La soda is the word for a casual restaurant in Costa Rica.

7

Tomás: La comida aquí es muy buena. Ahora no tengo hambre. ¿Y tú?

Raúl: ¡Creo que no!

Gloria: Pues, **creo que** debemos ir a casa.

8

Mamá: ¡A comer **la cena**!

Los jóvenes: *¡Uf!*

▼3 Leer • Escribir

¿Quién dice . . . ?

Number your paper 1–6. Based on what you read in the *Videohistoria,* write the name(s) of the character(s) who would make each of these statements.

1. Prefiero el café de Costa Rica.
2. Creo que es bueno hacer ejercicio.
3. Prefiero jugo de fruta.
4. Creo que los refrescos en Costa Rica son sabrosos.
5. Creo que el café es malo para la salud.
6. No debemos comer la cena.

Raúl

Gloria

Tomás

▼4 Leer • Escribir

¿Estás de acuerdo?

Read each statement, and write *Cierto* if the statement is true, or *Falso* if it is not. Base your answers on what you read in the *Videohistoria.*

1. Raúl tiene sed.
2. Según Tomás, el café es bueno para la salud.
3. Un refresco en Costa Rica es un jugo de fruta.
4. Gloria bebe un refresco de mango con leche.
5. Tomás nada todos los días.
6. A Tomás no le gusta nada la comida de la soda.
7. Según Gloria, los jóvenes deben ir a casa.
8. La mamá de Raúl y Gloria no prepara *(doesn't prepare)* la cena.

Más práctica GO

realidades.com | print

Instant Check	✔	
Guided WB pp. 105–108	✔	✔
Core WB pp. 60–61	✔	✔
Comm. WB pp. 60–62, 63	✔	✔
Hispanohablantes WB p. 113		✔

Vocabulario en uso

▼**5** Leer • Escribir

¡Claro que no!

For each group of words, choose the word or expression that doesn't belong and write it on your paper. Then write one more word or expression that would fit with the group.

Modelo

la cebolla   la lechuga   las uvas
las uvas . . . las zanahorias

1. el pollo	el pescado	el arroz
2. las zanahorias	los pasteles	las judías verdes
3. caminar	correr	ver la televisión
4. comer mucho	levantar pesas	hacer ejercicio
5. los tomates	el pan	los espaguetis
6. el bistec	las papas	el pollo
7. la mantequilla	el helado	el pescado

▼**6** | 👥 | Escribir • Leer

Juego

❶ Working in a group, make one large food plate identical to the one you see on the right.

❷ Cut or tear a sheet of paper into ten small pieces, and write the word for one food or drink item on each piece of paper. Exchange the pieces of paper with another group.

❸ When your teacher tells you to start, correctly place each of the vocabulary words in the appropriate spot on the food plate you have created. The first group to fill in a correct plate wins!

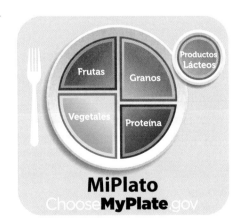

MiPlato
Choose **MyPlate**.gov

▼ Fondo Cultural | Argentina | Paraguay | Uruguay

El mate is the national beverage of Argentina, Paraguay, and Uruguay. This herbal tea is shared among family and friends. It is served hot in a hollow gourd, also called *un mate,* with a straw called *una bombilla.*

- What national beverage does the United States have that compares to *mate?*

Una mujer toma mate, Buenos Aires, Argentina.

---

 7 **Escribir**

La fiesta

You and a friend are preparing a surprise meal for your parent's birthday, using what's already in your kitchen. Look in the refrigerator at right, and make a list of eight items that you would use to prepare the meal. Be creative!

▼**8** | 😀👥 | **Hablar**

¿Qué comemos en la fiesta?

Compare your list from Actividad 7 with your partner's list. Tell your partner what you think you need for the party. Your partner will agree or disagree.

▶️ **Modelo**

A —*Creo que necesitamos queso.*
B —*Estoy de acuerdo. ¡Me encanta!*
o:—*No estoy de acuerdo. ¡Qué asco!*

▼9 | ♻ | Escribir

Menú del día

You're in charge of the menu! Decide what you would serve your family for each meal. Copy the chart below on a sheet of paper, and fill in items that you would serve. Be sure to include at least five logical items for each one.

el desayuno	el almuerzo	la cena

Una cena para toda la familia

▼10 | 👥 | ♻ | Pensar • Hablar

¿Sí o no?

With a partner, talk about the things that you should eat and drink in order to be healthy.

▶ **Modelo**

A —¿Debo *beber leche* cada día para mantener la salud?

B —Creo que sí.

o:—Creo que no.

Estudiante A

Estudiante B

Creo que . . .

▼**11** | (Talk!) 👥 | **Hablar**

¿Qué prefieres?

Ask your partner which of two foods he or she prefers. Your partner will answer and ask you which one you prefer.

▶️ **Modelo**

A —*¿Qué prefieres, <u>carne</u> o <u>pescado</u>?*
B —*Prefiero <u>carne</u>. Y tú, ¿qué prefieres?*
o:—*No como ni <u>carne</u> ni <u>pescado</u>. Y tú, ¿qué prefieres?*
A —*Prefiero <u>pescado</u>.*

Estudiante A

1.
2.
3.
4.
5.
6.
7.

Estudiante B

¡Respuesta personal!

En este mercado de la Ciudad de México, hay muchas frutas y verduras.

¿Hay algo para comer?

Working with a partner, talk about what you should
eat and drink at the following times.

Para decir más ...
de la **mañana**	in the morning
de la **tarde**	in the afternoon
de la **noche**	in the evening

▶ **Modelo**

A —*Son las ocho de la mañana y tengo hambre y sed.
¿Qué debo comer y beber?*

B —*Debes comer cereal y debes beber té.*

Estudiante A

1.   2.   3.

4.   5.   6.

Estudiante B

¡Respuesta personal!

▼**13** **Leer · Escribir**

Los buenos consejos

Give advice about what's good or bad
for your health. Copy and complete
each sentence.

1. Para mantener la salud, debes ____
   todos los días.

2. Necesitas beber ____ cada día.

3. Debes comer ____ en la cena.

4. ____ es malo para la salud.

5. El jugo de zanahoria es ____.

6. Debes comer ____ todos los días.

7. Nunca debes comer ____.

▼**14** | (Talk!) 👥 | **Hablar**

Compartir consejos

Compare the advice you gave in Actividad 13
with the advice your partner gave. If you
disagree with your partner's advice, suggest
something else.

▶ **Modelo**

A —*Para mantener la salud, debes practicar
deportes todos los días.*

B —*Estoy de acuerdo.*

o:—*No estoy de acuerdo. Debes correr todos
los días.*

También se dice ...

los guisantes = los chícharos
(México);
las arvejas
(Argentina, Bolivia)
las papas = las patatas (España)
el tomate = el jitomate (México)

▼15 | (Talk?) | ♻ | Leer • Escribir • Hablar

Un *quiz* para la salud

❶ Take the following quiz on healthy activities. Write your answers in complete sentences on a sheet of paper.

❷ Get together with a partner and ask each other all of the questions on the quiz. Keep track of your partner's *sí* and *no* answers and see how he or she scored.

❸ Write five recommendations suggesting what your partner should do every day to have a healthier lifestyle.

Modelo
Debes hacer ejercicio todos los días.

¿Qué haces para mantener la salud?

Contesta las preguntas según las actividades que haces cada día. Cada "sí" = 1 punto.

sí   no

1. ¿Haces ejercicio?
2. ¿Practicas deportes?
3. ¿Comes verduras?
4. ¿Comes frutas?
5. ¿Caminas o corres?
6. ¿Comes un buen desayuno?
7. ¿Comes comida que es buena para la salud?
8. ¿Bebes cinco vasos* de agua?
9. ¿Pasas tiempo con amigos?
10. ¿Ves tres horas o menos de televisión?

9–10 puntos *¡Felicidades! ¡Haces mucho para mantener la salud!*

6–8 puntos *Bueno, pero debes hacer más para mantener la salud.*

0–5 puntos *¡Ay, ay, ay! Necesitas hacer algo para mantener la salud.*

*glasses

| ▼ **Objectives**

▸ **Express opinions about food and describe people**
▸ **Discuss and compare food and beverage preferences with classmates**

Gramática

The plurals of adjectives

Just as adjectives agree with a noun depending on whether it's masculine or feminine, they also agree according to whether the noun is singular or plural. To make adjectives plural, just add an *-s* after the vowel at the end of the adjective. If the adjective ends in a consonant, add *-es*.

> La hamburguesa es sabrosa. Las hamburguesas son sabrosas.
>
> El pastel es muy popular. Los pasteles son muy populares.

When an adjective describes a group including both masculine and feminine nouns, use the masculine plural form.

> La lechuga, las zanahorias y los tomates son buenos para la salud.

Don't forget that in the singular form, *mucho(a)* means "much," but in the plural form, *muchos(as)* means "many."

> No como mucha carne, pero como muchas verduras.

> **¿Recuerdas?**
> Adjectives agree in gender with the masculine or feminine nouns they modify:
> - **El** bistec es sabro**so**.
> - **La** ensalada es sabro**sa**.

Más ayuda   **realidades.com**

▶ *GramActiva* Video

◀)) *Canción de hip hop:* ¿Sabroso o malo?

✎ *GramActiva* Activity

▼16 | ♻ | Pensar · Leer · GramActiva

¿Sabroso o sabrosa?

Your teacher will give you a GramActiva worksheet. Tear or cut apart the different adjective stems and endings that are printed on the sheet. Then your teacher will show you pictures of several foods. Show how you feel about each food item by holding up the appropriate adjective stem and the appropriate ending.

▼17 Escribir

Exageramos un poco

Exaggerate a little by rewriting the following sentences in plural form.

Modelo
La hamburguesa es sabrosa.
Todas las hamburguesas son sabrosas.

1. La estudiante es deportista.
2. El helado es muy popular.
3. La bebida es horrible.
4. El pastel es malo para la salud.
5. La fruta es buena para la salud.
6. El refresco es sabroso.

▼**18** | (Talk!) | **Hablar** _____

En el club deportivo

In many parts of Latin America, young people exercise, practice sports, and get together for after-school activities at sports clubs. Work with a partner to describe the following kids who go to the Club Deportivo Águila.

Luis y Ricardo

▶ **Modelo**

A —*¿Cómo son Luis y Ricardo?*
B —*Ellos son atrevidos.*

Estudiante A

Flor y Carlos

Lisa y Pilar

Andrés y Carmen

Marco y Tomás

Paqui y Ramón

Micaela y Luisa

Estudiante B

perezoso	serio
artístico	atrevido
gracioso	talentoso
deportista	

Más práctica   GO

realidades.com | print

Instant Check	✔	
Guided WB pp. 109–110	✔	✔
Core WB p. 62	✔	✔
Comm. WB pp. 64, 67	✔	✔
Hispanohablantes **WB** pp. 114–117		✔

▼ **Pronunciación** | 🔊 | (Talk!)

The letters *l* and *ll*

In Spanish, the letter *l* is pronounced much like the letter *l* in the English word *leaf*. Listen to and say these words:

lechuga	lunes	pasteles	helado
almuerzo	sol	abril	difícil

For most Spanish speakers, the letter combination *ll* is similar to the sound of the letter *y* in *yes*. Listen to and say these words:

llamo	silla	allí	llueve
cebolla	pollo	ella	mantequilla

Try it out!
Listen to this song and then sing it.

Canta el gallo, canta el gallo
con el kiri, kiri, kiri, kiri, kiri;
La gallina, la gallina
con el cara, cara, cara, cara, cara;
Los polluelos, los polluelos
con el pío, pío, pío, pío, pío, pío, pí.

Gramática

▼ **Objectives**

▶ **Listen to descriptions of food in a market**
▶ **Describe people, places, and foods**
▶ **Compare opinions about food with a classmate**
▶ **Read and write about a Spanish festival and pizza**

The verb *ser*

Ser, which means "to be," is an irregular verb. Use *ser* to describe what a person or thing is like. Here are the present-tense forms:

(yo)	soy	(nosotros) (nosotras)	somos
(tú)	eres	(vosotros) (vosotras)	sois
Ud. (él) (ella)	es	Uds. (ellos) (ellas)	son

¿Recuerdas?

In previous chapters, you learned how to talk about what a person is like.

—Tú **eres** muy deportista, ¿no?

—Sí, **soy** deportista.

—Mi amigo Pablo **es** deportista también.

Más ayuda   **realidades.com**

▶ *GramActiva* **Video Tutorial:** *ser* **Animated Verbs**

✎ *GramActiva* **Activity**

▼19 Escribir

Amigos deportistas

Juan Pablo thinks that he and his friends are very athletic. Find out why by combining the appropriate phrases. Write the completed sentences on a sheet of paper.

1. Es muy deportista . . .
2. Somos muy deportistas . . .
3. Son muy deportistas . . .
4. Soy muy deportista . . .
5. Eres muy deportista . . .

a. porque ellos caminan todos los días.
b. porque yo corro cada tarde.
c. porque ella hace mucho ejercicio.
d. porque tú levantas pesas.
e. porque nosotros nadamos todas las noches.

▼20 Leer • Escribir

En el mercado de frutas

Rafe's mother is explaining to him how she likes to buy fruit at the local market. Complete her explanation by using the correct form of the verb *ser*. Write your answers on a separate sheet of paper.

Yo __1.__ muy práctica. Me gusta mucho comprar la fruta en el mercado Zarzalejos. La fruta nunca __2.__ mala. Los plátanos __3.__ sabrosos y las fresas __4.__ muy buenas también. La Sra. Zarzalejos y yo __5.__ buenas amigas. Ella trabaja en el mercado y __6.__ muy trabajadora. El Sr. y la Sra. Zarzalejos __7.__ muy simpáticos. Rafe, tú __8.__ muy trabajador, ¿por qué no trabajas en el mercado con ellos en el verano?

Fondo Cultural | El mundo hispano

Los mercados, or open-air markets, are common throughout Latin America. Many towns have a central market, held on a given day of the week, where people come from all around to buy and sell food, as well as flowers, crafts, and clothing.

• How does this market compare with the ways in which fruits and vegetables are bought in your community?

Un mercado guatemalteco

▼21 | 🔊 | Escuchar • Escribir

Escucha y escribe

You will hear comments from five customers about the food being sold in a market. On a sheet of paper, write the numbers 1–5. As you listen, write the comments next to the numbers.

Un mercado de frutas

▼22 Escribir

En la cafetería

Write eight original sentences to describe the following people and things that you see while eating lunch in the cafeteria. Your sentences all need to make sense!

yo		inteligente	sabroso
el almuerzo		deportista	malo para la salud
las verduras		talentoso	horrible
mis amigos y yo	ser	simpático	perezoso
la leche		popular	bueno para la salud
los profesores			
tú			
el helado			

¡Respuesta personal!

Where did it come from?

The names of many foods in Spanish come from Latin as well as from other languages as diverse as Arabic, Italian, Greek, Turkish, and English. While it's clear that the word *espaguetis* comes from the Italian word *spaghetti,* it's not obvious that the word *zanahoria* comes from the Arabic word *safunariya.*

Try it out! Read the Spanish words on the left and match them up to their counterparts in their language of origin on the right.

agua	*piscatu* (Latin)
arroz	*aqua* (Latin)
pan	*beefsteak* (English)
bistec	*panis* (Latin)
salchichas	*pullu* (Latin)
pescado	*kahvé* (Turkish)
café	*salciccia* (Italian)
pollo	*óryza* (Greek)

▼**23**  | **Hablar**

¿Sabroso u horrible?

Work with a partner and express your opinions on various foods and beverages.

🎥 **Modelo**

A —*¿Comes <u>zanahorias en la cena</u>?*
B —*No, no como <u>zanahorias en la cena</u> porque <u>son horribles</u>.*
o:—*Sí, como zanahorias en la cena porque <u>son buenas para la salud</u>.*

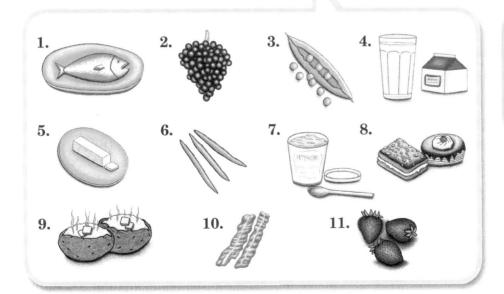

Estudiante A

1.   2.   3.   4.

5.   6.   7.   8.

9.   10.   11.

Estudiante B

(muy) sabroso
bueno para la salud
malo para la salud
horrible
¡Respuesta personal!

▼Fondo Cultural | España

La Tomatina How would you like to attend a festival where a gigantic food fight with tomatoes is the highlight of the day? That's what happens at the annual *Fiesta de la Tomatina* in Buñol, Spain. After the town council distributes more than 130 tons of ripe tomatoes to participants, the hour-long tomato-throwing festival begins.

• Describe any festivals unique to your community or your state. How do they compare to *La Tomatina*?

La Tomatina, en Buñol, España

▼24 Leer • Escribir

En el festival

Your friend Juanito has just attended the *Tomatina* festival and has written a postcard to tell you all about it. However, there were so many tomatoes flying around that some got on the postcard, and now you have to figure out what it says.

1 Number your paper 1–5 and write the forms of the verb *ser* that best complete the postcard.

2 Write your own postcard to a friend and describe people you know and things you are familiar with. Use Juanito's postcard as a model.

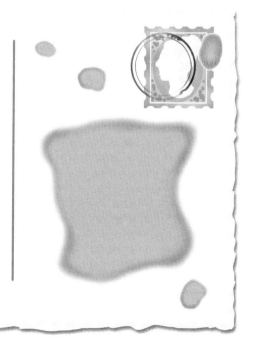

¡Hola!

Estoy en la Fiesta de la Tomatina en España. El festival __1.__ muy divertido. Yo __2.__ amigo de unos estudiantes en la escuela en Buñol. Nosotros __3.__ atrevidos y participamos[1] todos los años. Creo que los tomates __4.__ horribles. ¡No me gustan nada! Nunca como tomates, prefiero tirarlos.[2] Tú __5.__ atrevido, ¿verdad? Debes visitar Buñol.

Hasta pronto,

Juanito

[1]we participate   [2]to throw them

▼25 | ♻ | Leer • Escribir

Una pizza para la buena salud

Read this ad for pizza and answer the questions that follow.

¡Pizzas saludables!

A veces la pizza tiene muchas calorías y grasas que no son buenas para la salud.

La Pizzería Lilia tiene una variedad de pizzas con ingredientes que son buenos y saludables.

- Menos queso
- Usamos ingredientes nutritivos
  - Más verduras (tienen pocas calorías y son muy nutritivas)
- Evita[1] la combinación de carnes
  - Las carnes tienen mucho sodio y grasas
  - El pollo o el jamón son mejores[2] que las salchichas

¡Llámanos!

¡Estamos aquí para servirte!

372 42 89

Calle Independencia 28

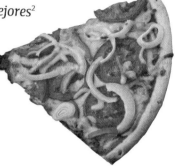

[1]Avoid [2]better

1. Find and list three cognates in this ad.
2. Write three recommendations for a healthier pizza.

▼26 | (talk!) | Escribir • Hablar

Y tú, ¿qué dices?

1. ¿Qué prefieres en tu pizza, cebolla o pollo?
2. Describe tu pizza favorita.
3. ¿Crees que la pizza es buena o mala para la salud? ¿Por qué?
4. ¿Qué verduras prefieres? ¿Qué verduras no te gustan?
5. ¿Qué comes cuando tienes hambre?

El español en el mundo del trabajo

Rick Bayless's career as a world-class Mexican chef began at the age of 14, when he visited Mexico and decided to study Spanish. Since 1987, Rick has opened gourmet Mexican restaurants, created and starred in cooking shows, written cookbooks, and won many awards.

- How would Rick's Spanish skills be helpful in his career?

Para decir más . . .

doscientos	two hundred	**seiscientos**	six hundred
trescientos	three hundred	**setecientos**	seven hundred
cuatrocientos	four hundred	**ochocientos**	eight hundred
quinientos	five hundred	**novecientos**	nine hundred

▼**27** | ♻ | Leer • Escribir

Las calorías y la salud

Conexiones | La salud

You've probably noticed that the nutritional labels on the bottle of juice that you drink, the energy bar that you eat, or even the gum that you chew all have a listing for calories. Our bodies burn calories even when we are sleeping. We can burn more or fewer calories depending on how much we weigh and what kind of activities we do. Look at the chart at right and answer the questions that follow.

Promedio[1] de calorías quemadas[2] en una hora de ejercicio

Actividad	Peso[3] 55–59 kg	Peso 77–82 kg
Básquetbol	170–515	400–800
Bailar	115–400	160–560
Correr 10 km/h	575	800
Fútbol	290–690	400–960
Nadar	230–690	320–900
Tenis	230–515	320–720
Caminar 6 km/h	250	340

[1]Average [2]burned (*quemar* = to burn) [3]weight

1. ¿En qué actividad quemas más calorías si pesas (*you weigh*) 78 kilogramos?

2. Pablo nada por una hora y Paco corre por una hora. Ellos queman el máximo (*maximum*) número de calorías. ¿Quién quema más calorías?

3. Tú pesas 55 kg. Bailas por dos horas y quemas el máximo número de calorías. ¿Cuántas quemas?

4. Una barra de chocolate (*chocolate bar*) tiene 320 calorías. Pesas 59 kg. ¿Por cuántos minutos tienes que caminar para quemar las calorías? ¿Es mucho?

Más práctica (GO) realidades.com | print

Instant Check	✔	
Guided WB pp. 111–112	✔	✔
Core WB pp. 63–64	✔	✔
Comm. WB pp. 65, 68, 145	✔	✔
Hispanohablantes WB pp. 118–121		✔

Lectura

La comida de los atletas

Lee este artículo *(article)* de una revista deportiva. ¿Qué comen y qué beben los atletas profesionales para mantener la salud y estar en buena forma?

Strategy

Skimming
List three things that you would expect to find in an article about athletes' eating habits. Skim the article to find the information.

¿Qué come un jugador de fútbol?

Los jugadores[1] de fútbol comen comidas equilibradas con muchos carbohidratos, minerales y vitaminas. Ellos consumen cerca de 5.000 calorías en total todos los días.

17% Proteínas

13% Grasas

70% Carbohidratos

Para el desayuno el día de un partido[2], un jugador típico come mucho pan con mantequilla y jalea[3], yogur y té.

Para el almuerzo antes del[4] partido, come pan, pasta, pollo sin grasa, verduras, frutas y una ensalada.

Para la cena después del[5] partido, el atleta come papas, carne sin grasa y más verduras y frutas.

También es muy importante beber muchos líquidos. La noche antes del partido, el jugador bebe un litro de jugo de naranja y durante el partido bebe hasta[6] dos litros de agua y bebidas deportivas.

[1]players [2]game [3]jam [4]before the [5]after the [6]up to

Nombre: Carlos Tévez
Fecha de nacimiento: 2/5/84
Lugar de nacimiento: Capital Federal
País de nacimiento: Argentina
Nacionalidad: argentino
Equipo[7]: Manchester City
Función: Ofensa

En esta foto, Tévez representa al equipo nacional de Argentina.

[7]**team**

¿Comprendes?

1. ¿Qué debe comer Carlos Tévez antes de un partido de fútbol?

2. ¿Qué debe beber?

3. ¿Qué comida no debe comer Carlos?

4. ¿Es tu dieta diferente de la dieta de un jugador de fútbol profesional? ¿Cómo?

5. ¿Cuál es la fecha de nacimiento (*birth date*) de Carlos? Escribe tu fecha de nacimiento como lo hacen en los países hispanohablantes.

Más práctica	GO
	**realidades.com	print**
Guided WB p. 113	✔ ✔
Comm. WB pp. 69, 146	✔ ✔
Hispanohablantes WB pp. 122–123	✔
Cultural Reading Activity	✔

 Fondo Cultural | El mundo hispano

¡Goooooooooooool! Scoring the winning *gol* is the most exciting moment of the game. *El fútbol* is the most popular sport in the world, and it has many *fanáticos* (fans) in every Spanish-speaking country. Every four years, teams throughout the world compete regionally in order to become one of the 32 teams to advance to the World Cup (*la Copa Mundial*) competition. Many Spanish-speaking countries compete in what has become the most widely watched sporting event in the world. Since the competition began in 1930, three Spanish-speaking countries have won the World Cup competition: Uruguay in 1930 and 1950, Argentina in 1978 and 1986, and Spain in 2010.

• How does the enthusiasm for soccer in the United States compare with the rest of the world's view of this sport? Why do you think this is so?

España gana la Copa Mundial, 2010.

Perspectivas del mundo hispano
¿Qué haces para mantener la salud?

Have you ever eaten chicken soup when you have a cold? How about putting aloe on a sunburn? In many countries, including those in the Spanish-speaking world, traditional remedies consisting of medicinal herbs have been used for centuries to treat common medical problems. In Mexico, a mint known as *yerbabuena* may be made into tea and given to someone with a stomachache. Remedies such as these may not be prescribed by licensed physicians, but people have confidence in them because they have been passed down through the generations. Many of those herbs are very safe, though some may have harmful side effects.

Researchers are studying traditional herbal remedies to find modern-day medical solutions. In the Amazon rainforest in South America, an amazing abundance of plant life may hold the key to treating a wide variety of common ailments and diseases. Drug companies are looking for cures found in these plants and herbs that could be reproduced in today's modern drugs.

Increasingly, medicinal herbs are accepted not only as the basis for pharmaceutical drugs, but also for their own inherent healing qualities. In many countries, including the United States, herbal remedies are sometimes used in combination with conventional healthcare.

Estos hombres estudian plantas medicinales en la selva *(jungle)* amazónica.

Check it out! What alternatives to conventional medical care are available in your community? Make a list of all the healthcare services you can think of that are not traditional physicians. Are there health stores that sell herbal medicines? What types of herbal medicines are being sold and what remedies are attributed to these medicines?

Think about it! In many Spanish-speaking cultures, herbal remedies have been accepted for centuries. Do you think that medicinal herbs can provide relief and cures? Why or why not?

En un mercado de Guanajuato, México

Presentación escrita

Para mantener la salud

Task
You are researching good eating and exercise habits for your health class. Make a poster in Spanish with five health suggestions.

1 Prewrite Ask people at school and home about good eating and exercise habits for teens. List their ideas under these headings to organize your information.

- *Debes comer . . .*
- *No debes comer mucho(a) . . .*
- *Debes . . . para mantener la salud*
- *Debes beber . . .*
- *No debes beber mucho(a) . . .*

Strategy

Gathering information
Gathering information from a variety of sources helps you create a more complete presentation on a topic.

2 Draft Decide how to present the information logically as you write your first draft. Use visuals for clarity and give your poster a title.

3 Revise Share your draft with a partner. Your partner should check the following:

- Have you communicated five suggestions well?
- Do the visuals convey meaning? Is the poster attractive?
- Are the vocabulary and grammar correct?

Revise your poster, making any necessary changes.

4 Publish Make a final copy for posting in the nurse's office, a community center, your classroom, or your portfolio.

5 Evaluation The following rubric will be used to grade your presentation.

Rubric	Score 1	Score 3	Score 5
Completion of task	You included at least three suggestions for a healthy lifestyle.	You included at least four suggestions for a healthy lifestyle.	You included five or more suggestions for a healthy lifestyle.
Accuracy of vocabulary and grammar	You had very little variation of vocabulary use with many grammar errors.	You had limited usage of vocabulary and some grammar errors.	You had extended use of a variety of vocabulary with very few grammar errors.
Effective use of visuals	You included only three visuals that clearly connect to information.	You included only four visuals that clearly connect to information.	You included five visuals that clearly connect to information.

América del Sur

Parte sur

A large proportion of the people of Argentina, Uruguay, and Chile live in cities. As in the United States, these cities have been shaped by mass immigration from southern and eastern Europe during the nineteenth and twentieth centuries. Many more Paraguayans, in contrast, live in the countryside.

In the early 1900s, the area of *las cataratas de Iguazú* was made an Argentine national park. Three countries—Brazil, Argentina, and Paraguay—meet at these spectacular falls, which are four times the width of Niagara Falls and 50 percent higher. Hundreds of species of insects, birds, and mammals are found in the area, and at least 500 species of butterflies. As many as 14,000 tourists a day visit the falls, a worrisome number for environmental groups, who continue to lobby against nearby hotel construction projects.

¿Sabes que . . . ?

At 22,840 feet (6,962 meters), Argentina's Cerro Aconcagua is the highest point in the Western Hemisphere, but it is considered a relatively easy climb. Chile's Torres del Paine, three granite towers, are nearly 6,000 feet lower, but their sheer cliffs, high winds, and extreme cold make them some of the most challenging climbs in the world. Both mountains are part of the Andes, a range that extends from Colombia to the southern tip of South America.

Para pensar

Think about what it would be like to be an immigrant arriving in one of the countries of southern South America. Would you prefer the city life of Buenos Aires, Argentina, Montevideo, Uruguay, or Santiago, Chile? Or would the countryside of Paraguay be more appealing? Why?

realidades.com GO

 Mapa global interactivo

 Reference Atlas

The Spanish were able to topple large, centralized empires such as those of the Aztecs and Incas quickly, but they were never able to conquer the smaller indigenous groups in the more remote regions. Chile's Pehuenche suffered defeats in the nineteenth century, but they still struggle to maintain their lands and culture. ▶

◀ Spain introduced horses, cows, sheep, and pigs to the Americas in the sixteenth century, transforming the ecology, culture, and economy of the region. In the nineteenth century, the growth of cities, the expansion of railways, and improvements in shipping created a worldwide market for South American meat and hides—and helped spur the development of the cowboy culture throughout the Americas. As on ranches in the western United States and northern Mexico, the main house of an Argentine or Uruguayan *estancia* served as a residence, office, and military stronghold.

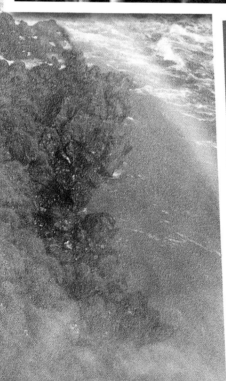

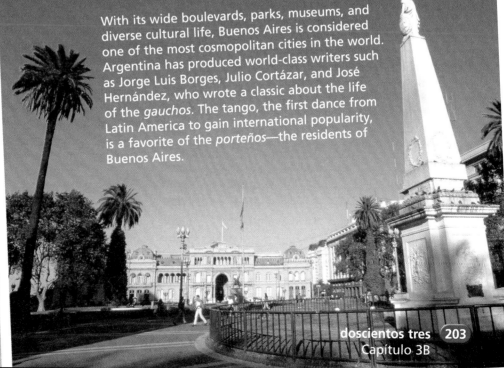

With its wide boulevards, parks, museums, and diverse cultural life, Buenos Aires is considered one of the most cosmopolitan cities in the world. Argentina has produced world-class writers such as Jorge Luis Borges, Julio Cortázar, and José Hernández, who wrote a classic about the life of the *gauchos*. The tango, the first dance from Latin America to gain international popularity, is a favorite of the *porteños*—the residents of Buenos Aires.

Repaso | 🔊 | ▶️ | 🖼️

▼ **Objectives**
▶ Review the vocabulary and grammar
▶ Demonstrate you can perform the tasks on p. 205

Repaso del capítulo
Vocabulario y gramática

to talk about food and beverages

la cena	dinner
el bistec	beefsteak
la carne	meat
el pescado	fish
el pollo	chicken
la cebolla	onion
los guisantes	peas
las judías verdes	green beans
la lechuga	lettuce
las papas	potatoes
los tomates	tomatoes
las uvas	grapes
las zanahorias	carrots
el arroz	rice
los cereales	grains
los espaguetis	spaghetti
las grasas	fats
la mantequilla	butter
el helado	ice cream
los pasteles	pastries
las bebidas	beverages

to talk about being hungry and thirsty

Tengo hambre.	I'm hungry.
Tengo sed.	I'm thirsty.

to discuss health

caminar	to walk
hacer ejercicio	to exercise
(yo) hago	I do
(tú) haces	you do
levantar pesas	to lift weights
para la salud	for one's health
para mantener la salud	to maintain one's health

to indicate a preference

(yo) prefiero	I prefer
(tú) prefieres	you prefer
deber	should, must

to indicate agreement or disagreement

Creo que . . .	I think (that) . . .
Creo que sí / no.	I (don't) think so.
(No) estoy de acuerdo.	I (don't) agree.

to express a question or an answer

¿Por qué?	Why?
porque	because

to express quantity

algo	something
muchos, -as	many
todos, -as	all

to describe something

horrible	horrible
malo, -a	bad
sabroso, -a	tasty, flavorful

other useful words

cada día	every day

plurals of adjectives

Masculine	Feminine
Singular/Plural	Singular/Plural
sabros**o**/sabros**os**	sabros**a**/sabros**as**
popular/popular**es**	popular/popular**es**

ser *to be*

soy	somos
eres	sois
es	son

For *Vocabulario adicional,* see pp. 268–269.

Más repaso GO   realidades.com | print

Instant Check	✔
Puzzles	✔
Core WB pp. 65–66	✔
Comm. WB pp. 147, 148–150	✔ ✔

Preparación para el examen

On the exam you will be asked to . . .	Here are practice tasks similar to those you will find on the exam . . .	For review go to your print or digital textbook . . .
1 Escuchar Listen and understand as people describe a healthy or unhealthy lifestyle	Listen as two people are interviewed about their habits. See if you can tell which one is an Olympic skier and which one is a drummer. Be prepared to explain your "educated guesses."	**pp. 178–183** *Vocabulario en contexto* **p. 179** Actividad 2
2 Hablar Express your opinion about food preferences	During a telephone survey, you are asked some questions in Spanish about your food preferences. Say whether you think each food choice is good or bad for your health.	**p. 187** Actividad 11 **p. 188** Actividades 12, 14 **p. 194** Actividad 23 **p. 197** Actividad 27
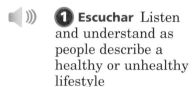 **3 Leer** Read and compare what people do and eat in order to determine whether they lead a healthy or unhealthy lifestyle	Read the online conversation that you have just joined in a chat room. Decide whether each person has a healthy or unhealthy lifestyle, based on what they tell each other. Chato: ¿Qué hago yo? Cuando hace buen tiempo, corro por treinta minutos. Cuando llueve, levanto pesas. Chispa: No me gusta hacer ejercicio. Prefiero comer papas fritas. Son muy sabrosas. Andrés: ¿Papas fritas? Son horribles para la salud. Para mantener la salud, nunca debes comer papas fritas.	**pp. 178–183** *Vocabulario en contexto* **p. 188** Actividad 13 **p. 189** Actividad 15 **p. 196** Actividad 25 **pp. 198–199** *Lectura*
4 Escribir Write a list of things a person should do to maintain a healthy lifestyle	Many people think that teens don't know anything about a healthy lifestyle. You and your friends are compiling a top-ten list of ways to improve teens' health. Write at least three suggestions for the list.	**p. 188** Actividad 13 **p. 189** Actividad 15 **p. 196** Actividad 25 **p. 201** *Presentación escrita*
5 Pensar Demonstrate an understanding of cultural perspectives regarding healthcare	Give an example of an herbal remedy that is accepted in a Spanish-speaking country as a remedy for a common ailment. Compare this with a similar herbal/natural remedy believed by many in the United States to be a cure for a common ailment.	**p. 200** *Perspectivas del mundo hispano*

Capítulo
4A ¿Adónde vas?

▼ Chapter Objectives

Communication
By the end of this chapter you will be able to:
- Listen to and read descriptions of leisure activities and schedules
- Talk and write about places to go and activities to do during free time
- Exchange information about weekend plans

Culture
You will also be able to:
- Understand the meaning and role of children's rhymes from the Spanish-speaking world
- Compare leisure activities in the Spanish-speaking world and the United States

You will demonstrate what you know and can do:
- Presentación oral, p. 233
- Preparación para el examen, p. 237

You will use:
Vocabulary
- Leisure activities
- Places in the community
- When things are done

Grammar
- The verb *ir*
- Asking questions

Exploración del mundo hispano

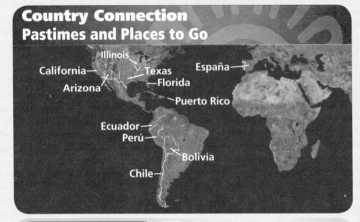

Country Connection
Pastimes and Places to Go

Illinois
California
Arizona
Texas
Florida
España
Puerto Rico
Ecuador
Perú
Bolivia
Chile

 realidades.com GO

 Reference Atlas

 Videocultura y actividad

 Mapa global interactivo

Arte y cultura | España

"El quitasol" is a work by Spanish painter Francisco de Goya (1746–1828). He made this painting in 1777 as a design to be used in the manufacture of a royal tapestry. At that time Goya was already famous for the elegance of his artwork and his ability to capture ordinary events in realistic detail. The brilliant colors of this painting suggest a happy moment of relaxation for two young people.

• Why do people who live in the city go out to the country to relax?

"El quitasol" (1777), Francisco de Goya ▼
Oil on canvas, 104 x 152 cm. Museo Nacional del Prado, Madrid, Spain.
Photo Credit: Scala / Art Resource, NY.

En el Parque Nacional Torres del Paine, Patagonia, Chile

Vocabulario en contexto

el gimnasio

el parque

el centro comercial

ir de compras

el trabajo

la lección de piano

el cine

ver una película

la biblioteca

la piscina

—En tu **tiempo libre después de** las clases, ¿qué haces?

—**Voy al** gimnasio **para** levantar pesas y al parque para correr. ¿Y tú?

—Hoy voy **a** mi trabajo. No voy a mi lección de piano.

—**¿Con quién** vas al centro comercial?

—Voy con Guillermo, y **después vamos** al cine. ¿Y tú?

—Voy a la biblioteca para estudiar. Después voy al **Café** del Mundo con Lucila.

la playa

el restaurante

el campo

las montañas

—¿Qué haces **los** domingos?

    —Voy **con mis amigos** a la playa.
    Allí comemos el almuerzo. Hay un
    restaurante muy bueno. ¿Y tú?

—**Generalmente** voy al campo o a las
montañas.

> **Más vocabulario**
>
> la iglesia   church
>
> la mezquita   mosque
>
> la sinagoga   synagogue
>
> el templo   temple;
>   Protestant church

▼**1** | 🔊))) | Escuchar

¿Estás de acuerdo?

You will hear Elena describe where she does
seven activities. If a statement is logical,
give a "thumbs-up" sign. If it is not logical, give
a "thumbs-down" sign.

▼**2** | 🔊))) | Escuchar

¡Muchas actividades!

Listen to Antonio describe his weekly list
of after-school activities. As he names his
activities, touch the corresponding picture(s).

Más práctica	GO	
	**realidades.com	print**	
Instant Check	✔	
Guided WB pp. 115–120	✔	✔
Core WB pp. 67–68	✔	✔
Comm. WB p. 75	✔	✔
Hispanohablantes **WB** p. 132	✔	

Un chico reservado

¿Qué pasa cuando Ignacio, Elena y Ana hablan con el estudiante nuevo *(new)?* Lee la historia.

España

Ignacio

Ana

Javier

Antes de leer

Strategy **Using visuals** You can use visuals to predict what might happen in a story.

  • Use the photos in the *Videohistoria* to predict what different activities Ana, Elena, Ignacio, and Javier are talking about. Then, look in the dialogues and find the corresponding word or phrase that describes each activity.

1. Does your school get many new students each year? If so, do you make a point to get to know them? Can you tell from the photos which person is the new student at this school?

2. What do you usually do after school? Do you have the same routine, or do your activities vary? Use the photos to compare the activities that these students participate in with your own pastimes.

Ignacio: Mira, el estudiante nuevo es un poco reservado, ¿verdad?

Elena: Ah sí . . . Está allí **solo.** ¿Por qué no hablamos con él?

Ignacio: Sí, ¡vamos!

Elena: Hola. Me llamo Elena. Él es Ignacio, y ella es Ana.

Javier: Mucho gusto. Me llamo Javier.

Elena: Encantada . . . **¿De dónde eres?**

Javier: Soy de Salamanca.

Ana: Pues, Javier, ¿vas después de las clases **con tus amigos?**

Javier: No, voy **a casa.**

Javier: **¿Adónde** vais* vosotros después de las clases?

Elena: Los lunes, miércoles y viernes voy a mi trabajo en el centro comercial.

Ignacio: Generalmente voy al gimnasio. Me gusta levantar pesas.

*Remember that in Spain, the *vosotros(as)* form of the verb is used when speaking to a group of people you would address individually with *tú.*

Ana: Los lunes voy a mi lección de piano y los martes, miércoles y jueves voy a la biblioteca para estudiar. Y Javier, ¿qué haces **los fines de semana?**

Javier: ¿Los fines de semana? **Me quedo en casa.** No tengo muchos amigos aquí.

Ignacio: ¿Qué te gusta hacer?

Javier: ¡Me gusta el fútbol!

Ana: ¡No me digas! Pues, nosotros vamos al parque para practicar fútbol.

Javier: ¿Cuándo?

Ana: El sábado.

Javier: Está bien.

Elena: Pero Ana, ¿fútbol?

Ana: ¿Por qué no? ¡No tiene muchos amigos y le gusta el fútbol!

▼**3** Leer • Escribir

¿Comprendes?

Number your paper 1–6. Based on the *Videohistoria*, choose the response that best completes each statement below. Write the completed sentences on your paper.

1. Javier es de . . .
   a. Madrid.
   b. Barcelona.
   c. Salamanca.

2. Después de las clases Javier va . . .
   a. a la biblioteca para estudiar.
   b. a casa.
   c. al cine.

3. Después de las clases Ignacio va . . .
   a. al gimnasio.
   b. al centro comercial.
   c. al restaurante.

4. El jueves Ana va . . .
   a. a la lección de piano.
   b. a la biblioteca.
   c. a la iglesia.

5. A Javier le gusta practicar . . .
   a. el fútbol.
   b. el golf.
   c. el español.

6. Todos van al parque el . . .
   a. martes.
   b. jueves.
   c. sábado.

▼**4** Leer • Escribir

La rutina de los estudiantes

You are trying to organize everybody's schedule. Copy the chart below onto a sheet of paper. Based on information in the *Videohistoria,* write what each person does on the various days of the week. Not all of the spaces on the chart will be filled.

	Ignacio	Elena	Ana	Javier
lunes				
martes				
miércoles				
jueves				
viernes				
sábado				
domingo				

Más práctica	GO
	realidades.com | print
Instant Check	✔
Guided WB pp. 121–124	✔ ✔
Core WB pp. 69–70	✔ ✔
Comm. WB pp. 70–71, 72	✔ ✔
Hispanohablantes WB p. 133	✔

| ▼ **Objectives**

▶ Write and talk about places you go in your free time
▶ Discuss and compare where you go and how often
▶ Listen to a description of a plaza
▶ Exchange information while reading a map

Vocabulario en uso

▼5 Escribir

¿Qué haces en . . . ?

Using the pictures at right, complete the following sentences logically. Write the completed sentences on your paper.

1. Hago ejercicio en . . .
2. Nado en . . .
3. Veo películas en . . .
4. Leo libros y revistas en . . .
5. Esquío en . . .
6. Como el desayuno en . . .

¡Respuesta personal!

▼6 | ♻ | Escribir

¿Vas mucho a . . . ?

On a sheet of paper, copy the diagram below and write the names of the places you go under the appropriate time expressions.

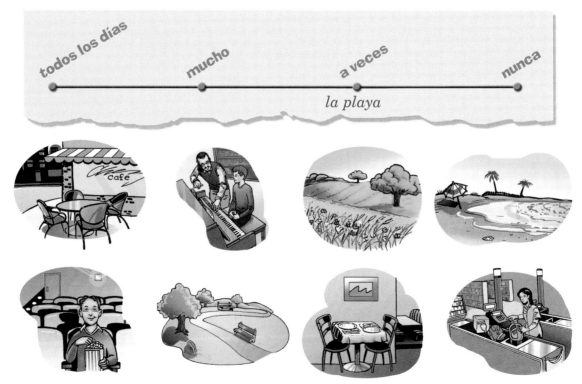

todos los días   mucho   a veces   nunca

la playa

▼7 | Hablar

¡No me digas!

Work with a partner. Using what you wrote for Actividad 6, take turns saying where you go and how often. React to your partner's statements. Follow the model.

▶ Modelo

A —*Voy a la playa a veces.*

B —*¡No me digas! Yo voy a la playa a veces también.*

o: *¡No me digas! Yo nunca voy a la playa.*

o: *Pues, yo voy a la playa todos los días.*

> ### Nota
>
> When *a* is used before *el,* the two words form the contraction *al (to the):*
>
> $$a + el = al$$
>
> • Voy **al** centro comercial a veces pero voy **a la** piscina mucho.

> ### También se dice . . .
>
> **la piscina** la alberca *(México);* la pileta *(América del Sur)*
>
> **el restaurante** el restaurán *(América del Sur)*

▼8 | Escuchar • Escribir

Escucha y escribe

Look at this painting of the plaza below. You will hear six statements about the painting. Number your paper from 1–6 and write what you hear.

▼ Fondo Cultural | El mundo hispano

La plaza Strolling through the main square, *la plaza mayor,* of most towns and cities in Spanish-speaking countries is a popular activity for young and old alike. The *plaza mayor* is typically ringed by stores, cafés, churches, and government buildings. Here people go to eat, shop, worship, and conduct business, and gather for festivals and celebrations. This painting by Pedro Lázaro (1956–) celebrates the beauty and importance of the *plaza* in Hispanic culture.

• What social gathering place in your community is similar to *la plaza?*

"La plaza" (1981), Pedro Lázaro ▶

Lázaro, Pedro born 1956. "La plaza" (The Plaza), 1981. Painting. Madrid, Private Collection. Copyright akg-images/Joseph Martin/Newscom.

Origins of the Spanish days of the week

The word *sábado*, like many Spanish words, is based on Latin. The Spanish days of the week come from the Latin names for the gods, planets, sun, and moon, all of which were important in Roman daily life.

Try it out! Match the Spanish days of the week with their Latin origins.

1. lunes	**a.** *dies Mercurii:* named after Mercury, the god of commerce and travelers
2. martes	**b.** *dies Veneris:* named after Venus, the goddess of beauty and love
3. miércoles	**c.** *dies lunae:* the day dedicated to the moon *(luna)*
4. jueves	**d.** *dies solis:* named after the sun *(sol)*, but later changed to *dies Dominicus*, which means "the Lord's day"
5. viernes	**e.** *dies Martis:* dedicated to Mars, the god of war
6. sábado	**f.** *dies Saturni:* named after Saturn; also called *dies Sabbati*, based on the Hebrew word *shabbath*, or "day of rest"
7. domingo	**g.** *dies Jovis:* named after Jove, or Jupiter, the ruler of the gods

- Since you know *día* means "day" in Spanish, what is the word for "day" in Latin?

▼**9** |  | **Hablar**

¿Adónde vas?

With a partner, talk about the places you go at different times during the week.

 Modelo

los lunes

A —*¿Adónde vas los lunes?*
B —*Generalmente voy a la lección de piano.*
o: *Generalmente me quedo en casa.*

> **Nota**
>
> To say that something usually happens on a certain day every week, use *los* with the plural of the day of the week:
>
> - Generalmente ellos van al campo **los viernes** o **los sábados**.

Estudiante A

1. los miércoles
2. los viernes
3. los sábados
4. los domingos
5. los fines de semana
6. después de las clases

Estudiante B

¡**Respuesta personal!**

▼10 |  | Pensar • Hablar

Leer un mapa no es difícil

When you visit a new city or town in a Spanish-speaking country, you will often use a map to help you get to where you want to go. Although maps may vary from place to place, you will usually find some standard features that will help you find your way around. You should always look for the key *(la clave)*. This will give you the symbols and other information that you need to read the map. Some maps are set up as a grid so that you can use an index to help you find streets or places of interest.

Conexiones | La geografía

You are visiting Madrid. With a partner, take turns asking and answering where you are going, based on the grid locations and the map.

1. F4   **2.** B7   **3.** E1   **4.** B8   **5.** E9   **6.** C10

▶ **Modelo**

D9

A —*Estoy en D9. ¿Adónde voy?*

B —*Vas al restaurante.*

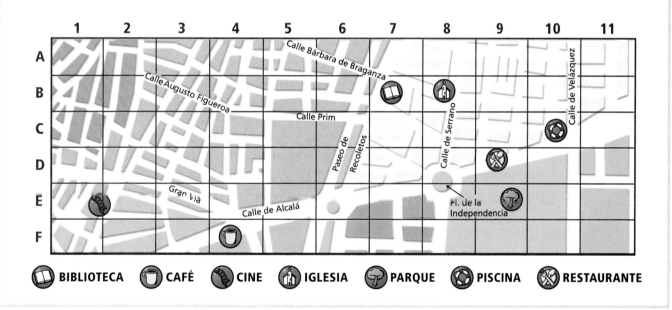

BIBLIOTECA   CAFÉ   CINE   IGLESIA   PARQUE   PISCINA   RESTAURANTE

▼11 | Talk! | Escribir • Hablar

Y tú, ¿qué dices?

1. ¿Dónde ves más películas, en casa o en el cine?

2. Cuando vas de compras, ¿adónde vas?

3. ¿Adónde vas los fines de semana? ¿Vas solo(a) o con tus amigos?

Gramática

The verb *ir*

To say where someone is going, use the verb *ir*. Here are its present-tense forms:

(yo)	**voy**	(nosotros) (nosotras)	**vamos**
(tú)	**vas**	(vosotros) (vosotras)	**vais**
Ud. (él) (ella)	**va**	Uds. (ellos) (ellas)	**van**

The verb *ir* is almost always followed by *a*. To ask where someone is going, use *¿Adónde?*

¿Adónde vas? *Where are you going?*

• You will often hear people say *¡Vamos!* This means, "Let's go!"

¿Recuerdas?

You have used the infinitive *ir* to talk about going to school.

• Me gusta **ir** a la escuela.

Más ayuda — **realidades.com**

▶ **GramActiva Video**
   Animated verbs

🔊 **Canción de hip hop:** *¿Adónde vas?*

GramActiva Activity

▼12 Escribir

¿Adónde va la familia?

The members of the Li family are always busy. They have to leave messages on the refrigerator to let the others know where they are going. Find out where everyone is going by putting the messages together. Write the complete sentences on a separate sheet of paper.

Mario

Luisa y Carlos

Papá y yo

Tú

Yo

vamos al templo.

vas al café.

va a la lección de piano.

voy a casa después del templo.

van a la biblioteca.

▼13 Leer • Escribir

Un año en Chile

María, a student from Corpus Christi, Texas, is spending a year with a family in Santiago, Chile. Read the letter that she wrote to her friends back home and write the correct forms of the verb *ir* on a separate sheet of paper.

Chile

17 de julio

Querida Sonia:

¿Cómo estás? Yo, bien. Generalmente, paso tiempo en casa los fines de semana, pero a veces yo __1.__ a Portillo con mi familia para esquiar. Hace mucho frío allí y por eso la mamá no __2.__ siempre con nosotros. En Portillo hay una escuela para los esquiadores y muchos chicos simpáticos __3.__ a las lecciones. También hay un cibercafé con computadoras. Muchas personas __4.__ allí para pasar tiempo con los amigos. Nosotros __5.__ el domingo. Y tú, ¿ __6.__ a la playa todos los días con tus amigos?

Hasta luego,

María

▼14 Leer • Hablar

La carta

Read the letter in Actividad 13 again and answer the following questions about María's experience in Chile.

1. ¿Quién no va siempre con la familia a Portillo?
2. ¿Por qué a María le gusta ir a las lecciones de esquí?
3. ¿Adónde van para usar las computadoras?
4. ¿Cuándo van al cibercafé?
5. ¿Adónde van muchas personas para pasar tiempo con los amigos?

Portillo, Chile

▼15 Escribir

¿Adónde van todos?

Look at the pictures below. Number your paper 1–6 and, using the places in the word bank, write complete sentences telling where the following people are going.

Elena

Modelo
Elena va a la biblioteca.

la piscina	el cine	la biblioteca
el restaurante	el centro comercial	el parque
el gimnasio		

1.

Luis

2.

yo

3.

Carlitos y Sandrina

4.

nosotros

5.

tú

6.

Uds.

▼16 | ♻ | Escribir

¿Por qué van allí?

Where you go often depends on what you like to do. Using the sentences you wrote in Actividad 15, explain why the people go to those places.

Modelo
Elena va a la biblioteca porque lee muchos libros.

▼17 | Hablar

Voy allí porque me gusta . . .

Choose five of the following places. Working in pairs, ask your partner if he or she goes there and why.

▶ Modelo

A —¿Vas al café?

B —Sí, por supuesto.

o: —Claro que no.

A —¿Por qué (no) vas al café?

B —Voy porque me gusta pasar tiempo con mis amigos.

o: —No voy porque no me gusta beber café.

Estudiante A

el café	la casa
la playa	el cine
la biblioteca	la escuela
las montañas	el centro comercial
el parque	el restaurante

Estudiante B

comer	ver
beber	hablar
pasar tiempo con mis amigos	comprar
	nadar
estudiar	esquiar
leer	

¡Respuesta personal!

▼Fondo Cultural | El mundo hispano

Sports clubs and gyms are very popular in Spanish-speaking countries. Since there are few school-based sports teams, many young people join private gyms for individual exercise, or play for privately sponsored teams, in order to compete in their favorite sports.

• What do you think students would do if your school did not offer opportunities for playing and competing in sports?

Estudiantes en el gimnasio

▼18 | (Talk!) | Escribir • Hablar

Juego

❶ With a partner, write five sentences telling what the two of you do in your free time and when. On a separate sheet of paper, write sentences telling where you go to do these activities.

Modelo

Nosotros corremos después de las clases.
Vamos al gimnasio.

❷ Get together with another pair of students and tell them what you and your partner do in your free time. Be sure not to tell them where you go! It's their job to guess where you go. If they guess correctly, their team gets a point. The team that earns the most points wins.

▶️ Modelo

A —*Nosotros corremos después de las clases.*

B —*Uds. van al gimnasio, ¿verdad?*

A —*Sí, vamos al gimnasio para correr.*

o: —*No, no vamos al gimnasio para correr. Vamos al parque.*

🌎 El español en la comunidad

In many businesses and neighborhoods in the United States, you can hear Spanish being spoken. For example, the Pilsen neighborhood in Chicago, Illinois, is home to one of the nation's largest Mexican communities. Colorful murals, thriving businesses, and popular restaurants give Pilsen its character.

● Are there areas near you where you can see expressions of community for Spanish speakers like those in Pilsen? What are they?

Un mural en la comunidad de Pilsen, en Chicago

Más práctica [GO]

realidades.com | print

Instant Check	✔	
Guided WB pp. 125–126	✔	✔
Core WB p. 71	✔	✔
Comm. WB pp. 73, 76	✔	✔
Hispanohablantes **WB** pp. 134–137		✔

▼ Pronunciación | 🔊 | 💬

Stress and accents

How can you tell which syllable to stress, or emphasize, when you see words written in Spanish? Here are some general rules.

1. **When words end in a vowel, *n,* or *s*** place the stress on the **next-to-last syllable.** Copy each of these words and draw a line under the next-to-last syllable. Then listen to and say these words, making sure you stress the underlined syllable:

centro	pasteles	piscina
computadora	trabajo	parque
mantequilla	escriben	generalmente

2. **When words end in a consonant (except *n* or *s*)** place the stress on the **last syllable.** Listen to and say these words, making sure you stress the last syllable:

señor	nariz	escribir
profesor	reloj	arroz
español	trabajador	comer

3. **When a word has a written accent** place the stress on the **accented syllable.** One reason for written accents is to indicate exceptions to the first two rules. Listen to and say these words. Be sure to emphasize the accented syllable:

café	número	teléfono
difícil	película	lápiz
fácil	plátano	artístico

Try it out! Listen to the first verse of the song "La Bamba" and say each word with the stress on the correct syllable. Then listen to the recording again and see if you can sing along with the first verse.

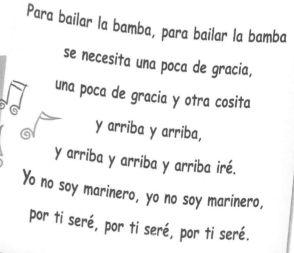

Para bailar la bamba, para bailar la bamba
se necesita una poca de gracia,
una poca de gracia y otra cosita
y arriba y arriba,
y arriba y arriba y arriba iré.
Yo no soy marinero, yo no soy marinero,
por ti seré, por ti seré, por ti seré.

Gramática

Asking questions

You use interrogative words (*who, what, where,* and so on) to ask questions.

¿Qué?	What?	¿Dónde?	Where?	¿Cuál?	Which?, What?
¿Cómo?	How?, What?	¿Cuántos, -as?	How many?	¿Por qué?	Why?
¿Quién?	Who?	¿Adónde?	(To) Where?	¿Cuándo?	When?
¿Con quién?	With whom?	¿De dónde?	From where?		

In Spanish, when you ask a question with an interrogative word, you put the verb before the subject.

¿Qué **come Elena** en el restaurante?

*What **does Elena eat** at the restaurant?*

¿Adónde **van Uds.** después de las clases?

*Where **do you go** after classes?*

¿Por qué **va Ignacio** a la playa todos los días?

*Why **does Ignacio go** to the beach every day?*

You have already used several interrogative words. Notice that all these words have a written accent mark.

For simple questions that can be answered by *sí* or *no,* you can indicate with your voice that you're asking a question:

¿**Ana va a la biblioteca?**

OR: ¿**Ana va a la biblioteca?**

OR: Ana va a la biblioteca, ¿**verdad?**

Más ayuda · **realidades.com**

▶ *GramActiva* **Video**
Tutorials: Questions with Interrogative Words, Question-word Questions, Formation of yes-no questions

GramActiva **Activity**

▼19 Leer · Escribir

Un chico curioso

Joaquín is always asking you questions. Read his questions. Then, number your paper from 1–6 and write the appropriate responses.

1. ¿Qué haces tú después de las clases?
2. ¿Adónde van tú y tus amigos los sábados?
3. ¿Con quién comes tú en la cafetería?
4. ¿Por qué vas tú al gimnasio todos los días?
5. ¿Cuándo estudias tú?
6. ¿Quién es tu profesor favorito?

a. Yo estudio después de la cena.
b. Como el almuerzo con mis amigos.
c. Los sábados nosotros vamos a la biblioteca.
d. Generalmente yo voy al gimnasio.
e. Mi profesor favorito es el señor Rodríguez.
f. Voy porque me gusta mantener la salud.

▼20 Pensar • Escribir

Preguntas revueltas

Your new pen pal from Bolivia has sent you an e-mail, but all of his questions are scrambled. Unscramble the words and write the questions in a logical order on a separate sheet of paper. Then answer your pen pal's questions.

1. ¿eres / de dónde / tú?

2. ¿clases / tienes / cuántas?

3. ¿Uds. / adónde / van / los fines de semana?

4. ¿tú / qué / después de las clases / haces?

5. ¿al centro comercial / cuándo / van / Uds.?

6. ¿vas / tú / con quién / al centro comercial?

▼21 Leer • Pensar • Escribir

¿Cómo es el cine?

Read the advertisement for the *Cine Parque Arauco*. Then read the questions and answers below the advertisement. Number your paper from 1–5 and write the appropriate question words, based on what you read.

Cine Parque Arauco

Excelente calidad de proyección	Diariamente funciones continuadas desde el mediodía
Estacionamientos iluminados, gratis	Funciones de trasnoche los miércoles, viernes y sábados
Para su comodidad, aire acondicionado	Palomitas recién preparadas
Las únicas butacas reclinables de la ciudad	Servicio amable y eficiente
Excelentes instalaciones para discapacitados	Precios especiales para grupos y arriendos de salas de cine

Situado delante del Centro Comercial Gigante

1. ¿ ___ es la calidad de la proyección en el cine? *Es excelente.*

2. ¿ ___ comen muchas personas allí? *Comen palomitas.*

3. ¿ ___ es el nombre del cine? *Es el Cine Parque Arauco.*

4. ¿ ___ van las personas a ver películas muy tarde *(late)* en la noche? *Van los miércoles, viernes y sábados.*

5. ¿ ___ está el cine? *Está delante del Centro Comercial Gigante.*

Cuándo	Cuál
Por qué	Dónde
Cómo	Qué

▼22 | (Talk!) 👥 | Escribir · Hablar

Los fines de semana

1 Copy a chart like this one on a separate sheet of paper. Write *yo* in the first column, and the name of a place that you go on the weekends in the second column. If there are people who go with you, write their names in the third column.

Nombre	¿Adónde vas?	¿Con quién?
yo	a la lección de guitarra	solo(a)
Laura	al centro comercial	con Selena

2 Follow the model to find out the same information about three of your classmates. Write the information on your chart.

▶ Modelo

A —¿*Adónde vas los fines de semana?*
B —*Voy al centro comercial.*
A —¿*Con quién vas?*
B —*Voy con Selena.*
o: —*Voy solo(a).*

3 Report the information you find to the class.

▶ Modelo

Yo voy a mi lección de guitarra solo(a).
Laura va al centro comercial con Selena.

▼23 | (Talk!) 👥 | Leer · Escribir · Hablar

Una estrella de cine

1 *Estrella* magazine interviewed Luis Ramos, a famous movie star. Read the interview, then answer the questions below.

¿Comprendes?

1. What city is Luis Ramos from?
2. What is happening on September 15?
3. Who are María Rúa and Lorena Herrera?
4. What does Luis Ramos like to do in his free time?
5. Why is he an actor?

2 Write two additional questions that you might add to the interview with Luis Ramos.

3 Work with a partner to take turns playing the role of Luis or his co-star María. Ask him or her the additional questions that you wrote.

Entrevista[1] con **Luis Ramos**

¿De dónde eres?
Soy de San Juan, Puerto Rico.

¿Cuándo vamos a ver tu nueva[2] película?
El 15 de septiembre.

¿Con quién trabajas en la película Y tú también?
Trabajo con María Rúa y Lorena Herrera.

¿Cuándo tienes tiempo libre?
No trabajo los fines de semana ni en diciembre.

¿Qué haces en tu tiempo libre?
Generalmente yo voy al gimnasio todos los días. También me gusta ir a los restaurantes. Me quedo en casa cuando no trabajo en una nueva película.

¿Por qué eres actor?
Soy actor porque me encantan las películas, y creo que soy talentoso.

¡Gracias!

¡Gracias a usted! ¡Nos vemos!

[1]Interview   [2]new

▼24 Leer • Escribir

Estudiantes desordenados

At the Colegio de Ponce, a public school in Puerto Rico, the school newspaper staff is extremely disorganized today. They have the answers to the questions that they asked in an interview with a new student, but they lost the questions. Help them complete the article by reading the answers at right and then writing a logical question for each one.

Modelo

Me llamo Juliana Ramírez.
¿Cómo te llamas?

Me llamo Juliana Ramírez.

Yo soy de San Juan.

Yo estudio con mis amigos.

Mi clase favorita es matemáticas.

Después de las clases, voy al centro comercial.

Porque soy deportista y me gusta mucho
   practicar deportes.

Los sábados, voy a la playa o voy al cine para
   ver una película.

▼25 | Hablar • Escribir

Una entrevista con un amigo

Use the questions that you wrote for Actividad 24 to interview a partner. Present the information you find out to the class.

Modelo

Jaime es de Houston. Él va a la lección de piano después de las clases . . .

▼26 | Escribir • Hablar • GramActiva

Juego

Modelo

❶ With a partner, cut a sheet of blank paper into twelve squares, making sure that each square is the same size.

❷ Write six questions, each on a different square. Use a different question word for each one. On the remaining six squares of paper, write a logical answer for each question.

¿Cómo es Ana?

Ella es inteligente.

❸ Mix up the questions and answers, and spread them out facedown on the desk. Take turns turning two cards faceup, and read what they say aloud. If the cards are a logical question and answer match, pick them up and take another turn. If not, turn them facedown again and let your partner take a turn. The person with the most pairs wins. When you finish your game, switch cards with another pair of students.

Y tú, ¿qué preguntas?

1 Look at the photo and write four questions about the beach, the people, and the activities.

2 Ask your partner your questions and he or she will respond. Then switch roles.

> **Para decir más . . .**
>
> **el hombre** man
> **la mujer** woman
> **la persona** person
> **tomar el sol** to sunbathe

Muchas personas pasan el día en la playa de Aguadilla, Puerto Rico.

▼ Fondo Cultural

La música puertorriqueña In Puerto Rico, as in much of the Caribbean, music is an extremely important part of the identity of the people. Two of the musical styles that are often associated with Puerto Rico are *bomba* and *plena*. *Bomba* is a style of music with African roots where various people tend to call out and respond to the accompaniment of drums. *Plena* is a style of music where a singer tells a story or recounts an event to a musical accompaniment.

• What style of music do you listen to that is similar to *bomba* or *plena?*

▼28 Leer • Escribir

¡Vamos al Viejo San Juan!

Puerto Rico has been a commonwealth of the United States since 1952. It is an island with a fascinating past. Look at the pictures and read about a historic section of Puerto Rico's capital. Then answer the questions below.

 Conexiones | La historia

El Viejo[1] San Juan es una zona histórica, pintoresca,[2] colonial y muy popular en la capital de Puerto Rico. Los jóvenes[3] pasan el tiempo con sus amigos en los parques, cafés y plazas. Allí cantan, bailan y comen en los restaurantes típicos.

El Morro fue construido[6] en el siglo[7] XVI para combatir los ataques de los piratas ingleses y franceses.[8]

Datos importantes:

- Cristóbal Colón llega[4] aquí durante su segunda visita a las Américas en 1493.
- El Viejo San Juan llega a ser[5] la capital de Puerto Rico en 1521.

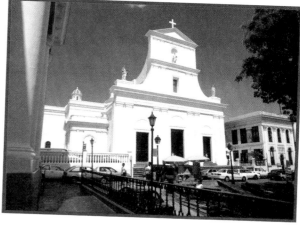

La Catedral de San Juan tiene muchas obras de arte.[9] Allí descansan[10] los restos[11] de Juan Ponce de León, famoso explorador de la Florida.

[1]Old [2]picturesque [3]young people [4]arrives [5]becomes [6]was constructed [7]century [8]French [9]works of art [10]lie [11]remains

¿Comprendes?

1. For how many years has San Juan been the capital of Puerto Rico?
2. On which of his voyages did Christopher Columbus land on Puerto Rico?
3. Why did the Spaniards build *El Morro?*
4. What are two things you'll see when you visit the cathedral?

Más práctica	GO
	realidades.com	print
Guided WB pp. 127–129	✔ ✔
Core WB pp. 72–73	
Comm. WB pp. 74, 77, 151	✔ ✔
Hispanohablantes **WB** pp. 138–141	✔

▶ Read about after-school and weekend activities at a mall
▶ Use prior knowledge to better understand what you read
▶ Compare the instruments used in Andean music to those used in music you enjoy

Lectura

Al centro comercial

Lee las actividades diferentes que puedes hacer en la semana del 11 al 17 de enero durante tu tiempo libre.

Strategy

Using prior knowledge
Think about what you know about special-event weeks at shopping centers. List events from this calendar that you think might be offered at a mall.

¡Vamos a la Plaza del Sol!

Aquí en la Plaza del Sol, ¡siempre hay algo que hacer!

Actividades para el 11 al 17 de enero

11 lunes
7.00 p.m. Música andina

12 martes
7.00 P.M. Clase de yoga

13 miércoles
8.00 P.M. Noche de jazz

14 jueves
7.00 P.M. Clase de repostería[1]

15 viernes
8.00 P.M. Música andina

16 sábado
1.30 P.M. Exposición de fotografía
2.00 P.M. Show infantil
4.00 P.M. Exhibición de yoga
8.00 P.M. Sábado flamenco

17 domingo
1.30 P.M. Exposición de fotografía
2.00 P.M. Show infantil
4.00 P.M. Exhibición de yoga
8.00 P.M. Noche de tango

Música andina
El grupo Sol Andino toca música andina fusionada con bossa nova y jazz el lunes a las 8.00 P.M. Abierto[2] al público.

Clase de yoga
La práctica de yoga es todos los martes desde las 7.00 hasta las 9.00 P.M. La instructora Lucía Gómez Paloma enseña los secretos de esta disciplina. Inscríbase[3] al teléfono 224-24-16. Vacantes limitadas.

[1]pastry making [2]Open [3]Register

Sábado flamenco

El Sábado flamenco es el programa más popular de la semana. María del Carmen Ramachi baila acompañada por el guitarrista Ernesto Hermoza el sábado a las 8.00 P.M. Es una noche emocionante y sensacional de música y danza. Abierto al público.

Clase de repostería

Inscríbase gratis[4] en la clase de repostería programada para el jueves a las 7.00 P.M. Preparamos unos pasteles deliciosos gracias a la Repostería Ideal y al maestro Rudolfo Torres. Inscríbase al teléfono 224-24-16. Vacantes limitadas.

[4]free

¿Comprendes?

1. You will be in town from January 9 through February 2. Will you be able to take part in these activities?

2. Which events require you to sign up in advance? Which don't?

3. You have to baby-sit your six-year-old sister. Which day(s) would be best to go?

4. According to the interests of these people, to what events mentioned in the *Lectura* are they going?

   Raquel: Me gusta mucho hacer ejercicio.

   Roberto: Me encantan los pasteles.

   Teresa: Estudio baile. Tomo lecciones todos los jueves.

   Alejandro: Me gusta escuchar música ... toda clase de música.

5. What activities mentioned interest you the most?

Más práctica GO

realidades.com | print

Guided WB pp. 130–131	✔	✔
Comm. WB pp. 77–78, 152	✔	✔
Hispanohablantes WB pp. 142–143		✔
Cultural Reading Activity		✔

▼ Fondo Cultural | Bolivia • Chile · Ecuador • Perú

Andean music Andean music has become popular worldwide. This style originated in the Andes mountains of Peru, Ecuador, Bolivia, and Chile. The music has a slightly haunting sound. Performers often wear typical Andean attire. Instruments commonly used in Andean music include the *quena* flute, *siku* panpipes, and a small guitar called a *charango*.

- The Andean sound is created using a particular set of instruments. What Instruments define the music you enjoy?

La cultura en vivo

Rimas infantiles

Can you remember the chants and songs you learned as a child? Or do you remember the rhymes you or your friends recited while jumping rope?

Here are some chants and songs that children in the Spanish-speaking world use when they play. The first one is a Spanish-language equivalent to "Eenie, meenie, minie, moe . . ." It is a nonsense rhyme used to select the person who will be "It" in various games.

Tin Marín de dopingüé
cucaramanga titirifuera.
Yo no fui,
fue Teté.
Pégale, pégale,
que ella fue.

Niña saltando a la cuerda

Here's a chant for jumping rope:

Salta, salta la perdiz	**The partridge jumps and jumps**
por los campos de maíz.	**Through the cornfields.**
Ten cuidado, por favor,	**Be careful, please!**
¡porque viene el cazador!	**Here comes the hunter!**

(The jump rope then turns faster.)

Try it out! Here's a traditional game that combines Spanish, math, and hopping over a board. Place a long, narrow board on the floor. Take turns hopping with both feet from one side of the board to the other. Go forward as you hop. When you get to the end of the board, jump and turn in the air, facing the direction you came from. Continue hopping from side to side back to the other end. Be very careful! Try this in an area where you won't hurt yourself. As you are hopping, sing this song:

Brinca la tablita	**Jump over the board**
que yo la brinqué.	**That I already jumped.**
Bríncala tú ahora	**Now you jump**
que yo me cansé.	**Since I'm tired.**
Dos y dos son cuatro,	**Two and two are four,**
cuatro y dos son seis.	**Four and two are six.**
Seis y dos son ocho,	**Six and two are eight,**
y ocho dieciséis,	**And eight are sixteen,**
y ocho veinticuatro,	**And eight are twenty-four,**
y ocho treinta y dos.	**And eight are thirty-two.**
Y diez que le sumo	**And ten that I add**
son cuarenta y dos.	**Equals forty-two.**

Think about it! What rhymes and songs do you know? What purpose do they serve in play?

Presentación oral

Un estudiante nuevo

▼ **Objectives**

▶ Role-play a conversation with another student about how you spend your free time
▶ Use models to prepare for your performance

Aplicación

Task
This is a new student's first day at school. You and a partner will play the roles of a new student and a student who has been at the school for a while. Find out information about the new student.

1 **Prepare** You will need to prepare for both roles.

Current student: List at least four questions. Greet the student and introduce yourself. Find out where the new student is from, what activities he or she likes to do and on what days, and where he or she goes and with whom.

New student: Look at the questions the current student will ask you and note your answers.

2 **Practice** Work with a partner to practice different questions and responses. Be sure you are comfortable in both roles as you go through your presentation. Use your notes in practice, but not to present. Try to:

• get and give information
• keep the conversation going
• speak clearly

3 **Present** You will be paired with another student and your teacher will assign roles. The current student begins by greeting the new student. Listen to your partner's questions and responses and keep the conversation going.

4 **Evaluation** The following rubric will be used to grade your presentation.

> ### Strategy
>
> **Using models**
> It helps to go back and review models that prepare you for a task like this role-play. Reread *A primera vista* (pp. 208–213). Pay attention to the different questions and answers that will help you with this task.

Rubric	Score 1	Score 3	Score 5
Completion of task	You ask or answer two questions.	You ask or answer three questions.	You ask or answer four or more questions.
Your ability to keep the conversation going	You have no response or follow-up to what your partner says.	You have frequent responses or follow-ups to what your partner says.	You always respond to your partner and ask follow-up questions.
How easily you are understood	You are very difficult to understand. The teacher could only recognize isolated words and phrases.	You are understandable, but have frequent errors in vocabulary and/or grammar that hinder understanding.	You are easily understood. Your teacher does not have to "decode" what you are trying to say.

El mundo hispano

Estados Unidos

Histórico

The oldest permanent European settlement in the United States, St. Augustine, Florida, was established by Spain in 1565—55 years before the Pilgrims landed at Plymouth Rock. For more than two centuries after that, the Spanish controlled a large territory in North America that included what is now Mexico, parts of the southern United States, the states of Texas, New Mexico, Arizona, California, and Nevada, and parts of Colorado and Utah.

Constructed as a mission in 1718, the Alamo (in San Antonio, Texas) today is best known as a key battleground in the secession of Texas from Mexico in 1836. The defeat of the Texans at the Alamo became a rallying cry for Texas independence, and Texas gained its freedom from Mexico two months later. ▶

¿Sabes que . . . ?

The language of the Nahua peoples of central Mexico, which included the Aztecs, is related to the languages of the Shoshone, Comanche, and Hopi tribes in the United States. When Spaniards pushed north from the newly conquered central Mexico, they often followed ancient Native American trade routes and used Nahua people as guides.

Para pensar

You can find many Spanish names of cities, counties, and states in the United States. Work with a partner and write a list of at least ten places with Spanish names and then try to guess what they mean in English.

realidades.com GO

 Mapa global interactivo

DK Reference Atlas

The French Quarter in New Orleans was named after the French who first settled here. In spite of its name, most of the buildings date to when Spain ruled Louisiana (1763–1803). Fires ravaged the area in 1788 and 1794, so when the rebuilding was done, the architectural style was Spanish. This can be seen in the landscaped patios and iron grillwork on balconies. Despite the destruction caused by Hurricane Katrina, the French Quarter remains.

A network of Spanish Catholic missions once extended throughout the Americas. Many cities in the southwestern United States, including San Francisco, San Diego, and Santa Fe, were originally built around Catholic missions, which in turn were often located at Native American villages or religious sites. The Mission San Xavier del Bac, in Arizona, combines the name of a Catholic saint (San Xavier) with the name of the Papago village where it was built (Bac, which means "where the water emerges"). Constructed in the early 1700s, the mission is still used by the Papago people and is considered one of the world's architectural treasures. ▼

Spain built the Castillo de San Marcos to protect both St. Augustine (Florida) and the sea routes for ships returning to Spain from enemy attacks. This fort was started in 1672 and took 23 years to build. When Spain sold Florida to the United States in 1821, the fort was renamed Fort Marion. The Castillo has been a National Monument since 1924.

Repaso del capítulo

Vocabulario y gramática

to talk about leisure activities

ir de compras	to go shopping
ver una película	to see a movie
la lección de piano	piano lesson (class)
Me quedo en casa.	I stay at home.

to talk about places

la biblioteca	library
el café	café
el campo	countryside
la casa	home, house
en casa	at home
el centro comercial	mall
el cine	movie theater
el gimnasio	gym
la iglesia	church
la mezquita	mosque
las montañas	mountains
el parque	park
la piscina	swimming pool
la playa	beach
el restaurante	restaurant
la sinagoga	synagogue
el templo	temple, Protestant church
el trabajo	work, job

to ask and tell where you go

a	to (*prep.*)
a la, al (*a + el*)	to the
¿Adónde?	(To) Where?
a casa	(to) home

to ask and tell with whom you go

con mis/tus amigos	with my/your friends
¿Con quién?	With whom?
solo, -a	alone

to talk about when things are done

¿Cuándo?	When?
después	afterwards
después (de)	after
los fines de semana	on weekends
los lunes,	on Mondays,
los martes…	on Tuesdays…
tiempo libre	free time

to talk about where someone is from

¿De dónde eres?	Where are you from?
de	from, of

to indicate how often

generalmente	generally

other useful words and expressions

¡No me digas!	You don't say!
para + *infinitive*	in order to + *infinitive*

ir *to go*

voy	vamos
vas	vais
va	van

For *Vocabulario adicional,* see pp. 268–269.

Más repaso (GO)	realidades.com | print
Instant Check	✔
Puzzles	✔
Core WB pp. 74–75	✔ ✔
Comm. WB pp. 153, 154–156	✔ ✔

Preparación para el examen

On the exam you will be asked to . . .	Here are practice tasks similar to those you will find on the exam . . .	For review go to your print or digital textbook . . .
1 Escuchar Listen and understand as people ask questions about weekend events	Two friends are trying to make plans for the weekend. Based on their dialogue, what do they finally agree on? a) who is going b) where they are going c) when they are going	**pp. 208–213** *Vocabulario en contexto* **p. 226** Actividad 22
2 Hablar Talk about places to go and things to do on the weekend	Your parents want to know what you're doing this weekend. Mention at least three places you plan to go or things you plan to do. For example, you might say *Voy de compras con mis amigos.*	**pp. 208–213** *Vocabulario en contexto* **p. 215** Actividad 7 **p. 216** Actividad 9 **p. 221** Actividad 17 **p. 222** Actividad 18 **p. 226** Actividad 22
3 Leer Read about what a person does on particular days of the week	Someone has left his or her planner at your house. Read the schedule for two days to try to figure out what type of person owns it. Indicate whether you agree or disagree with the statements about the person. MARTES: 6:00 Desayuno 4:00 Lección de piano 5:00 Trabajo 8:30 Clase aeróbica JUEVES: 3:30 Gimnasio 4:30 Piscina 6:00 Trabajo 8:00 Biblioteca *¿Estás de acuerdo o no?* *a) Es muy perezoso(a).* *b) Es atlético(a).* *c) Le gusta ir de compras.*	**pp. 208–213** *Vocabulario en contexto* **p. 214** Actividad 5 **p. 219** Actividad 13 **pp. 230–231** *Lectura*
4 Escribir Write a short note to a friend to let him or her know where you are going after school	Your friend is taking a make-up test after school, so you need to write her a short note to tell her what you are doing after school today. In the note, tell her where you are going and then at what time you are going home.	**p. 214** Actividad 5 **p. 217** Actividad 11 **p. 220** Actividad 15 **p. 222** Actividad 18 **p. 228** Actividad 27
5 Pensar Demonstrate an understanding of rhymes, songs, and games from Spanish-speaking cultures	Think about your favorite childhood game. How does it compare to the children's games you learned about in this chapter? Describe a traditional game from a Spanish-speaking country.	**p. 232** *La cultura en vivo*

▼ Chapter Objectives

Communication

By the end of this chapter you will be able to:

- Listen to and read invitations and responses
- Discuss and write an invitation and an activity plan
- Exchange information while responding to an invitation

Culture

You will also be able to:

- Understand cultural differences regarding extracurricular activities
- Compare and contrast the careers of two athletes

You will demonstrate what you know and can do:

- Presentación escrita, p. 263
- Preparación para el examen, p. 267

You will use:

Vocabulary

- Sports and activities outside of school
- Feelings
- Extending, accepting, and declining invitations
- Telling time

Grammar

- *Ir* + *a* + infinitive
- The verb *jugar*

Exploración del mundo hispano

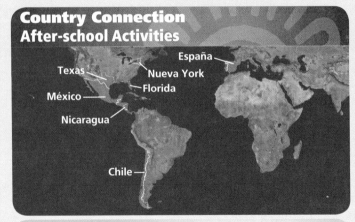

Country Connection
After-school Activities

Texas
España
Nueva York
Florida
México
Nicaragua
Chile

realidades.com **GO**

 Reference Atlas

 Videocultura y actividad

 Mapa global interactivo

En los Juegos Paralímpicos de Atlanta, Georgia

Arte y cultura | El mundo hispano

Los Juegos Paralímpicos Starting with
the first Paralympic Games in Rome in 1960,
the International Paralympic Committee has
organized summer and winter games that
follow the Olympic Games and are hosted
by the same city. Athletes with all types of
disabilities compete in the Paralympics. In the
most recent Summer and Winter Paralympics,
more than 150 nations participated, with
over 4,200 athletes worldwide.

• How do you think athletes benefit from
competing in the Paralympics or in similar
local events?

Vocabulario en contexto

Club Deportivo León

Parque de la Independencia

¿Te gustan los deportes? ¡**Puedes** practicar con uno de nuestros expertos! ¿**Juegas** bien o juegas mal? ¡No importa! Hay un deporte para ti.

8.00	🏃	el fútbol
8.00	🏐	el vóleibol
10.00	🏌️	el golf
10.00	🎾	el tenis
13.00	⚾	el béisbol
13.00	🏀	el básquetbol
16.00	🏈	el fútbol americano

—¿Qué **quieres** hacer a las ocho de la mañana, jugar al fútbol o al vóleibol?

—A ver . . . No **quiero** jugar al fútbol. **Juego** muy **mal**. Prefiero jugar al vóleibol. Necesito practicar más. ¿Y qué **te gustaría** hacer a las cuatro **esta tarde?**

—**Me gustaría** jugar al fútbol americano.

el concierto

la fiesta

el baile

el partido

—¡Hola! Soy Rosa. ¿Quieres hacer algo **conmigo este fin de semana?** Hay un concierto en el parque.

—**Lo siento,** pero no **puedo.** Estoy **demasiado ocupado** y tengo mucha tarea.

—No puedo porque **tengo que trabajar.** Trabajo **esta noche** a las siete y mañana trabajo **a la una de la tarde. Voy a estar** un poco **cansada.** ¡Ay! ¡Qué pena!

—¡Qué **triste!** No, no puedo ir **contigo.** Estoy **un poco enferma.**

ir de cámping

ir de pesca

—**¡Qué buena idea!** Pero no me gustan los conciertos. Prefiero ir de cámping. Siempre estoy muy **contenta** cuando voy de cámping. **¿A qué hora?** ¿Mañana a las cinco de la tarde? **Entonces,** nos vemos.

▼**1** | 🔊 | Escuchar

¡Deportemanía!

Marcela is a sports fanatic! As she lists the days on which she will play the various sports, touch the picture of each sport.

▼**2** | 🔊 | Escuchar

¿Cómo estás?

You will hear how five people are feeling. Act out the adjectives that you hear.

Más práctica	GO	
realidades.com	print	
Instant Check	✔	
Guided WB pp. 133–138	✔	✔
Core WB pp. 76–77	✔	✔
Comm. WB p. 84	✔	✔
Hispanohablantes WB p. 152		✔

¡A jugar!

Ignacio, Javier, Ana y Elena están en el Parque del Retiro en Madrid.
¿Qué van a jugar y hacer? ¿De qué hablan? Lee la historia.

España

Javier

Ana

Elena

Ignacio

Antes de leer

Strategy **Look to find key questions** Before you read the story, skim to find where the characters are asking questions. The answers may point to important information in the story.

- Look at the questions. Which characters are offering invitations? What do you think they will do?

1. Look through the text for words that you already know. What clues do they give you about how the students are spending their weekend?

2. Think about how you spend your weekends. How does your weekend compare with what you see the students doing in the pictures?

3. Using the pictures, try to determine what each person is like. What can you tell about each student's interests based on what you see?

1

Hoy es sábado y hace buen tiempo. Ignacio, Javier, Ana y Elena están en el parque para jugar al fútbol.

2

Ignacio: ¡Oye, Javier! ¡Sabes jugar muy bien al fútbol!

Javier: Y tú también . . . pero necesito practicar más. Ana, ¿quieres jugar?

Ana: ¡Por supuesto! Vamos a jugar.

3

Elena: Estoy demasiado cansada y tengo sed. ¿Por qué no tomamos un refresco?

Ignacio: ¡Genial! Yo también estoy un poco cansado.

4

Ana: ¿Juegas al vóleibol esta tarde?
Elena: Sí, a las seis.

Ignacio: Oye, hay una fiesta esta noche. Ana, tú y Elena vais, ¿verdad?

Ana: ¡Claro!

Elena: Javier, ¿quieres ir con nosotros a la fiesta?

Ana: ¡Qué buena idea!

Javier: ¿A qué hora es la fiesta?

Ana: A las nueve **de la noche,** en la escuela.

Javier: ¿Tengo que bailar?

Ana: Pues, sí. Puedes bailar conmigo y con Elena.

Javier: No **sé** bailar muy bien.

Ana: ¡Vamos, Javier!

Javier: Bien, voy.

Javier: Hasta las nueve entonces.

Ignacio: ¡Genial! Hasta más tarde.

▼3 Leer • Escribir

Una postal de Javier

Before going to the party, Javier decides to write a postcard to his friend in Salamanca, telling him about his new friends in Madrid. Number your paper from 1–6. Use the words in the box to complete his postcard. Base your answers on the *Videohistoria*.

fiesta	bailar
Elena	fútbol
sábado	nueve

Querido José:

¿Cómo estás? Estoy bien en mi nueva¹ escuela. Tengo tres amigos: Ignacio, Ana y __1.__. Ellos son muy divertidos. Hoy es __2.__, y fuimos² al parque para jugar al __3.__. Esta noche, vamos a una __4.__. Vamos a las __5.__ de la noche. Según mi amiga, yo tengo que __6.__. ¡Pero no sé bailar muy bien! Bueno, son las ocho y media y debo ir.

¡Hasta pronto!
Javier

José Romero-Manterola
15-D, c/Luchana
37008 Salamanca

¹new ²we went

▼4 Escribir • Hablar

¿Quién habla?

Who is speaking: Ana, Ignacio, Elena, or Javier?

Ana   **Ignacio**   **Elena**   **Javier**

1. No sé bailar bien.
2. Juego al vóleibol a las seis.
3. Necesito beber algo después de jugar al fútbol.
4. Necesito practicar más el fútbol.
5. Voy a la fiesta a las nueve.
6. Sé jugar al fútbol muy bien.

Más práctica	GO	
realidades.com	print	
Instant Check	✔	
Guided WB pp. 139–142	✔	✔
Core WB pp. 78–79	✔	✔
Comm. WB pp. 79–80, 81	✔	✔
Hispanohablantes WB p. 153		✔

Vocabulario en uso

▼**5** Hablar

Me gustaría ir . . .

Say whether or not you would like to do these things this weekend.

Modelo

Me gustaría ir a una fiesta este fin de semana.

o: *No me gustaría ir a una fiesta este fin de semana.*

1.
2.
3.
4.
5.

▼**6** Escribir • Hablar

No sé jugar . . .

Number your paper from 1–6. Indicate whether or not you know how to play the sports pictured below.

Modelo

Sé jugar al béisbol muy bien.

o: *No sé jugar al béisbol.*

1.
2.
3.

4.
5.
6.

▼**7** Hablar

¿Qué deportes practicas?

Using the information from Actividad 6, ask and tell about which sports you know, or don't know, how to play.

 Modelo

A —*¿Sabes jugar al béisbol?*

B —*¡Por supuesto! Sé jugar al béisbol muy bien.*

o:—*No, no sé jugar al béisbol.*

▼**8** Escribir

La fiesta de Marta

Marta is having a party, and many of her classmates are there. While some people are having a great time, others are not. Number your paper from 1–6. Use the adjectives in the word bank to write six sentences describing the people in the picture below.

triste
ocupado, -a
cansado, -a
contento, -a
enfermo, -a
mal

Modelo

Felipe y María están contentos.

Fondo Cultural | México

La Noche de los Rábanos is just one of the many kinds of *fiestas* in the Spanish-speaking world. On the evening of December 23, people set up booths around the *zócalo* (town square) of Oaxaca, Mexico, to display and sell radishes *(los rábanos)* sculpted into a fantastic array of shapes. *Oaxaqueños* and visitors alike crowd the square to view the amazing creations.

• Do you know communities or regions in the United States that are known for particular crafts or products?

Rábanos esculpidos *(sculpted)*, Oaxaca, México

9 | Hablar

Lo siento

Ask your partner if he or she wants to do these activities with you. Your partner can't go and will offer excuses to explain why.

Modelo

A —¡Oye! ¿Quieres <u>patinar</u> conmigo esta tarde?

B —Lo siento. Hoy no puedo. Estoy <u>demasiado enfermo(a)</u>.

Estudiante A

1.
2.
3.
4.
5.

Estudiante B

muy	ocupado, -a
demasiado	enfermo, -a
un poco	cansado, -a
	triste
	mal

¡Respuesta personal!

10 | Escuchar • Escribir

Escucha y escribe

You will hear three invitations to events and the responses given. On a sheet of paper, write the numbers 1–3. As you listen, write what each invitation is for and whether the person accepted it (write *sí*) or turned it down (write *no*).

11 | Escribir

Un estudiante muy popular

You have a busy Saturday and your friends are asking you to do things. Respond by telling them why you cannot accept.

Modelo
¿Quieres ir al cine a la una y media de la tarde?
No puedo. Tengo que ir a la biblioteca con Ramón.

1. ¿Te gustaría ir al café a las diez de la mañana?
2. ¿Puedes jugar al vóleibol a las tres de la tarde?
3. ¿Quieres ir al concierto esta noche a las siete?
4. ¿Puedes ir al restaurante con la clase esta tarde?
5. ¿Quieres ir a la fiesta de Beto esta noche?
6. ¿Te gustaría ir de pesca a las doce del mediodía?

sábado: el 26 de abril	
10:00	ir a la lección de piano
12:00	jugar al fútbol americano con mis amigos
1:30	ir a la biblioteca con Ramón
3:00	jugar al básquetbol con Silvia y Jaime
5:30	comer en casa
7:00	ir al baile
9:30	ir a la fiesta de Julia

▼12 | Hablar

¿A qué hora?

Take turns asking and telling what
time the following activities take place.

 8:00

▶ Modelo
A —¿A qué hora es *la película?*
B —*A las ocho de la noche.*

1.  9:00

2.  2:30

3.  1:30

4.  8:30

5.  7:30

6.  7:00

Nota

To ask and tell what time something happens, you say:

- ¿A qué hora vas?
- Voy a la una.
- Voy a las tres y media.

To specify what part of the day, add:

de la mañana* in the morning (A.M.)
de la tarde in the afternoon (P.M.)
de la noche in the evening, at night (P.M.)

*Mañana means "tomorrow"; la mañana means "morning."

▼ Exploración del lenguaje

Spanish words borrowed from English

Languages often borrow words from one
another. For example, *rodeo* and *patio*
are Spanish words that have found their
way into English. There are also many
examples of English words that have
entered Spanish. By recognizing these
familiar words, you can increase your
vocabulary in Spanish.

Try it out! Read the sentences and
identify the "borrowed words." Don't
forget to pronounce the words correctly
in Spanish.

Quiero hacer videos.
¿Quieres jugar al básquetbol conmigo?
Practico el rugby y el ráquetbol.
Juego al fútbol cuando voy de cámping.
¡Me encantan los sándwiches!

Una invitación para el sábado

Invite your partner to these places, and tell at what time you will
go. Your partner will accept or decline. Follow the model.

1:30

▶️ **Modelo**

A —*¿Te gustaría ir al concierto
el sábado?*

B —*¿A qué hora?*

A —*A la una y media de la tarde.*

B —*¡Genial! Nos vemos el sábado.*

Estudiante A

Estudiante B

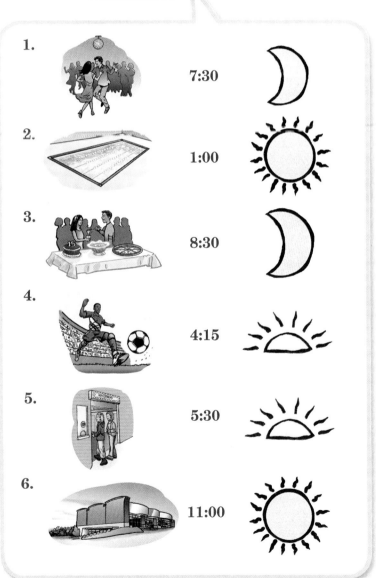

1. 7:30

2. 1:00

3. 8:30

4. 4:15

5. 5:30

6. 11:00

¡Por supuesto! Me
gustaría mucho.

Lo siento, pero no puedo.

¡Ay! ¡Qué pena! Tengo
quc trabajar.

¡Genial! Nos vemos el
sábado.

¡Qué buena idea! ¡Gracias!

¡Respuesta personal!

▼14 | (Talk!) 👥 | Escribir • Hablar

Una invitación para mi amigo

viernes, el _____ de _____

  la mañana _____
  la tarde _____
  la noche _____

sábado, el _____ de _____

  la mañana _____
  la tarde _____
  la noche _____

domingo, el _____ de _____

  la mañana _____
  la tarde _____
  la noche _____

1 Copy this page of an agenda book onto a sheet of paper. Then, fill in each space with what you will be doing this weekend. Try to include specific times whenever possible.

2 After you have completed your schedule, work with a partner to invite him or her to various activities. Your partner will accept or decline, based on the information in his or her agenda book.

▼15 | (Talk!) | Escribir • Hablar

Y tú, ¿qué dices?

1. ¿Qué haces los fines de semana?

2. ¿Qué prefieres, practicar un deporte o ver la televisión? ¿Por qué?

3. ¿Cómo estás después de practicar tu deporte favorito? ¿Cómo estás cuando pasas tiempo con tus amigos?

4. ¿Qué te gustaría hacer esta noche? ¿Y mañana?

5. ¿Qué tienes que hacer este fin de semana?

▼ **Objectives**

▶ **Listen to phone messages about invitations**
▶ **Write about and discuss plans**
▶ **Read an ad and extend an invitation by phone**

Gramática

Ir + a + infinitive

Just as you use "going" + infinitive in English to say what you are going to do, in Spanish you use a form of the verb *ir + a +* an infinitive to express the same thing:

Voy a jugar al tenis hoy.
I'm going to play tennis today.

¿Tú **vas a jugar** al golf esta tarde?
Are you going to play golf this afternoon?

Mis amigas **van a ir** de cámping mañana.
My friends are going camping tomorrow.

Javier: ¿**Van a jugar** conmigo, o no?
Ana: Sí, **vamos a jugar** contigo.

Más ayuda **realidades.com**

 ***GramActiva* Video**
Tutorials: Future with *ir + a +* infinitive, Vamos a + infinitive

 Canción de hip hop: ¿Qué vas a hacer?

 ***GramActiva* Activity**

▼**16** Escribir

¿Qué van a hacer todos?

You and the people you know have a lot to do this weekend. Tell what everyone is going to do by matching the people in the first column with any of the activities in the third column. Use the appropriate form of the verb *ir*. Write the sentences you create on a sheet of paper.

1. yo
2. mis amigos
3. mi mamá
4. mi papá y yo
5. mi profesor(a) y director(a)
6. tú

ir a

ver una película
ir de pesca
jugar al golf
estudiar
trabajar
pasar tiempo con amigos
¡Respuesta personal!

▼**17** | 🔊 | Escuchar · Escribir

Escucha y escribe

Rosario and Pablo have left messages on your answering machine telling you what they are going to do and inviting you to join them. Copy this chart on your paper. As you listen to each message, complete the chart with information given in the message.

	Rosario	Pablo
1. ¿Adónde quiere ir?		
2. ¿Qué va a hacer?		
3. ¿A qué hora va a ir?		

▼**18** | ♻ | Escribir

Este fin de semana vamos a . . .

On your paper, write sentences telling what the Ríos family is going to do this weekend.

Esteban / / 8:00

Modelo
Esteban va a estudiar a las ocho de la noche.

1. Angélica /  / 3:30

4. Los señores Ríos / / 7:30

2. Angélica y el Sr. Ríos / / 7:00

5. Esteban y un amigo / / 10:00

3. yo /  / 4:00

6. Angélica, Esteban y yo /  / 8:00

▼**19** | 💬 | ♻ | Hablar

En mi tiempo libre voy a . . .

Work with a partner and talk about what you are going to do in your free time and when.

▶️ **Modelo**
A —¿*Cuándo vas a correr*?
B —*Voy a correr esta tarde.*
o:—*Nunca voy a correr.*

Estudiante A

correr en el parque
estudiar español
hacer ejercicio
trabajar
comer en un restaurante
ver una película
¡Respuesta personal!

Estudiante B

a la(s) . . .
esta tarde
esta noche
este fin de semana
nunca
¡Respuesta personal!

The letter *d*

In Spanish, the pronunciation of the letter *d* is determined by its location in a word. When *d* is at the beginning of a word, or when it comes after *l* or *n*, it sounds similar to the *d* in "dog." Listen to and say these words:

diccionario	doce	donde
domingo	desayuno	día
deportes	calendario	bandera

When *d* comes between vowels and after any consonant except *l* or *n,* it sounds similar to the *th* of "the." Listen to and say these words:

cansado	ocupado	puedes
idea	sábado	partido
tarde	ensalada	atrevido

Try it out! Here is a tongue twister to give you practice in pronouncing the letter *d,* and also to give you something to think about!

> **Porque puedo, puedes,
> porque puedes, puedo;
> Pero si no puedes,
> yo tampoco puedo.**

▼**20** | 💬 👥 | ♻ | **Escribir • Hablar**

¿Qué vas a hacer?

1 Make a chart like this one to describe five things you're going to do, when you're going to do them, and with whom. Use the following words to say when you're going to do these things: *esta tarde, esta noche, mañana, el (jueves), este fin de semana.*

¿Qué?	¿Cuándo?	¿Con quién?
tocar la guitarra	esta tarde	mis amigos

2 Ask your partner what his or her plans are.

▶ **Modelo**

A —*¿Qué vas a hacer esta tarde?*
B —*Esta tarde mis amigos y yo vamos a tocar la guitarra.*

Mañana voy a tocar la guitarra.

▼21 Leer • Escribir

El teléfono celular

Answer the following questions about this ad for a cellular phone. Then create your own ad by writing at least five things that you want to do.

1. ¿Por qué es bueno tener un teléfono celular?

2. ¿Te gusta hablar por teléfono celular? ¿Con quién?

3. ¿Crees que es bueno o malo usar un teléfono celular en un restaurante? ¿Por qué?

¿Te gustaría...

pasar más tiempo con tus amigos?

ir de compras?

ir al cine?

escribir un mensaje?

escuchar música?

jugar un juego?

¡Por supuesto!

¡Con un teléfono celular puedes hacer planes para hacerlo todo!

▼22  Hablar

Una conversación por teléfono celular

You're calling a friend to invite him or her to do something. Your friend turns down the invitation and explains why. Make at least three invitations each.

▶ **Modelo**

A —Hola, <u>Sara</u>. Soy <u>Rosa</u>. ¿Puedes <u>jugar al tenis</u> conmigo <u>esta tarde</u>?

B —Lo siento, hoy no puedo. Voy a <u>estudiar para mi clase de inglés</u>.

A —¡Ay! ¡Qué pena!

▼23 | Escribir • Hablar

Y tú, ¿qué dices?

1. ¿Con quién te gustaría ir a una fiesta? ¿Por qué?

2. ¿Qué prefieres: ir de pesca o ir a un baile?

3. ¿Qué vas a hacer mañana a las ocho de la noche?

4. ¿Qué vas a hacer este fin de semana?

5. ¿Te gustaría ver un partido de fútbol o ir a un concierto?

Más práctica		
realidades.com	print		
Instant Check	✔	
Guided WB pp. 143–144	✔	✔
Core WB pp. 80–81	✔	✔
Comm. WB pp. 82, 85	✔	✔
Hispanohablantes WB pp. 154–157		✔

▼ **Objectives**

▸ Read, write, and talk about sports and athletes
▸ Exchange information about sports while playing a game
▸ Read and write about camping in Spain

Gramática

The verb *jugar*

Use the verb *jugar* to talk about playing a sport or a game. Even though *jugar* uses the same endings as the other *-ar* verbs, it has a different stem in some forms. For those forms, the *u* becomes *ue*. This kind of verb is called a "stem-changing verb." Here are the present-tense forms:

(yo)	juego	(nosotros) (nosotras)	jugamos
(tú)	juegas	(vosotros) (vosotras)	jugáis
Ud. (él) (ella)	juega	Ud. (ellos) (ellas)	juegan

Nota

Many Spanish speakers always use *jugar a* and the name of the sport or game:

• ¿Juegas **al** vóleibol?

Others do not use the *a:*

• ¿Juegas vóleibol?

Más ayuda   **realidades.com**

▸ *GramActiva* Video
Animated Verbs

✎ *GramActiva* Activity

▼**24** Escribir

¿A qué juegan?

Write sentences telling what sports the following people play.

Modelo
Alejandro juega al béisbol.

Alejandro

También se dice...

el básquetbol = el baloncesto *(muchos países)*

el fútbol = el balompié *(muchos países)*

el vóleibol = el balonvolea *(España)*

1.

Natalia

2.

los estudiantes en mi clase

3.

nosotros

4.

Sara

5.

Uds.

6.

tú

▼**25** | 👥 | **Dibujar • Escribir • Hablar • GramActiva**

Juego

1 On each of two index cards, draw a picture that represents a sport or game and write *muy bien, bien,* or *mal* to show how well you play that sport or game. Don't let your classmates see your cards.

2 Get together with five other students. Put all the cards face down in the center of your group. Choose a card and try to identify who drew it by asking the others how well they play what is pictured. Keep track of what you learn about your classmates.

▶️ **Modelo**

A —*Enrique, ¿juegas bien al tenis?*
B —*No, juego muy mal al tenis.*

3 Write six sentences describing the sports and games the students in your group play.

Modelo

Óscar y Nacho juegan muy bien al fútbol.
Teresa y yo jugamos bien al béisbol.

Estos jugadores de Managua, Nicaragua, juegan muy bien al béisbol.

26 Leer • Escribir • Hablar

La ciudad deportiva

Read about Iván Zamorano's dream and answer the questions.

1. ¿Cuál es el sueño de Iván Zamorano?
2. ¿Qué deportes juegan en la Ciudad Deportiva de Iván?
3. ¿Qué día empieza *(begins)* la inscripción para las escuelas? ¿A qué hora?
4. ¿A qué hora empiezan las actividades?
5. ¿Te gustaría ir a la Ciudad Deportiva de Iván Zamorano? ¿Por qué?

Mi sueño[1]

Quiero una ciudad[2] dedicada al deporte, a la familia y a los niños.[3] Quiero servicios de calidad internacional, con profesores de excelencia. En mi sueño, los niños y jóvenes juegan y practican deportes para ser mejores[4]. Este sueño ya es realidad y quiero compartirlo contigo.

El lugar[5] para hacer deporte en familia.

Escuelas de Fútbol, Tenis, Hockey

Inicio de Inscripción[6]: 23 de marzo, a las 8
Inicio de Actividades: 1 de abril, a las 14 horas

Avenida Pedro Hurtado 2650, Las Condes, Santiago, Chile
Teléfono: 212 2711

[1]dream	[3]children	[5]place
[2]city	[4]better	[6]Registration

El español en el mundo del trabajo

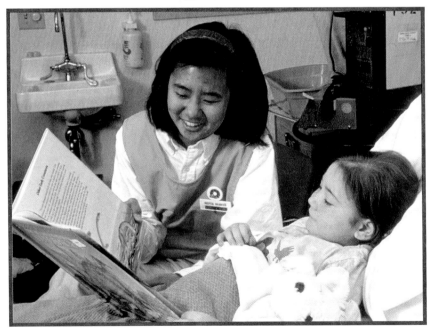

Una voluntaria en un hospital de niños

There are many opportunities to use Spanish in the health care field—in hospitals, emergency rooms, and neighborhood clinics. This young woman volunteers in a California hospital. Since many of the patients come from Spanish-speaking homes, she is able to speak with them and their families in Spanish. *"Para mí, trabajar como voluntaria es una de mis actividades favoritas. Creo que mi trabajo es importante."*

- What opportunities are there in your community to do volunteer work where speaking Spanish is helpful?

▼27 Leer • Pensar • Escribir

¡Vamos de cámping!

Tourism is an important industry in Spain. Many tourists prefer to go camping rather than stay in hotels. Read the following brochure about a campground and then answer the questions.

Conexiones | Las matemáticas

Camping Las Palmas

Miramar
Teléfono: 462 41 42 73   Fax: 964 01 55 05

85 kilómetros al sur de Valencia
110 kilómetros al norte de Alicante

- Un camping ideal
- Muchas actividades para todos
- Una buena opción para sus vacaciones

Con bellas palmas que dan[1] mucha sombra,[2] directamente sobre una bella playa. Ideal para toda la familia. Un sitio excelente para pescar.

[1]give   [2]shade

1. ¿Qué distancia en millas[3] hay entre[4] Valencia y el Camping Las Palmas?

2. ¿Qué distancia hay entre Alicante y el Camping Las Palmas?

   Para convertir kilómetros en millas, es necesario dividir el número de kilómetros por 1.6.

[3]miles   [4]between

> **Para decir más . . .**
> **200**   doscientos

▼28 Escribir • Hablar

Y tú, ¿qué dices?

1. ¿Qué deporte juegas bien? ¿Qué deporte juegas mal?
2. ¿Quién juega al básquetbol muy bien? ¿Al golf?
3. ¿Dónde juegan tú y tus amigos al vóleibol?
4. ¿Qué deportes juegan tú y tus amigos para la escuela?
5. ¿Qué deportes juegan tú y tus amigos en invierno?

Más práctica	GO

realidades.com | print

Instant Check	✔	
Guided WB pp. 145–146	✔	✔
Core WB p. 82	✔	✔
Comm. WB pp. 82–83, 86, 157	✔	✔
Hispanohablantes WB pp. 158–161		✔

▶ **Read about and compare the lives of two famous athletes**

▶ **Use cognates to understand new words**

▶ **Learn more about an Hispanic athlete and role model**

Lectura

Sergio y Paola: Dos deportistas dotados[1]

Lee este artículo de una revista deportiva.
Vas a conocer a[2] Sergio García y a Paola
Espinosa, dos atletas famosos.

> ### Strategy
> **Cognates**
> Use the cognates in the following articles to help you understand what is being said about the athletes.

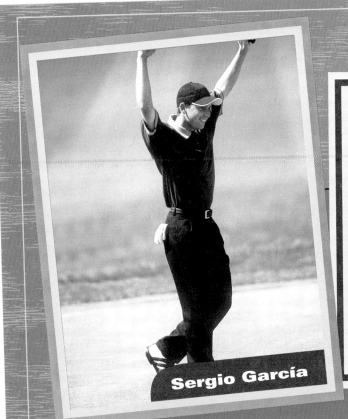

Sergio García

Nombre: Sergio García

Fecha de nacimiento: 9/1/80

**Lugar de nacimiento:
Borriol, Castellón (España)**

**Club: Club de Campo
del Mediterráneo**

**Su objetivo: Ser el mejor
del mundo**

**Profesional: Desde abril
del 99**

**Aficiones[3]: Real Madrid,
tenis, fútbol, videojuegos,
carros rápidos**

Sergio García es uno de los golfistas profesionales más populares del mundo.

Sergio juega para el Club de Campo del Mediterráneo en Borriol, Castellón, donde su padre Víctor es golfista profesional. Juega al golf desde la edad[4] de tres años y a los 12 años es campeón[5] del Club de Campo. Es el golfista más joven en participar[6] en el campeonato PGA desde 1921. En el campeonato gana[7] el segundo lugar[8]. Tiene el nombre "El niño." A los 15 años, juega en un torneo europeo de profesionales. Y a la edad de 17 años gana su primer torneo profesional.

Hoy Sergio García es uno de los 10 mejores golfistas del mundo.

[1]gifted [2]You will meet [3]Interests [4]age [5]champion [6]to participate [7]he wins [8]second place

Paola Espinosa

Nombre:
Paola Milagros Espinosa Sánchez

Fecha de nacimiento:
31/7/86

Su objetivo: Ser la clavadista[9] número uno del mundo

Lugar de nacimiento:
La Paz, Baja California (México)

Aficiones: Nadar, practicar gimnasia, viajar, pasar tiempo con su familia

Paola Espinosa es la mejor[10] clavadista de saltos[11] en plataforma y en saltos sincronizados de México. Tiene el nombre de "la princesa mexicana del clavado" y es una heroína nacional.

De niña, le gusta nadar y hacer gimnasia. Compite[12] como clavadista desde la edad de 10 años. A los 18 años, participa en sus primeros Juegos Olímpicos. ¡Y a los 22 años gana la medalla de bronce en los Juegos Olímpicos de Beijing!

Paola dice que es necesario practicar todos los días. Su meta[13] es ganar la medalla de oro en los próximos Juegos Olímpicos.

[9]diver   [10]best   [11]dives   [12]competes   [13]goal

¿Comprendes?

Copy this Venn diagram on a sheet of paper. Make a list in English of at least eight facts that you learned about Sergio and Paola. Write the facts on your Venn diagram. Include information about Sergio in the left oval, information about Paola in the right oval, and any fact that applies to both of them in the overlapping oval.

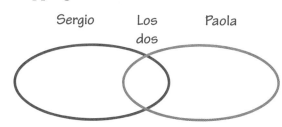

Sergio   Los   Paola
             dos

Más práctica (GO)   realidades.com | print

Guided WB p. 147   ✔ ✔
Comm. WB pp. 87, 158   ✔ ✔
Hispanohablantes WB pp. 162–163   ✔
Cultural Reading Activity   ✔

▼ Fondo Cultural | Estados Unidos

Una jugadora profesional Rebecca Lobo, former professional basketball player, won a gold medal in the 1996 Olympics. She became one of the WNBA's original players. Rebecca wrote a book called *The Home Team,* which tells about her life and her mother's struggle against breast cancer. In 2001, she established a college scholarship fund for minority students who plan to enter the healthcare field. Today, Rebeccca is an announcer for the WNBA.

• Rebecca Lobo is a popular motivational speaker. What message do you think she gives to her audiences?

Perspectivas del mundo hispano

¿Qué haces en tu tiempo libre?

In many Spanish-speaking countries, extracurricular activities traditionally play a much smaller role in school life than in the United States. Students usually participate in activities such as music and athletics at clubs and institutions outside of school.

¿Te gusta jugar al ajedrez?

Although some schools have teams, many students who are interested in sports attend clubs such as el Club Deportivo General San Martín. At these clubs teens practice and compete on teams. They also participate in individual sports such as tennis. The competition between clubs is sometimes more intense than the competition between schools.

Students with artistic talents often go to a private institute to take music, dance, or art lessons. They might attend el Instituto de Música Clásica or el Instituto de Danza Julio Bocca.

Many students spend their time outside of classes studying a foreign language. They might learn English at la Cultura Inglesa or French at la Alianza Francesa.

In general, students do not hold jobs. They spend their time studying, being with family and friends, and participating in different activities.

Check it out! Take a survey of your friends to find out what they do after school. Do they work a part-time job? Do they participate in a sport with a school team or in extracurricular activities at school? Do they belong to a club or organization outside of school?

Trabajando después de las clases

Think about it! How do the practices in your community compare with what you have learned about young people's after-school activities in Spanish-speaking countries?

Presentación escrita

Una invitación

Task
Invite a friend to go to a special event with you.

❶ **Prewrite** Think of an event to invite a friend to, such as a concert, game, or party. Write an invitation that includes:

- the name of the event
- the day, time, and location
- who is going

❷ **Draft** Use the information from Step 1 to write a first draft. Begin your invitation with *¡Hola . . . !* and close with *Tu amigo(a)* and your name.

❸ **Revise** Check your note for spelling and grammar, then share with a partner. Your partner should check the following:

- Did you give all the necessary information?
- Is there anything to add or change?
- Are there any errors?

❹ **Publish** Write a final copy of your invitation. You might give it to your friend or include it in your portfolio.

❺ **Evaluation** The following rubric will be used to grade your invitation.

> **Strategy**
>
> **Organizing information**
> Thinking about the correct format and necessary information beforehand will help you create a better invitation.

Rubric	Score 1	Score 3	Score 5
Amount of information	You give very few or no details or examples about locations and activities.	You give only a few details or examples about locations and activities.	You consistently give many details and examples about locations, times, and activities.
Use of vocabulary expressions	You have very little variation of vocabulary usage with frequent incorrect usage.	You have limited usage of vocabulary; some usage errors.	You have extended use of a variety of vocabulary; few usage errors.
Accuracy of sentence structures	You have at least three sentences; many grammar errors.	You have at least three sentences; some grammar errors.	You have at least three sentences; very few grammar errors.

Estados Unidos

Contemporáneo

According to the 2010 census, 50,477,594 people (about 16 percent of the total population of the United States) classified themselves as being of Spanish or Hispanic descent. Out of that number, 39,412,310 indicated that they were of either Mexican, Puerto Rican, Cuban, or Dominican descent. The remaining 11,065,384 people checked "Other Hispanic/Latino" on their census questionnaires. This broad category included people who came from or who had ancestral ties to other Spanish-speaking countries in the Caribbean, Central and South America, or Spain.

Born in Costa Rica, Dr. Franklin Chang-Díaz (left) was the first Hispanic astronaut to fly in space. He was selected by NASA in 1980 and is a veteran of seven space flights. In 1990, Californian Dr. Ellen Ochoa (right) became the first Hispanic female astronaut. Since then she has logged more than 978 hours in space. Her dream is to help build a space station, which she considers "critical . . . to human exploration in space." Both Dr. Ochoa and Dr. Chang-Díaz are the recipients of many honors for their technical contributions and their scholarship. ▶

¿Sabes que . . . ?

The influence of Spanish-speaking cultures is evident throughout the United States. Musical artists such as Enrique Iglesias, Shakira, and Marc Anthony sell millions of CDs. Actors such as Salma Hayek, Jennifer López, Cameron Díaz, and Martin Sheen earn great acclaim for their work. And in politics, Spanish-speaking Americans serve in Congress and top-level Cabinet posts.

Para pensar

Work with a partner and interview a classmate, friend, or acquaintance who is Spanish-speaking or who has ties to a Spanish-speaking country. What is the person's name? Where did the family come from, and when? Why did the family move to your community? If this person had one thing to say to you and your classmates about the immigrant experience and cultural differences, what might that be? Write a short account of the interview and present it to your class or to a small group.

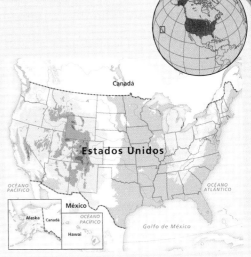

Canadá

Estados Unidos

OCÉANO PACÍFICO

OCÉANO ATLÁNTICO

México

Alaska | Canadá

Hawai

Golfo de México

 realidades.com GO

 Mapa global interactivo

DK **Reference Atlas**

The music and poetry of New York City's Puerto Rican community are a creative blend of English and Spanish. *Nuyoricans* of the *Loisaida* (Lower East Side) rub shoulders with people of diverse ethnic backgrounds creating sounds and rhythms unlike any other in the world. The Nuyorican Poets Café has become an institution on the *Loisaida*, where poets, writers, performance artists, musicians, and visual artists of all nationalities can find an outlet for their work.

More than half of Miami's population is of Spanish-speaking descent. Calle Ocho is the heart of Little Havana, the largest Cuban American community in the United States. The Calle Ocho Festival, which takes place at the end of Carnaval Miami, is a great time to sample Cuban food and dance to some of the world's greatest salsa artists.

More Mexicans visit the border town of Laredo, Texas, than any other city in the United States; and more United States citizens visit the Mexican border town of Tijuana than any other foreign city. Most of the visitors come from nearby areas and stay for only a few hours to visit or shop.

Repaso del capítulo

Vocabulario y gramática

to talk about leisure activities

el baile	dance
el concierto	concert
la fiesta	party
ir + a + *infinitive*	to be going + infinitive
ir de cámping	to go camping
ir de pesca	to go fishing
jugar al básquetbol	to play basketball
jugar al béisbol	to play baseball
jugar al fútbol	to play soccer
jugar al fútbol americano	to play football
jugar al golf	to play golf
jugar al tenis	to play tennis
jugar al vóleibol	to play volleyball
el partido	game, match
(yo) sé	I know (how)
(tú) sabes	you know (how)

to describe how someone feels

cansado, -a	tired
contento, -a	happy
enfermo, -a	sick
mal	bad, badly
ocupado, -a	busy
triste	sad

to extend, accept, or decline invitations

conmigo	with me
contigo	with you
(yo) puedo	I can
(tú) puedes	you can
¡Ay! ¡Qué pena!	Oh! What a shame!
¡Genial!	Great!
lo siento	I'm sorry
¡Oye!	Hey!
¡Qué buena idea!	What a good/nice idea!
(yo) quiero	I want
(tú) quieres	you want
¿Te gustaría?	Would you like?
Me gustaría	I would like
Tengo que ___.	I have to ___.

to tell what time something happens

¿A qué hora?	(At) what time?
a la una	at one (o'clock)
a las ocho	at eight (o'clock)
de la mañana	in the morning
de la noche	in the evening, at night
de la tarde	in the afternoon
esta noche	this evening
esta tarde	this afternoon
este fin de semana	this weekend

other useful words and expressions

demasiado	too
entonces	then
un poco (de)	a little

jugar (a) *to play (games, sports)*

juego	jugamos
juegas	jugáis
juega	juegan

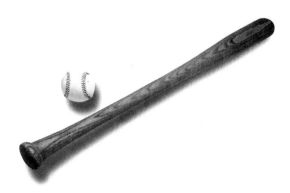

For *Vocabulario adicional,* see pp. 268–269.

Más repaso (GO) **realidades.com | print**

Instant Check	✔
Puzzles	✔
Core WB pp. 83–84	✔
Comm. WB pp. 159, 160–162	✔ ✔

Preparación para el examen

On the exam you will be asked to . . .	Here are practice tasks similar to those you will find on the exam . . .	For review go to your print or digital textbook . . .
1 Escuchar Listen to and understand messages that give information about when and where to meet someone	On your answering machine, you hear your friend asking if you can go somewhere with her this weekend. Based on her message, try to tell: a) where she is going; b) what she is going to do; and c) what time she wants to go.	**pp. 240–245** *Vocabulario en contexto* **p. 248** Actividad 10 **p. 252** Actividad 17
2 Hablar Make excuses for not accepting an invitation	You and a friend have planned a camping trip this weekend, but another friend now wants you to do something with him. With a partner, take turns rehearsing excuses for declining his invitation.	**p. 246** Actividad 5 **p. 248** Actividad 9 **p. 250** Actividad 13 **p. 255** Actividad 22
3 Leer Read and understand short messages about accepting or declining invitations	You find notes under your desk that were written to the person who was sitting there before you. Read them to see why people declined an invitation to a party: (a) Me gustaría, pero no puedo. Tengo que estudiar para un examen. (b) ¡Genial! ¡Una fiesta! Ay, pero no puedo. Voy de cámping. (c) ¿A las siete? No puedo. Juego un partido de vóleibol a las siete y media. Lo siento.	**pp. 240–245** *Vocabulario en contexto* **pp. 260–261** *Lectura*
4 Escribir Write a short note telling what you are going to do during the week	As a counselor for an after-school program for children, you must write a note to the parents telling them at least three things their children are going to do during the week. (Hint: Start your note with *¡Hola! Esta semana . . .*)	**pp. 240–245** *Vocabulario en contexto* **p. 253** Actividad 18 **p. 254** Actividad 20 **p. 263** *Presentación escrita*
5 Pensar Demonstrate an understanding of cultural differences regarding extracurricular activities	Think about what you and your friends typically do after school. Are your activities usually school-related? How would you compare what you do to what some Spanish-speaking teens do in their after-school time?	**p. 262** *Perspectivas del mundo hispano*

Vocabulario adicional

Tema 1

Las actividades

coleccionar sellos / monedas to collect stamps / coins

jugar al ajedrez to play chess

patinar sobre hielo to ice-skate

practicar artes marciales *(f.)* to practice martial arts

tocar to play *(an instrument)*

    el bajo bass

    la batería drums

    el clarinete clarinet

    el oboe oboe

    el saxofón, *pl.* **los saxofones** saxophone

    el sintetizador synthesizer

    el trombón, *pl.* **los trombones** trombone

    la trompeta trumpet

    la tuba tuba

    el violín, *pl.* **los violines** violin

Tema 2

Las clases

el alemán German

el álgebra *(f.)* algebra

el anuario yearbook

la banda band

la biología biology

el cálculo calculus

el drama drama

la fotografía photography

el francés French

la geografía geography

la geometría geometry

el latín Latin

la química chemistry

la trigonometría trigonometry

Las cosas para la clase

la grapadora stapler

las grapas staples

el sujetapapeles, *pl.* **los sujetapapeles** paper clip

las tijeras scissors

Tema 3

Las comidas

Las frutas

el aguacate avocado

la cereza cherry

la ciruela plum

el coco coconut

el durazno peach

la frambuesa raspberry

el limón, *pl.* **los limones** lemon

el melón, *pl.* **los melones** melon

la pera pear

la sandía watermelon

la toronja grapefruit

Las verduras

el apio celery

el brócoli broccoli

la calabaza pumpkin

el champiñón, *pl.* **los champiñones** mushroom

la col cabbage

la coliflor cauliflower

los espárragos asparagus

las espinacas spinach

el pepino cucumber

La carne

la chuleta de cerdo pork chop

el cordero lamb

la ternera veal

Los condimentos

la mayonesa mayonnaise

la mostaza mustard

la salsa de tomate ketchup

Otro tipo de comidas

los fideos noodles

Tema 4

Los lugares y actividades

el banco bank

el club club

el equipo de . . . ___ team

la farmacia pharmacy

la oficina office

la práctica de . . . ___ practice

la reunión, *pl.* **las reuniones de . . . ___** meeting

el supermercado supermarket

Resumen de gramática
Grammar Terms

Adjectives describe nouns: *a **red** car.*

Adverbs usually describe verbs; they tell when, where, or how an action happens: *He read it **quickly.*** Adverbs can also describe adjectives or other adverbs: ***very tall, quite well.***

Articles are words in Spanish that can tell you whether a noun is masculine, feminine, singular, or plural. In English, the articles are ***the, a,*** and ***an.***

Commands are verb forms that tell people to do something: ***Study!, Work!***

Comparatives compare people or things.

Conjugations are verb forms that add endings to the stem in order to tell who the subject is and what tense is being used: *escrib**o**, escrib**iste.***

Conjunctions join words or groups of words. The most common ones are ***and, but,*** and ***or.***

Direct objects are nouns or pronouns that receive the action of a verb: *I read the **book.** I read **it.***

Gender in Spanish tells you whether a noun, pronoun, or article is masculine or feminine.

Indirect objects are nouns or pronouns that tell you to whom / what or for whom / what something is done: *I gave **him** the book.*

Infinitives are the basic forms of verbs. In English, infinitives have the word "to" in front of them: ***to walk.***

Interrogatives are words that ask questions: ***What** is that? **Who** are you?*

Nouns are people, places, or things: ***students, Mexico City, books.***

Numbers tell you if a noun, pronoun, article, or verb is singular or plural.

Prepositions show the relationship between an object and another word in the sentence: *He is **in** the classroom.*

Present tense is used to talk about actions that always take place, or that are happening now: *I always **take** the bus; I **study** Spanish.*

Present progressive tense is used to emphasize that an action is happening *right now: I **am doing** my homework; he **is finishing** dinner.*

Preterite tense is used to talk about actions that were completed in the past: *I **took** the train yesterday; I **studied** for the test.*

Pronouns are words that take the place of nouns: ***She** is my friend.*

Subjects are the nouns or pronouns that perform the action in a sentence: ***John** sings.*

Superlatives describe which things have the most or least of a given quality: *She is the **best** student.*

Verbs show action or link the subject with a word or words in the predicate (what the subject does or is): *Ana **writes;** Ana **is** my sister.*

Nouns, Number, and Gender

Nouns refer to people, animals, places, things, and ideas. Nouns are singular or plural. In Spanish, nouns have gender, which means that they are either masculine or feminine.

Singular Nouns	
Masculine	Feminine
libro	carpeta
pupitre	casa
profesor	noche
lápiz	ciudad

Plural Nouns	
Masculine	Feminine
libros	carpetas
pupitres	casas
profesores	noches
lápices	ciudades

Definite Articles

El, la, los, and *las* are definite articles and are the equivalent of "the" in English. *El* is used with masculine singular nouns; *los* with masculine plural nouns. *La* is used with feminine singular nouns; *las* with feminine plural nouns. When you use the words *a* or *de* before *el,* you form the contractions *al* and *del: Voy **al** centro; Es el libro **del** profesor.*

Masculine	
Singular	**Plural**
el libro	los libros
el pupitre	los pupitres
el profesor	los profesores
el lápiz	los lápices

Feminine	
Singular	**Plural**
la carpeta	las carpetas
la casa	las casas
la noche	las noches
la ciudad	las ciudades

Indefinite Articles

Un and *una* are indefinite articles and are the equivalent of "a" and "an" in English. *Un* is used with singular masculine nouns; *una* is used with singular feminine nouns. The plural indefinite articles are *unos* and *unas.*

Masculine	
Singular	**Plural**
un libro	unos libros
un escritorio	unos escritorios
un baile	unos bailes

Feminine	
Singular	**Plural**
una revista	unas revistas
una mochila	unas mochilas
una bandera	unas banderas

Pronouns

Subject pronouns tell who is doing the action. They replace nouns or names in a sentence. Subject pronouns are often used for emphasis or clarification: *Gregorio escucha música.* *Él escucha música.*

After most prepositions, you use *mí* and *ti* for "me" and "you." The forms change with the preposition *con: conmigo, contigo.* For all other persons, you use subject pronouns after prepositions.

Subject Pronouns		Objects of Prepositions	
Singular	**Plural**	**Singular**	**Plural**
yo	nosotros, nosotras	(para) mí, conmigo	nosotros, nosotras
tú	vosotros, vosotras	(para) ti, contigo	vosotros, vosotras
usted (Ud.)	ustedes (Uds.)	Ud.	Uds.
él, ella	ellos, ellas	él, ella	ellos, ellas

Interrogative Words

You use interrogative words to ask questions. When you ask a question with an interrogative word, you put the verb before the subject. All interrogative words have a written accent mark.

¿Adónde?	¿Cuándo?	¿Dónde?
¿Cómo?	¿Cuánto, -a?	¿Por qué?
¿Con quién?	¿Cuántos, -as?	¿Qué?
¿Cuál?	¿De dónde?	¿Quién?

Adjectives

Words that describe people and things are called adjectives. In Spanish, most adjectives have both masculine and feminine forms, as well as singular and plural forms. Adjectives must agree with the noun they describe in both gender and number. When an adjective describes a group including both masculine and feminine nouns, use the masculine plural form.

Masculine	
Singular	Plural
alto	altos
inteligente	inteligentes
trabajador	trabajadores
fácil	fáciles

Feminine	
Singular	Plural
alta	altas
inteligente	inteligentes
trabajadora	trabajadoras
fácil	fáciles

Shortened Forms of Adjectives

When placed before masculine singular nouns, some adjectives change into a shortened form.

bueno	→	buen chico
malo	→	mal día
primero	→	primer trabajo
tercero	→	tercer plato
grande	→	gran señor

One adjective, **grande,** changes to a shortened form before any singular noun: *una **gran** señora, un **gran** libro.*

Possessive Adjectives

Possessive adjectives are used to tell what belongs to someone or to show relationships. Like other adjectives, possessive adjectives agree in number with the nouns that follow them.

Only *nuestro* and *vuestro* have different masculine and feminine endings. *Su* and *sus* can have many different meanings: *his, her, its, your,* or *their.*

Singular	Plural
mi	mis
tu	tus
su	sus
nuestro, -a	nuestros, -as
vuestro, -a	vuestros, -as
su	sus

Demonstrative Adjectives

Like other adjectives, demonstrative adjectives agree in gender and number with the nouns that follow them. Use *este, esta, estos, estas* ("this" / "these") before nouns that name people or things that are close to you. Use *ese, esa, esos, esas* ("that" / "those") before nouns that name people or things that are at some distance from you.

Singular	Plural
este libro	estos libros
esta casa	estas casas

Singular	Plural
ese niño	esos niños
esa manzana	esas manzanas

Verbos

Regular Present Tense

Here are the conjugations for regular -ar, -er, and -ir verbs in the present tense.

Infinitive	Present	
estudiar	estudio	estudiamos
	estudias	estudiáis
	estudia	estudian
correr	corro	corremos
	corres	corréis
	corre	corren
escribir	escribo	escribimos
	escribes	escribís
	escribe	escriben

Stem-changing Verbs

Here is an alphabetical list of the stem-changing verbs.

Infinitive	Present	
doler (o → ue)	duele	duelen
dormir (o → ue)	duermo	dormimos
	duermes	dormís
	duerme	duermen
empezar (e → ie)	empiezo	empezamos
	empiezas	empezáis
	empieza	empiezan
jugar (u → ue)	juego	jugamos
	juegas	jugáis
	juega	juegan
llover (o → ue)	llueve	
nevar (e → ie)	nieva	
pensar (e → ie)	pienso	pensamos
	piensas	pensáis
	piensa	piensan
preferir (e → ie)	prefiero	preferimos
	prefieres	preferís
	prefiere	prefieren

Irregular Verbs

These verbs have irregular patterns.

Infinitive	Present	
estar	estoy	estamos
	estás	estáis
	está	están
hacer	hago	hacemos
	haces	hacéis
	hace	hacen
ir	voy	vamos
	vas	vais
	va	van
poder	puedo	podemos
	puedes	podéis
	puede	pueden
querer	quiero	queremos
	quieres	queréis
	quiere	quieren
saber	sé	sabemos
	sabes	sabéis
	sabe	saben
ser	soy	somos
	eres	sois
	es	son
tener	tengo	tenemos
	tienes	tenéis
	tiene	tienen
ver	veo	vemos
	ves	veis
	ve	ven

Expresiones útiles para conversar

The following are expressions that you can use when you find yourself in a specific situation and need help to begin, continue, or end a conversation.

Greeting Someone

Buenos días. Good morning.

Buenas tardes. Good afternoon.

Buenas noches. Good evening. Good night.

Making Introductions

Me llamo . . . My name is . . .

Soy . . . I'm . . .

¿Cómo te llamas? What's your name?

Éste es mi amigo m. **. . .** This is my friend . . .

Ésta es mi amiga f. **. . .** This is my friend . . .

Se llama . . . His / Her name is . . .

¡Mucho gusto! It's a pleasure!

Encantado, -a. Delighted.

Igualmente. Likewise.

Asking How Someone Is

¿Cómo estás? How are you?

¿Cómo andas? How's it going?

¿Cómo te sientes? How do you feel?

¿Qué tal? How's it going?

Estoy bien, gracias. I'm fine, thank you.

Muy bien. ¿Y tú? Very well. And you?

Regular. Okay. Alright.

Más o menos. More or less.

(Muy) mal. (Very) bad.

¡Horrible! Awful!

¡Excelente! Great!

Talking on the Phone

Aló. Hello.

Diga. Hello.

Bueno. Hello.

¿Quién habla? Who's calling?

Habla . . . It's [name of person calling].

¿Está . . . , por favor? Is . . . there, please?

¿De parte de quién? Who is calling?

¿Puedo dejar un recado? May I leave a message?

Un momento. Just a moment.

Llamo más tarde. I'll call later.

¿Cómo? No le oigo. What? I can't hear you.

Making Plans

¿Adónde vas? Where are you going?

Voy a . . . I'm going to . . .

¿Estás listo, -a? Are you ready?

Tengo prisa. I'm in a hurry.

¡Date prisa! Hurry up!

Sí, ahora voy. OK, I'm coming.

Todavía necesito . . . I still need . . .

¿Te gustaría . . . ? Would you like to . . . ?

Sí, me gustaría . . . Yes, I'd like to . . .

¡Claro que sí (no)! Of course (not)!

¿Quieres . . . ? Do you want to . . . ?

Quiero . . . I want to . . .

¿Qué quieres hacer hoy? What do you want to do today?

¿Qué haces después de las clases? What do you do after school (class)?

¿Qué estás haciendo? What are you doing?

Te invito. It's my treat.

¿Qué tal si . . . ? What about . . . ?

Primero . . . First . . .

Después . . . Later . . .

Luego . . . Then . . .

Making an Excuse

Estoy ocupado, -a. I'm busy.

Lo siento, pero no puedo. I'm sorry, but I can't.

¡Qué lástima! What a shame!

Ya tengo planes. I already have plans.

Tal vez otro día. Maybe another day.

Being Polite

Con mucho gusto. With great pleasure.

De nada. You're welcome.

Disculpe. Excuse me.

Lo siento. I'm sorry.

Muchísimas gracias. Thank you very much.

Te (Se) lo agradezco mucho. I appreciate it a lot.

Muy amable. That's very kind of you.

Perdón. Pardon me.

¿Puede Ud. repetirlo? Can you repeat that?

¿Puede Ud. hablar más despacio? Can you speak more slowly?

Keeping a Conversation Going

¿De veras? Really?

¿Verdad? Isn't that so? Right?

¿En serio? Seriously?

¡No lo puedo creer! I don't believe it!

¡No me digas! You don't say!

Y entonces, ¿qué? And then what?

¿Qué hiciste? What did you do?

¿Qué dijiste? What did you say?

¿Crees que . . . ? Do you think that . . . ?

Me parece bien. It seems alright.

Perfecto. Perfect.

¡Qué buena idea! What a good idea!

¡Cómo no! Of course!

De acuerdo. Agreed.

Está bien. It's all right.

Giving a Description When You Don't Know the Name of Someone or Something

Se usa para . . . It's used to / for . . .

Es la palabra que significa . . . It's the word that means . . .

Es la persona que . . . It's the person who . . .

Ending a Conversation

Bueno, tengo que irme. Well, I have to go.

Chao. (Chau.) Bye.

Hasta pronto. See you soon.

Hasta mañana. See you tomorrow.

Vocabulario español-inglés

The *Vocabulario español-inglés* contains all active vocabulary from the text, including vocabulary presented in the grammar sections.

A dash (—) represents the main entry word. For example, **pasar la —** after **la aspiradora** means **pasar la aspiradora.**

The number following each entry indicates the chapter in which the word or expression is presented. The letter *P* following an entry refers to the *Para empezar* section.

The following abbreviations are used in this list: *adj.* (adjective), *dir. obj.* (direct object), *f.* (feminine), *fam.* (familiar), *ind. obj.* (indirect object), *inf.* (infinitive), *m.* (masculine), *pl.* (plural), *prep.* (preposition), *pron.* (pronoun), *sing.* (singular).

A

a to *(prep.)* (4A)
   — casa (to) home (4A)
   — la una de la tarde at one (o'clock) in the afternoon (4B)
   — las ocho de la mañana at eight (o'clock) in the morning (4B)
   — las ocho de la noche at eight (o'clock) in the evening / at night (4B)
   — mí también I do (like to) too (1A)
   — mí tampoco I don't (like to) either (1A)
   ¿— qué hora? (At) what time? (4B)
   — veces sometimes (1B)
   — ver Let's see (2A)
   al *(a + el)*, **a la,** to the (4A)
   al lado de next to (2B)
abril April (P)
aburrido, -a boring (2A)
acuerdo:
   Estoy de —. I agree. (3B)
   No estoy de —. I don't agree. (3B)
¡Adiós! Good-bye! (P)

¿Adónde? (To) where? (4A)
agosto August (P)
el **agua** *f.* water (3A)
al *(a + el)*, **a la,** to the (4A)
   — lado de next to (2B)
algo something (3B)
allí there (2B)
el **almuerzo** lunch (2A)
   en el — for lunch (3A)
el **amigo, la amiga** friend (1B)
el **año** year (P)
aquí here (2B)
el **arroz** rice (3B)
el **arte:**
   la clase de — art class (2A)
   artístico, -a artistic (1B)
   asco:
   ¡Qué —! How awful! (3A)
   atrevido, -a daring (1B)
   ¡Ay! ¡Qué pena! Oh! What a shame / pity! (4B)

B

bailar to dance (1A)
el **baile** dance (4B)
la **bandera** flag (2B)
el **básquetbol: jugar al —** to play basketball (4B)
beber to drink (3A)
las **bebidas** beverages (3B)
   béisbol: jugar al — to play baseball (4B)
la **biblioteca** library (4A)
bien well (P)
el **bistec** beefsteak (3B)
la **boca** mouth (P)
el **bolígrafo** pen (P)
el **brazo** arm (P)
bueno (buen), -a good (1B)
   Buenas noches. Good evening. (P)
   Buenas tardes. Good afternoon. (P)
   Buenos días. Good morning. (P)

C

la **cabeza** head (P)
   cada día every day (3B)
el **café** coffee (3A); café (4A)
la **calculadora** calculator (2A)
   calor: Hace —. It's hot. (P)
   caminar to walk (3B)
el **campo** countryside (4A)
   cansado, -a tired (4B)
   cantar to sing (1A)
la **carne** meat (3B)
la **carpeta** folder (P)
   la — de argollas three-ring binder (2A)
el **cartel** poster (2B)
la **casa** home, house (4A)
   a — (to) home (4A)
   en at home (4A)
   catorce fourteen (P)
la **cebolla** onion (3B)
la **cena** dinner (3B)
el **centro: el — comercial** mall (4A)
el **cereal** cereal (3A)
los **cereales** grains (3B)
   cero zero (P)
la **chica** girl (1B)
el **chico** boy (1B)
   cien one hundred (P)
las **ciencias:**
   la clase de — naturales science class (2A)
   la clase de — sociales social studies class (2A)
   cinco five (P)
   cincuenta fifty (P)
el **cine** movie theater (4A)
la **clase** class (2A)
   la sala de clases classroom (P)
   comer to eat (3A)
la **comida** food, meal (3A)
   ¿Cómo?:
   ¿— eres? What are you like? (1B)

¿— es? What is he / she like? (1B)

¿— está Ud.? How are you? *formal* (P)

¿— estás? How are you? *fam.* (P)

¿— se dice . . . ? How do you say . . . ? (P)

¿— se escribe . . . ? How is . . . spelled? (P)

¿— se llama? What's his / her name? (1B)

¿— te llamas? What is your name? (P)

compartir to share (3A)

compras: ir de — to go shopping (4A)

comprender to understand (3A)

la **computadora** computer (2B)

    usar la — to use the computer (1A)

con with (3A)

    — mis / tus amigos with my / your friends (4A)

    ¿— quién? With whom? (4A)

el **concierto** concert (4B)

conmigo with me (4B)

contento, -a happy (4B)

contigo with you (4B)

correr to run (1A)

creer:

    Creo que . . . I think . . . (3B)

    Creo que no. I don't think so. (3B)

    Creo que sí. I think so. (3B)

el **cuaderno** notebook (P)

¿Cuál? Which?, What? (3A)

    ¿— es la fecha? What is the date? (P)

¿Cuándo? When? (4A)

¿Cuántos, -as? How many? (P)

cuarenta forty (P)

cuarto, -a fourth (2A)

    y — quarter past *(in telling time)* (P)

    menos — *(time)* quarter to (P)

cuatro four (P)

D

de of (2B); from (4A)

    ¿— dónde eres? Where are you from? (4A)

    — la mañana / la tarde / la noche in the morning / afternoon / evening (4B)

debajo de underneath (2B)

deber should, must (3B)

décimo, -a tenth (2A)

decir to say, to tell

    ¿Cómo se dice . . . ? How do you say . . . ? (P)

    ¡No me digas! You don't say! (4A)

    ¿Qué quiere — . . . ? What does . . . mean? (P)

    Quiere — . . . It means . . . (P)

    Se dice . . . You say . . . (P)

el **dedo** finger (P)

delante de in front of (2B)

demasiado too (4B)

deportista athletic, sports-minded (1B)

el **desayuno** breakfast (3A)

    en el — for breakfast (3A)

desordenado, -a messy (1B)

después (de) after, afterwards (4A)

detrás de behind (2B)

el **día** day (P)

    Buenos —s. Good morning. (P)

    cada — every day (3B)

    ¿Qué — es hoy? What day is today? (P)

    todos los —s every day (3A)

dibujar to draw (1A)

el **diccionario** dictionary (2A)

diciembre December (P)

diecinueve nineteen (P)

dieciocho eighteen (P)

dieciséis sixteen (P)

diecisiete seventeen (P)

diez ten (P)

difícil difficult (2A)

divertido, -a amusing, fun (2A)

doce twelve (P)

domingo Sunday (P)

dónde:

    ¿—? Where? (2B)

    ¿De — eres? Where are you from? (4A)

dos two (P)

E

educación física: la clase de — physical education class (2A)

el **ejercicio: hacer —** to exercise (3B)

el the *m. sing.* (1B)

él he (1B)

ella she (1B)

ellas they *f. pl.* (2A)

ellos they *m. pl.* (2A)

en in, on (2B)

    — casa at home (4A)

    — la . . . hora in the . . . hour (class period) (2A)

encantado, -a delighted (P)

encantar to please very much, to love

    me / te encanta(n) . . . I / you love . . . (3A)

encima de on top of (2B)

enero January (P)

enfermo, -a sick (4B)

la **ensalada** salad (3A)

    la — de frutas fruit salad (3A)

enseñar to teach (2A)

entonces then (4B)

¿Eres . . . ? Are you . . . ? (1B)

es is (P); (he / she / it) is (1B)

    — el *(number)* **de** *(month)* it is the . . . of . . . *(in telling the date)* (P)

    — el primero de *(month)*. It is the first of . . . (P)

    — la una. It is one o'clock. (P)

    — un(a) . . . it's a . . . (2B)

escribir:

¿Cómo se escribe . . . ? How is . . . spelled? (P)

— cuentos to write stories (1A)

Se escribe . . . It's spelled . . . (P)

el **escritorio** desk (2B)

escuchar música to listen to music (1A)

los **espaguetis** spaghetti (3B)

el **español: la clase de —** Spanish class (2A)

esquiar (i → í) to ski (1A)

la **estación,** *pl.* **las estaciones** season (P)

estar to be (2B)

¿Cómo está Ud.? How are you? *formal* (P)

¿Cómo estás? How are you? *fam.* (P)

Estoy de acuerdo. I agree. (3B)

No estoy de acuerdo. I don't agree. (3B)

este, esta this

esta noche this evening (4B)

esta tarde this afternoon (4B)

este fin de semana this weekend (4B)

el **estómago** stomach (P)

estos, estas these

¿Qué es esto? What is this? (2B)

Estoy de acuerdo. I agree. (3B)

el/la **estudiante** student (P)

estudiar to study (2A)

estudioso, -a studious (1B)

F

fácil easy (2A)

favorito, -a favorite (2A)

febrero February (P)

la **fecha: ¿Cuál es la —?** What is the date? (P)

la **fiesta** party (4B)

el **fin de semana:**

este — this weekend (4B)

los fines de semana on weekends (4A)

las **fresas** strawberries (3A)

frío: Hace —. It's cold. (P)

el **fútbol: jugar al —** to play soccer (4B)

el **fútbol americano: jugar al —** to play football (4B)

G

la **galleta** cookie (3A)

generalmente generally (4A)

¡Genial! Great! (4B)

el **gimnasio** gym (4A)

el **golf: jugar al —** to play golf (4B)

gracias thank you (P)

gracioso, -a funny (1B)

las **grasas** fats (3B)

los **guisantes** peas (3B)

gustar:

(A mí) me gusta . . . I like to . . . (1A)

(A mí) me gusta más . . . I like to . . . better (I prefer to . . .) (1A)

(A mí) me gusta mucho . . . I like to . . . a lot (1A)

(A mí) no me gusta . . . I don't like to . . . (1A)

(A mí) no me gusta nada . . . I don't like to . . . at all. (1A)

Le gusta . . . He / She likes . . . (1B)

Me gusta . . . I like . . . (3A)

Me gustaría . . . I would like . . . (4B)

No le gusta . . . He / She doesn't like . . . (1B)

¿Qué te gusta hacer? What do you like to do? (1A)

¿Qué te gusta hacer más? What do you like better (prefer) to do? (1A)

Te gusta . . . You like . . . (3A)

¿Te gusta . . . ? Do you like to . . . ? (1A)

¿Te gustaría . . . ? Would you like . . . ? (4B)

H

hablar to talk (2A)

— por teléfono to talk on the phone (1A)

hacer to do (3B)

Hace calor. It's hot. (P)

Hace frío. It's cold. (P)

Hace sol. It's sunny. (P)

Hace viento. It's windy. (P)

— ejercicio to exercise (3B)

¿Qué tiempo hace? What's the weather like? (P)

(yo) hago I do (3B)

(tú) haces you do (3B)

hambre: Tengo —. I'm hungry. (3B)

la **hamburguesa** hamburger (3A)

hasta:

— luego. See you later. (P)

— mañana. See you tomorrow. (P)

Hay There is, There are (P)

el **helado** ice cream (3B)

la **hoja de papel** sheet of paper (P)

¡Hola! Hello! (P)

la **hora:**

en la . . . — in the . . . hour (class period) (2A)

¿A qué hora? (At) what time? (4B)

el **horario** schedule (2A)

horrible horrible (3B)

hoy today (P)

los **huevos** eggs (3A)

I

la **iglesia** church (4A)

igualmente likewise (P)

impaciente impatient (1B)

el **inglés: la clase de —** English class (2A)

inteligente intelligent (1B)

interesante interesting (2A)

el **invierno** winter (P)

ir to go (4A)

— **a** + *inf.* to be going to + *verb* (4B)

— **a la escuela** to go to school (1A)

— **de cámping** to go camping (4B)

— **de compras** to go shopping (4A)

— **de pesca** to go fishing (4B)

J

el **jamón** ham (3A)

las **judías verdes** green beans (3B)

jueves Thursday (P)

jugar (a) (u → ue) to play *(games, sports)* (4B)

— **al básquetbol** to play basketball (4B)

— **al béisbol** to play baseball (4B)

— **al fútbol** to play soccer (4B)

— **al fútbol americano** to play football (4B)

— **al golf** to play golf (4B)

— **al tenis** to play tennis (4B)

— **al vóleibol** to play volleyball (4B)

— **videojuegos** to play video games (1A)

el **jugo:**

— **de manzana** apple juice (3A)

— **de naranja** orange juice (3A)

julio July (P)

junio June (P)

L

la the *f. sing.* (1B)

lado: al — de next to, beside (2B)

el **lápiz,** *pl.* **los lápices** pencil (P)

las the *f. pl.* (2B)

le (to / for) him, her

— **gusta . . .** He / She likes . . . (1B)

No — gusta . . . He / She doesn't like . . . (1B)

la **lección,** *pl.* **las lecciones de piano** piano lesson (class) (4A)

la **leche** milk (3A)

la **lechuga** lettuce (3B)

leer revistas to read magazines (1A)

levantar pesas to lift weights (3B)

el **libro** book (P)

la **limonada** lemonade (3A)

llamar:

¿Cómo se llama? What's his / her name? (1B)

¿Cómo te llamas? What is your name? (P)

Me llamo . . . My name is . . . (P)

llover (o → ue): Llueve. It's raining. (P)

lo it, him

— **siento.** I'm sorry. (4B)

los the *m. pl.* (2B)

— **fines de semana** on weekends (4A)

— **lunes, los martes . . .** on Mondays, on Tuesdays . . . (4A)

lunes Monday (P)

los lunes on Mondays (4A)

M

mal bad, badly (4B)

malo, -a bad (3B)

la **mano** hand (P)

mantener: para — la salud to maintain one's health (3B)

la **mantequilla** butter (3B)

la **manzana** apple (3A)

el jugo de — apple juice (3A)

mañana tomorrow (P)

la **mañana:**

a las ocho de la — at eight (o'clock) in the morning (4B)

de la — in the morning (4B)

martes Tuesday (P)

los martes on Tuesdays (4A)

marzo March (P)

más more (1A)

— **. . . que** more . . . than (2A)

— **o menos** more or less (3A)

las **matemáticas: la clase de —** mathematics class (2A)

mayo May (P)

me (to / for) me

— **gusta** I like (1A)

— **gustaría** I would like (4B)

— **llamo . . .** My name is . . . (P)

— **quedo en casa.** I stay at home. (4A)

media, -o half (P)

y — thirty, half past *(in telling time)* (P)

menos:

— until *(in telling time)* (P)

— **cuarto** quarter to *(in telling time)* (P)

— **más o —** more or less (3A)

el **mes** month (P)

la **mesa** table (2B)

la **mezquita** mosque (4A)

mi my (2B)

mí:

a — también I do (like to) too (1A)

a — tampoco I don't (like to) either (1A)

miércoles Wednesday (P)

la **mochila** bookbag, backpack (2B)

las **montañas** mountains (4A)

montar:

— **en bicicleta** to ride a bicycle (1A)

— **en monopatín** to skateboard (1A)

mucho, -a a lot (2A)

— **gusto** pleased to meet you (P)

muchos, -as many (3B)

muy very (1B)

— **bien** very well (P)

N

nada nothing (P)

    (A mí) no me gusta — . . . I don't like to . . . at all. (1A)

nadar to swim (1A)

la **naranja: el jugo de —** orange juice (3A)

la **nariz,** *pl.* **las narices** nose (P)

necesitar:

    (yo) necesito I need (2A)

    (tú) necesitas you need (2A)

nevar (e → ie) Nieva. It's snowing. (P)

ni . . . ni neither . . . nor, not . . . or (1A)

No estoy de acuerdo. I don't agree. (3B)

¡No me digas! You don't say! (4A)

noche:

    a las ocho de la — at eight (o'clock) in the evening, at night (4B)

    Buenas —s. Good evening. (P)

    de la — in the evening, at night (4B)

    esta — this evening (4B)

nos (to / for) us

    ¡— vemos! See you later! (P)

nosotros, -as we (2A)

noveno, -a ninth (2A)

noventa ninety (P)

noviembre November (P)

nueve nine (P)

nunca never (3A)

O

o or (1A)

ochenta eighty (P)

ocho eight (P)

octavo, -a eighth (2A)

octubre October (P)

ocupado, -a busy (4B)

el **ojo** eye (P)

once eleven (P)

ordenado, -a neat (1B)

el **otoño** fall, autumn (P)

¡Oye! Hey! (4B)

P

paciente patient (1B)

el **pan** bread (3A)

    el — tostado toast (3A)

la **pantalla** (computer) screen (2B)

las **papas** potatoes (3B)

    las — fritas French fries (3A)

la **papelera** wastepaper basket (2B)

para for (2A)

    — + *inf.* in order to (4A)

    — la salud for one's health (3B)

    — mantener la salud to maintain one's health (3B)

el **parque** park (4A)

el **partido** game, match (4B)

pasar:

    — tiempo con amigos to spend time with friends (1A)

    ¿Qué pasa? What's happening? (P)

los **pasteles** pastries (3B)

patinar to skate (1A)

la **película: film, movie**

    ver una — to see a movie (4A)

pena: ¡Qué —! What a shame/pity! (4B)

perezoso, -a lazy (1B)

pero but (1B)

el **perrito caliente** hot dog (3A)

pesas: levantar — to lift weights (3B)

el **pescado** fish (3B)

el **piano: la lección de —** piano lesson (4A)

el **pie** foot (P)

la **pierna** leg (P)

la **piscina** pool (4A)

la **pizza** pizza (3A)

el **plátano** banana (3A)

la **playa** beach (4A)

    poco: un — (de) a little (4B)

poder (o → ue) to be able

    (yo) puedo I can (4B)

    (tú) puedes you can (4B)

el **pollo** chicken (3B)

por:

    — favor please (P)

    ¿— qué? Why? (3B)

    — supuesto of course (3A)

porque because (3B)

practicar deportes to play sports (1A)

práctico, -a practical (2A)

preferir (e → ie) to prefer

    (yo) prefiero I prefer (3B)

    (tú) prefieres you prefer (3B)

la **primavera** spring (P)

primer (primero), -a first (2A)

el **profesor, la profesora** teacher (P)

puedes: (tú) — you can (4B)

puedo: (yo) — I can (4B)

la **puerta** door (2B)

pues well *(to indicate pause)* (1A)

el **pupitre** student desk (P)

Q

Qué:

    ¡— asco! How awful! (3A)

    ¡— buena idea! What a good / nice idea! (4B)

    ¿— día es hoy? What day is today? (P)

    ¿— es esto? What is this? (2B)

    ¿— hora es? What time is it? (P)

    ¿— pasa? What's happening? (P)

    ¡— pena! What a shame / pity! (4B)

    ¿— quiere decir . . . ? What does . . . mean? (P)

    ¿— tal? How are you? (P)

    ¿— te gusta hacer? What do you like to do? (1A)

¿— te gusta hacer más?
What do you like better
(prefer) to do? (1A)

¿— tiempo hace? What's the
weather like? (P)

quedo: Me — en casa. I stay at
home. (4A)

querer (e → ie) to want

¿Qué quiere decir . . . ?
What does . . . mean? (P)

Quiere decir . . .
It means . . . (P)

(yo) quiero I want (4B)

(tú) quieres you want (4B)

el **queso** cheese (3A)

¿Quién? Who? (2A)

quince fifteen (P)

quinto, -a fifth (2A)

R

el **ratón,** *pl.* **los ratones**
(computer) mouse (2B)

el **refresco** soft drink (3A)

regular okay, so-so (P)

el **reloj** clock (2B)

reservado, -a reserved, shy (1B)

el **restaurante** restaurant (4A)

S

sábado Saturday (P)

saber to know (how)

(yo) sé I know (how to) (4B)

(tú) sabes you know (how to)
(4B)

sabroso, -a tasty, flavorful (3B)

el **sacapuntas,** *pl.* **los sacapuntas**
pencil sharpener (2B)

la **sala de clases** classroom (P)

la **salchicha** sausage (3A)

la **salud:**

para la — for one's health (3B)

para mantener la — to
maintain one's health (3B)

el **sándwich de jamón y queso**
ham and cheese sandwich (3A)

Se dice . . . You say . . . (P)

Se escribe . . . It's spelled . . . (P)

sé: (yo) — I know (how to) (1B)

sed: Tengo —. I'm thirsty. (3B)

según according to (1B)

— mi familia according to
my family (1B)

segundo, -a second (2A)

seis six (P)

la **semana** week (P)

este fin de — this weekend
(4B)

los fines de — on weekends
(4A)

señor (Sr.) sir, Mr. (P)

señora (Sra.) madam, Mrs. (P)

señorita (Srta.) miss, Miss (P)

septiembre September (P)

séptimo, -a seventh (2A)

ser to be (3B)

¿Eres . . . ? Are you . . . ? (1B)

es he / she is (1B)

no soy I am not (1B)

soy I am (1B)

serio, -a serious (1B)

sesenta sixty (P)

setenta seventy (P)

sexto, -a sixth (2A)

sí yes (1A)

siempre always (3A)

siento: lo — I'm sorry (4B)

siete seven (P)

la **silla** chair (2B)

simpático, -a nice, friendly (1B)

sin without (3A)

la **sinagoga** synagogue (4A)

sociable sociable (1B)

el **sol: Hace —.** It's sunny. (P)

solo, -a alone (4A)

Son las . . . It is . . . *(in telling*
time) (P)

la **sopa de verduras** vegetable
soup (3A)

soy I am (1B)

supuesto: por — of course (3A)

T

tal: ¿Qué —? How are you? (P)

talentoso, -a talented (1B)

también also, too (1A)

a mí — I do (like to) too (1A)

tampoco: a mí — I don't (like
to) either (1A)

la **tarde** afternoon (4B)

a la una de la — at one
(o'clock) in the afternoon (4B)

Buenas —s. Good afternoon.
(P)

de la tarde in the afternoon
(4B)

esta — this afternoon (4B)

la **tarea** homework (2A)

te (to / for) you

¿— gusta . . . ? Do you like
to . . . ? (1A)

¿— gustaría . . . ? Would you
like . . . ? (4B)

el **té** tea (3A)

el — helado iced tea (3A)

el **teclado** (computer) keyboard (2B)

la **tecnología** technology /
computers (2A)

la clase de — technology /
computer class (2A)

el **templo** temple; Protestant
church (4A)

tener to have

(yo) tengo I have
(2A)

(tú) tienes you have
(2A)

Tengo hambre. I'm hungry.
(3B)

Tengo que . . .
I have to . . . (4B)

Tengo sed. I'm thirsty. (3B)

el **tenis: jugar al —** to play tennis
(4B)

tercer (tercero), -a third (2A)

ti you *fam. after prep.*

¿Y a —? And you? (1A)

el **tiempo:**

el **— libre** free time (4A)

pasar — con amigos to spend time with friends (1A)

¿Qué — hace? What's the weather like? (P)

tocar la guitarra to play the guitar (1A)

el **tocino** bacon (3A)

todos, -as all (3B)

— los días every day (3A)

los **tomates** tomatoes (3B)

trabajador, -ora hardworking (1B)

trabajar to work (1A)

el **trabajo** work, job (4A)

trece thirteen (P)

treinta thirty (P)

treinta y uno thirty-one (P)

tres three (P)

triste sad (4B)

tu your (2B)

tú you *fam.* (2A)

U _____

Ud. (usted) you *formal sing.* (2A)

Uds. (ustedes) you *formal pl.* (2A)

un, una a, an (1B)

un poco (de) a little (4B)

la **una: a la —** at one o'clock (4B)

uno one (P)

unos, -as some (2B)

usar la computadora to use the computer (1A)

usted (Ud.) you *formal sing.* (2A)

ustedes (Uds.) you *formal pl.* (2A)

las **uvas** grapes (3B)

V _____

veinte twenty (P)

veintiuno (veintiún) twenty-one (P)

la **ventana** window (2B)

ver:

a — Let's see (2A)

¡Nos vemos! See you later! (P)

— la tele to watch television (1A)

— una película to see a movie (4A)

el **verano** summer (P)

¿Verdad? Really?, Right? (3A)

la **vez,** *pl.* **las veces:**

a veces sometimes (1B)

los **videojuegos: jugar —** to play video games (1A)

el **viento: Hace —.** It's windy. (P)

viernes Friday (P)

el **vóleibol: jugar al —** to play volleyball (4B)

vosotros, -as you *pl.* (2A)

Y _____

y and (1A)

¿— a ti? And you? (1A)

— cuarto quarter past *(in telling time)* (P)

— media thirty, half past *(in telling time)* (P)

¿— tú? And you? *fam.* (P)

¿— usted (Ud.)? And you? *formal* (P)

yo I (1B)

el **yogur** yogurt (3A)

Z _____

las **zanahorias** carrots (3B)

English-Spanish Vocabulary

The *English-Spanish Vocabulary* contains all active vocabulary from the text, including vocabulary presented in the grammar sections.

A dash (—) represents the main entry word. For example, **to play —** after **baseball** means **to play baseball.**

The number following each entry indicates the chapter in which the word or expression is presented. The letter *P* following an entry refers to the *Para empezar* section.

The following abbreviations are used in this list: *adj.* (adjective), *dir. obj.* (direct object), *f.* (feminine), *fam.* (familiar), *ind. obj.* (indirect object), *inf.* (infinitive), *m.* (masculine), *pl.* (plural), *prep.* (preposition), *pron.* (pronoun), *sing.* (singular).

A

a, an un, una (1B)

  a little un poco (de) (4B)

  a lot mucho, -a (2A)

according to según (1B)

  — my family según mi familia (1B)

after después de (4A)

afternoon:

  at one (o'clock) in the afternoon a la una de la tarde (4B)

  Good —. Buenas tardes. (P)

  in the — de la tarde (4B)

  this — esta tarde (4B)

afterwards después (4A)

agree:

  I —. Estoy de acuerdo. (3B)

  I don't —. No estoy de acuerdo. (3B)

all todos, -as (3B)

alone solo, -a (4A)

also también (1A)

always siempre (3A)

am:

  I — (yo) soy (1B)

  I — not (yo) no soy (1B)

amusing divertido, -a (2A)

and y (1A)

¿— you? ¿Y a ti? *fam.* (1A); ¿Y tú? *fam.* (P); ¿Y usted (Ud.)? *formal* (P)

apple la manzana (3A)

  — juice el jugo de manzana (3A)

April abril (P)

Are you . . . ? ¿Eres . . . ? (1B)

arm el brazo (P)

art class la clase de arte (2A)

artistic artístico, -a (1B)

at:

  — eight (o'clock) a las ocho (4B)

  — eight (o'clock) at night a las ocho de la noche (4B)

  — eight (o'clock) in the evening a las ocho de la noche (4B)

  — eight (o'clock) in the morning a las ocho de la mañana (4B)

  — home en casa (4A)

  — one (o'clock) a la una (4B)

  — one (o'clock) in the afternoon a la una de la tarde (4B)

  — what time? ¿A qué hora? (4B)

athletic deportista (1B)

August agosto (P)

autumn el otoño (P)

awful: How —! ¡Qué asco! (3A)

B

backpack la mochila (2B)

bacon el tocino (3A)

bad malo, -a (3B); mal (4B)

badly mal (4B)

banana el plátano (3A)

baseball: to play — jugar al béisbol (4B)

basketball: to play — jugar al básquetbol (4B)

to be ser (3B); estar (2B)

  to — going to + *verb* ir a + *inf.* (4B)

beach la playa (4A)

because porque (3B)

beefsteak el bistec (3B)

behind detrás de (2B)

beside al lado de (2B)

beverages las bebidas (3B)

bicycle: to ride a — montar en bicicleta (1A)

binder: three-ring — la carpeta de argollas (2A)

book el libro (P)

bookbag la mochila (2B)

boring aburrido, -a (2A)

boy el chico (1B)

bread el pan (3A)

breakfast el desayuno (3A)

  for — en el desayuno (3A)

busy ocupado, -a (4B)

but pero (1B)

butter la mantequilla (3B)

C

café el café (4A)

calculator la calculadora (2A)

can:

  I — (yo) puedo (4B)

  you — (tú) puedes (4B)

carrots las zanahorias (3B)

cereal el cereal (3A)

chair la silla (2B)

cheese el queso (3A)

chicken el pollo (3B)

church la iglesia (4A)

  Protestant — el templo (4A)

class la clase (2A)

classroom la sala de clases (P)

clock el reloj (2B)

coffee el café (3A)

cold: It's —. Hace frío. (P)

computer la computadora (2A)

  — keyboard el teclado (2B)

  — mouse el ratón (2B)

  — screen la pantalla (2B)

  —s / technology la tecnología (2A)

  to use the — usar la computadora (1A)

concert el concierto (4B)

cookie la galleta (3A)

countryside el campo (4A)

D

dance el baile (4B)

to dance bailar (1A)

daring atrevido, -a (1B)

date: What is the —? ¿Cuál es la fecha? (P)

day el día (P)

    every — todos los días (3A); cada día (3B)

    What — is today? ¿Qué día es hoy? (P)

December diciembre (P)

delighted encantado, -a (P)

desk el pupitre (P); el escritorio (2B)

dictionary el diccionario (2A)

difficult difícil (2A)

dinner la cena (3B)

to do hacer (3B)

    — you like to … ? ¿Te gusta . . . ? (1A)

    I — (yo) hago (3B)

    you — (tú) haces (3B)

door la puerta (2B)

to draw dibujar (1A)

to drink beber (3A)

E

easy fácil (2A)

to eat comer (3A)

eggs los huevos (3A)

eight ocho (P)

eighteen dieciocho (P)

eighth octavo, -a (2A)

eighty ochenta (P)

either tampoco (1A)

    I don't (like to) — a mí tampoco (1A)

eleven once (P)

English class la clase de inglés (2A)

evening:

    Good —. Buenas noches. (P)

    in the — de la noche (4B)

    this — esta noche (4B)

every day cada día (3B); todos los días (3A)

to exercise hacer ejercicio (3B)

eye el ojo (P)

F

fall el otoño (P)

fats las grasas (3B)

favorite favorito, -a (2A)

February febrero (P)

fifteen quince (P)

fifth quinto, -a (2A)

fifty cincuenta (P)

finger el dedo (P)

first primer (primero), -a (2A)

fish el pescado (3B)

    to go —ing ir de pesca (4B)

five cinco (P)

flag la bandera (2B)

flavorful sabroso, -a (3B)

folder la carpeta (P)

food la comida (3A)

foot el pie (P)

football: to play — jugar al fútbol americano (4B)

for para (2A)

    — breakfast en el desayuno (3A)

    — lunch en el almuerzo (3A)

forty cuarenta (P)

four cuatro (P)

fourteen catorce (P)

fourth cuarto, -a (2A)

free time el tiempo libre (4A)

French fries las papas fritas (3A)

Friday viernes (P)

friend el amigo, la amiga (1B)

    with my/your —s con mis/tus amigos (4A)

friendly simpático, -a (1B)

from de (4A)

Where are you —? ¿De dónde eres? (4A)

front: in — of delante de (2B)

fruit salad la ensalada de frutas (3A)

fun divertido, -a (2A)

funny gracioso, -a (1B)

G

game el partido (4B)

generally generalmente (4A)

girl la chica (1B)

to go ir (4A)

    to be —ing to +*verb* ir a + *inf.* (4B)

    to — camping ir de cámping (4B)

    to — fishing ir de pesca (4B)

    to — shopping ir de compras (4A)

    to — to school ir a la escuela (1A)

golf: to play — jugar al golf (4B)

good bueno (buen), -a (1B)

    — afternoon. Buenas tardes. (P)

    — evening. Buenas noches. (P)

    — morning. Buenos días. (P)

Good-bye! ¡Adiós! (P)

grains los cereales (3B)

grapes las uvas (3B)

Great! ¡Genial! (4B)

green verde

    — beans las judías verdes (3B)

guitar: to play the — tocar la guitarra (1A)

gym el gimnasio (4A)

H

half media, -o (P)

    — past y media (*in telling time*) (P)

ham el jamón (3A)

ham and cheese sandwich el sándwich de jamón y queso (3A)

hamburger la hamburguesa (3A)

hand la mano (P)

happy contento, -a (4B)

hardworking trabajador, -ora (1B)

to have: I — tengo (2A)

I — to . . . tengo que + *inf.* (4B)

you — tienes (2A)

he él (1B)

he / she is es (1B)

head la cabeza (P)

health:

for one's — para la salud (3B)

to maintain one's — para mantener la salud (3B)

Hello! ¡Hola! (P)

here aquí (2B)

Hey! ¡Oye! (4B)

home la casa (4A)

at — en casa (4A)

(to) — a casa (4A)

homework la tarea (2A)

horrible horrible (3B)

hot:

— dog el perrito caliente (3A)

It's —. Hace calor. (P)

hour: in the . . . — en la . . . hora (class period) (2A)

house la casa (4A)

how: — awful! ¡Qué asco! (3A)

How? ¿Cómo? (P)

— are you? ¿Cómo está Ud.? *formal* (P); ¿Cómo estás? *fam.* (P); ¿Qué tal? *fam.* (P)

— do you say . . . ? ¿Cómo se dice . . . ? (P)

— is . . . spelled? ¿Cómo se escribe . . . ? (P)

— many? ¿Cuántos, -as? (P)

hundred: one — cien (P)

hungry: I'm —. Tengo hambre. (3B)

I

I yo (1B)

— am soy (1B)

— am not no soy (1B)

— don't think so. Creo que no. (3B)

— stay at home. Me quedo en casa. (4A)

— think . . . Creo que . . . (3B)

— think so. Creo que sí. (3B)

— would like Me gustaría (4B)

—'m hungry. Tengo hambre. (3B)

—'m sorry. Lo siento. (4B)

—'m thirsty. Tengo sed. (3B)

I do too a mí también (1A)

I don't either a mí tampoco (1A)

ice cream el helado (3B)

iced tea el té helado (3A)

impatient impaciente (1B)

in en (P, 2B)

— front of delante de (2B)

— order to para + *inf.* (4A)

— the . . . hour en la . . . hora (class period) (2A)

— the afternoon de la tarde (4B)

— the evening de la noche (4B)

— the morning de la mañana (4B)

intelligent inteligente (1B)

interesting interesante (2A)

is es (P)

he / she — es (1B)

it la, lo

— is . . . Son las *(in telling time)* (P)

— is one o'clock. Es la una. (P)

— is the . . . of . . . Es el *(number)* de *(month) (in telling the date)* (P)

— is the first of . . . Es el primero de *(month).* (P)

—'s a . . . es un / una . . . (2B)

—'s cold. Hace frío. (P)

—'s hot. Hace calor. (P)

—'s raining. Llueve. (P)

—'s snowing. Nieva. (P)

—'s sunny. Hace sol. (P)

—'s windy. Hace viento. (P)

J

January enero (P)

job el trabajo (4A)

juice:

apple — el jugo de manzana (3A)

orange — el jugo de naranja (3A)

July julio (P)

June junio (P)

K

keyboard (computer) el teclado (2B)

to know saber (4B)

I — (how to) (yo) sé (4B)

you — (how to) (tú) sabes (4B)

L

later: See you — ¡Hasta luego!, ¡Nos vemos! (P)

lazy perezoso, -a (1B)

leg la pierna (P)

lemonade la limonada (3A)

Let's see A ver . . . (2A)

lettuce la lechuga (3B)

library la biblioteca (4A)

to lift weights levantar pesas (3B)

to like:

Do you — to . . . ? ¿Te gusta . . . ? (1A)

He / She doesn't — . . . No le gusta . . . (1B)

He / She —s . . . Le gusta . . . (1B)

I don't — to . . . (A mí) no me gusta . . . (1A)

I don't — to . . . at all. (A mí) no me gusta nada . . . (1A)

I — . . . Me gusta . . . (3A)

I — to . . . (A mí) me gusta . . . (1A)

I — to . . . a lot (A mí) me gusta mucho . . . (1A)

I — to . . . better (A mí) me gusta más . . . (1A)

I would — Me gustaría (4B)

    What do you — better (prefer) to do? ¿Qué te gusta hacer más? (1A)

    What do you — to do? ¿Qué te gusta hacer? (1A)

    Would you —? ¿Te gustaría? (4B)

    You — . . . Te gusta . . . (3A)

likewise igualmente (P)

to **listen to music** escuchar música (1A)

little: a — un poco (de) (4B)

lot: a — mucho, -a (2A)

to **love** encantar

    I / You — . . . Me / Te encanta(n) . . . (3A)

lunch el almuerzo (2A)

    for — en el almuerzo (3A)

M

madam (la) señora (Sra.) (P)

magazines: to read — leer revistas (1A)

to **maintain one's health** para mantener la salud (3B)

mall el centro comercial (4A)

many muchos, -as (3B)

    How —? ¿Cuántos, -as? (P)

March marzo (P)

match el partido (4B)

mathematics class la clase de matemáticas (2A)

May mayo (P)

me me

    — neither. A mí tampoco. (1A)

    — too. A mí también. (1A)

    with — conmigo (4B)

meal la comida (3A)

to **mean:**

    It —s . . . Quiere decir . . . (P)

    What does . . . —? ¿Qué quiere decir . . . ? (P)

meat la carne (3B)

messy desordenado, -a (1B)

milk la leche (3A)

miss, Miss (la) señorita (Srta.) (P)

Monday lunes (P)

    on Mondays los lunes (4A)

month el mes (P)

more más (1A)

    — . . . than más . . . que (2A)

    — or less más o menos (3A)

morning:

    Good —. Buenos días. (P)

    in the — de la mañana (4B)

mosque la mezquita (4A)

mountains las montañas (4A)

mouse (computer) el ratón (2B)

mouth la boca (P)

movie la película

    to see a — ver una película (4A)

    — theater el cine (4A)

Mr. (el) señor (Sr.) (P)

Mrs. (la) señora (Sra.) (P)

music: to listen to — escuchar música (1A)

must deber (3B)

my mi (2B)

    — name is . . . Me llamo . . . (P)

N

name:

    My — is . . . Me llamo . . . (P)

    What is your —? ¿Cómo te llamas? (P)

    What's his / her —? ¿Cómo se llama? (1B)

neat ordenado, -a (1B)

to **need**

    I — necesito (2A)

    you — necesitas (2A)

neither . . . nor ni . . . ni (1A)

never nunca (3A)

next to al lado de (2B)

nice simpático, -a (1B)

night: at — de la noche (4B)

nine nueve (P)

nineteen diecinueve (P)

ninety noventa (P)

ninth noveno, -a (2A)

nose la nariz, *pl.* las narices (P)

not . . . or ni . . . ni (1A)

notebook el cuaderno (P)

nothing nada (P)

November noviembre (P)

O

o'clock:

    at eight — a las ocho (4B)

    at one — a la una (4B)

    It's one —. Es la una. (P)

October octubre (P)

of de (2B)

    — course por supuesto (3A)

Oh! What a shame / pity! ¡Ay! ¡Qué pena! (4B)

okay regular (P)

on en (2B)

    — Mondays, on Tuesdays . . . los lunes, los martes . . . (4A)

    — top of encima de (2B)

    — weekends los fines de semana (4A)

one uno (un), -a (P)

    at — (o'clock) a la una (4B)

one hundred cien (P)

onion la cebolla (3B)

or o (1A)

orange: — juice el jugo de naranja (3A)

P

paper: sheet of — la hoja de papel (P)

park el parque (4A)

party la fiesta (4B)

pastries los pasteles (3B)

patient paciente (1B)

peas los guisantes (3B)

pen el bolígrafo (P)

pencil el lápiz, *pl.* los lápices (P)

    — sharpener el sacapuntas, *pl.* los sacapuntas (2B)

phone: to talk on the — hablar por teléfono (1A)

physical education class la clase de educación física (2A)

piano lesson (class) la lección, *pl.* las lecciones de piano (4A)

pity: What a —! ¡Qué pena! (4B)

pizza la pizza (3A)

to play jugar (a) (u → ue) *(games, sports)* (4B); tocar *(an instrument)* (1A)

    to — baseball jugar al béisbol (4B)

    to — basketball jugar al básquetbol (4B)

    to — football jugar al fútbol americano (4B)

    to — golf jugar al golf (4B)

    to — soccer jugar al fútbol (4B)

    to — sports practicar deportes (1A)

    to — tennis jugar al tenis (4B)

    to — the guitar tocar la guitarra (1A)

    to — video games jugar videojuegos (1A)

    to — volleyball jugar al vóleibol (4B)

please por favor (P)

pleased to meet you mucho gusto (P)

pool la piscina (4A)

poster el cartel (2B)

potatoes las papas (3B)

practical práctico, -a (2A)

to prefer preferir (e → ie)

    I — (yo) prefiero (3B)

    I — to . . . (a mí) me gusta más . . . (1A)

    you — (tú) prefieres (3B)

Q

quarter past y cuarto *(in telling time)* (P)

quarter to menos cuarto *(in telling time)* (P)

R

rain: It's —ing. Llueve. (P)

to read magazines leer revistas (1A)

Really? ¿Verdad? (3A)

reserved reservado, -a (1B)

restaurant el restaurante (4A)

rice el arroz (3B)

to ride: to — a bicycle montar en bicicleta (1A)

Right? ¿Verdad? (3A)

to run correr (1A)

S

sad triste (4B)

salad la ensalada (3A)

    fruit — la ensalada de frutas (3A)

sandwich: ham and cheese — el sándwich de jamón y queso (3A)

Saturday sábado (P)

sausage la salchicha (3A)

to say decir

    How do you —? ¿Cómo se dice? (P)

    You — . . . Se dice . . . (P)

    You don't —! ¡No me digas! (4A)

schedule el horario (2A)

school: to go to — ir a la escuela (1A)

science: — class la clase de ciencias naturales (2A)

screen: computer — la pantalla (2B)

season la estación, *pl.* las estaciones (P)

second segundo, -a (2A)

to see ver

    Let's — A ver . . . (2A)

    — you! ¡Nos vemos! (P)

    — you later! ¡Nos vemos!, Hasta luego. (P)

    — you tomorrow. Hasta mañana. (P)

    to — a movie ver una película (4A)

September septiembre (P)

serious serio, -a (1B)

seven siete (P)

seventeen diecisiete (P)

seventh séptimo, -a (2A)

seventy setenta (P)

shame: What a —! ¡Qué pena! (4B)

to share compartir (3A)

she ella (1B)

sheet of paper la hoja de papel (P)

shopping: to go — ir de compras (4A)

should deber (3B)

shy reservado, -a (1B)

sick enfermo, -a (4B)

to sing cantar (1A)

sir (el) señor (Sr.) (P)

six seis (P)

sixteen dieciséis (P)

sixth sexto, -a (2A)

sixty sesenta (P)

to skate patinar (1A)

to skateboard montar en monopatín (1A)

to ski esquiar (i → í) (1A)

snow: It's —ing. Nieva. (P)

so-so regular (P)

soccer: to play — jugar al fútbol (4B)

sociable sociable (1B)

social studies class la clase de ciencias sociales (2A)

soft drink el refresco (3A)

some unos, -as (2B)

something algo (3B)

sometimes a veces (1B)

sorry: I'm —. Lo siento. (4B)

soup: vegetable — la sopa de verduras (3A)

spaghetti los espaguetis (3B)

Spanish class la clase de español (2A)

to spell:

    How is . . . spelled? ¿Cómo se escribe . . . ? (P)

    It's spelled . . . Se escribe . . . (P)

to spend time with friends pasar tiempo con amigos (1A)

sports:

> **to play —** practicar deportes (1A)

> **— -minded** deportista (1B)

spring la primavera (P)

to stay: I — at home. Me quedo en casa. (4A)

stomach el estómago (P)

stories: to write — escribir cuentos (1A)

strawberries las fresas (3A)

student el / la estudiante (P)

studious estudioso, -a (1B)

to study estudiar (2A)

summer el verano (P)

Sunday domingo (P)

sunny: It's —. Hace sol. (P)

to swim nadar (1A)

> **swimming pool** la piscina (4A)

> **synagogue** la sinagoga (4A)

T

table la mesa (2B)

talented talentoso, -a (1B)

to talk hablar (2A)

> **to — on the phone** hablar por teléfono (1A)

tasty sabroso, -a (3B)

tea el té (3A)

> **iced —** el té helado (3A)

to teach enseñar (2A)

teacher el profesor, la profesora (P)

technology / computers la tecnología (2A)

technology / computer class la clase de tecnología (2A)

television: to watch — ver la tele (1A)

temple el templo (4A)

ten diez (P)

tennis: to play — jugar al tenis (4B)

tenth décimo, -a (2A)

thank you gracias (P)

the el, la (1B); los, las (2B)

theater: movie — el cine (4A)

then entonces (4B)

there allí (2B)

> **— is / are** hay (P)

they ellos, ellas (2A)

to think pensar (e → ie)

> **I don't — so.** Creo que no. (3B)

> **I — . . .** Creo que . . . (3B)

> **I — so.** Creo que sí. (3B)

third tercer (tercero), -a (2A)

thirsty: I'm —. Tengo sed. (3B)

thirteen trece (P)

thirty treinta (P); y media *(in telling time)* (P)

thirty-one treinta y uno (P)

this este, esta

> **— afternoon** esta tarde (4B)

> **— evening** esta noche (4B)

> **— weekend** este fin de semana (4B)

> **What is —?** ¿Qué es esto? (2B)

three tres (P)

three-ring binder la carpeta de argollas (2A)

Thursday jueves (P)

time:

> **At what —?** ¿A qué hora? (4B)

> **free —** el tiempo libre (4A)

> **to spend — with friends** pasar tiempo con amigos (1A)

> **What — is it?** ¿Qué hora es? (P)

tired cansado, -a (4B)

to a *(prep.)* (4A)

> **in order —** para + *inf.* (4A)

> **— the** a la, al (4A)

toast el pan tostado (3A)

today hoy (P)

tomatoes los tomates (3B)

tomorrow mañana (P)

> **See you —.** Hasta mañana. (P)

too también (1A); demasiado (4B)

> **I do (like to) —** a mí también (1A)

> **me —** a mí también (1A)

top: on — of encima de (2B)

Tuesday martes (P)

> **on —s** los martes (4A)

twelve doce (P)

twenty veinte (P)

twenty-one veintiuno (veintiún) (P)

two dos (P)

U

underneath debajo de (2B)

to understand comprender (3A)

to use: to — the computer usar la computadora (1A)

V

vegetable soup la sopa de verduras (3A)

very muy (1B)

> **— well** muy bien (P)

video games: to play — jugar videojuegos (1A)

volleyball: to play — jugar al vóleibol (4B)

W

to walk caminar (3B)

to want querer (e → ie)

> **I —** (yo) quiero (4B)

> **you —** (tú) quieres (4B)

wastepaper basket la papelera (2B)

to watch television ver la tele (1A)

water el agua *f.* (3A)

we nosotros, -as (2A)

weather: What's the — like? ¿Qué tiempo hace? (P)

Wednesday miércoles (P)

week la semana (P)

weekend:

> **on —s** los fines de semana (4A)

> **this —** este fin de semana (4B)

weights: to lift weights levantar pesas (3B)

well bien (P); pues *(to indicate pause)* (1A)

> **very —** muy bien (P)

What? ¿Cuál? ¿Qué? (3A)

— are you like? ¿Cómo eres?
(1B)

(At) — time? ¿A qué hora? (4B)

— day is today? ¿Qué día es
hoy? (P)

**— do you like better (prefer)
to do?** ¿Qué te gusta hacer
más? (1A)

— do you like to do? ¿Qué te
gusta hacer? (1A)

— does . . . mean? ¿Qué quiere
decir . . . ? (P)

— is she / he like? ¿Cómo es?
(1B)

— is the date? ¿Cuál es la
fecha? (P)

— is this? ¿Qué es esto? (2B)

— is your name? ¿Cómo te
llamas? (P)

— time is it? ¿Qué hora es? (P)

—'s happening? ¿Qué pasa?
(P)

—'s his / her name? ¿Cómo se
llama? (1B)

—'s the weather like? ¿Qué
tiempo hace? (P)

What!:

— a good / nice idea! ¡Qué
buena idea! (4B)

— a shame / pity! ¡Qué pena!
(4B)

When? ¿Cuándo? (4A)

Where? ¿Dónde? (2B)

— are you from? ¿De dónde
eres? (4A)

(To) —? ¿Adónde? (4A)

Which? ¿Cuál? (3A)

Who? ¿Quién? (2A)

Why? ¿Por qué? (3B)

window la ventana (2B)

windy: It's —. Hace viento. (P)

winter el invierno (P)

with con (3A)

— me conmigo (4B)

— my / your friends con
mis / tus amigos (4A)

— whom? ¿Con quién? (4A)

— you contigo (4B)

without sin (3A)

work el trabajo (4A)

to work trabajar (1A)

Would you like . . . ?
¿Te gustaría . . . ? (4B)

to write: to — stories escribir
cuentos (1A)

Y

year el año (P)

yes sí (1A)

yogurt el yogur (3A)

you *fam. sing.* tú (2A); *formal
sing.* usted (Ud.) (2A); *fam. pl.*
vosotros, -as (2A); *formal pl.*
ustedes (Uds.) (2A); *fam. after
prep.* ti (1A)

And —? ¿Y a ti? (1A)

Are — . . . ? ¿Eres . . . ? (1B)

with — contigo (4B)

— don't say! ¡No me digas!
(4A)

— say . . . Se dice . . . (P)

your *fam.* tu (2B)

Z

zero cero (P)

Grammar Index

Structures are most often presented first in *A primera vista*, where they are practiced lexically. They are then explained later in a *Gramática* section or a *Nota*. Light face numbers refer to the pages where structures are initially presented or, after explanation, where student reminders occur. **Bold face numbers** refer to pages where structures are explained or are otherwise highlighted.

a 26–30, 218
+ definite article 208–209, **215**
after **jugar** 240, **256**
in time telling 240–241, **249**
with **ir** + infinitive 241, **252**
accent marks **13**, 38, **223**
in interrogative words **224**
adjectives:
agreement and formation 56–57, **64,** 82, **190,** 204
comparative 87
demonstrative 240–241
plural. *See* adjectives: agreement and formation
position of **72**
possessive 29, 118, 144
alphabet 12
-ar verbs 36
present 87, 89–90, **100,** 114, 160
articles:
definite **11, 70,** 82, **132,** 144
definite, with **a** 208–209, **215**
definite, with days of the week 216
definite, with **de 125**
definite, with titles of respect 94
indefinite **70,** 82, **132,** 144

cognates 40, 68
comparison 87
compound subject **98**

dates 14–15
de:
+ definite article 125
in compound nouns **156**
in prepositional phrases 119, 125
possessive 119, **135**
derivation of words 94, 194, 216, 249

encantar 149, **164**
-er verbs 36
present 148–149, **160,** 174
estar 118–119, **128,** 144
Exploración del lenguaje:
Cognates **40**
Cognates that begin with **es** + consonant **68**
Connections between Latin, English, and Spanish **94**
Language through gestures **127**
Origins of the Spanish days of the week **216**
Punctuation and accent marks **13**
Señor, señora, señorita **2**
Spanish words borrowed from English **249**
Tú vs. **usted 5**
Using a noun to modify another noun **156**
Where did it come from? **194**

gender **11**
of adjectives agreeing with nouns **64,** 82, **190,** 204
of articles **70,** 82
of pronouns **98**
gustar 26, 52, **164**

hacer 26, 179
use of in weather expressions 18
hay 14

infinitive **36**
after **ir a** 241, **252**
after **para** 208
after **tener que** 241
interrogative words **224**
ir 30, 208, **218,** 236
+ **a** + infinitive 241, **252**
with future meaning 241, **252**
-ir verbs 36
present 152, **160,** 174

jugar 27, 240, **256,** 266

negative 27, **42, 44,** 72, 105
nada used for emphasis 27, **42**
ni . . . ni 27, **42**
tampoco 27, **44**
nouns **11,** 64
compound **156**
plural **132,** 190
used with **gustar / encantar 164**
numbers 7
in dates 15
in telling time **8**
ordinal 86

plurals:
of adjectives **190,** 204
of nouns **132,** 190
poder 241
possession:
adjectives 29, 118, 144
with **de** 119, **135**
preferir 181
prepositions 119
present. *See individual verb listings*
pronouns:
conmigo / contigo 241
prepositional, used for agreement, clarity, or emphasis 26–27, **44**

Acknowledgments

Maps All maps created by XNR Productions.

Photographs Every effort has been made to secure permission and provide appropriate credit for photographic material. The publisher deeply regrets any omission and pledges to correct errors called to its attention in subsequent editions.

Unless otherwise acknowledged, all photographs are the property of Pearson Education, Inc.

Photo locators denoted as follows: Top (T), Center (C), Bottom (B), Left (L), Right (R), Background (Bkgd)

Cover (L) ColorBlind Images/Blend Images/Getty Images, (CL) nagelestock/Alamy Images, (CR) Yadid Levy/Alamy Images, (R) Michael Zysman/Shutterstock

Front Matter iv (TR) Kuttig—Travel—2/Alamy Images, (TL) Art Resource, NY, (BR) digital vision/Getty Images, (BL) Getty Images; **vi** (TR) Alamy, (BR, BC) NASA, (BL) StockTrek/SuperStock; **xii** (Inset) Bettmann/Corbis, (Bkgd) José Fusta Raga/Corbis; **xiii** (BR) ©Phil Schermeister/Corbis; **xiv** (Bkgd) Danny Lehman/Corbis; **xvi** (Bkgd) ©David Zimmerman/Corbis, (BL) Exactostock/SuperStock; **xviii** (Bkgd) Shutterstock; **xx** (Bkgd) Michael Hilton/Alamy Images; **xxii** (Inset) ©Mark L. Stephenson, (Bkgd) ©Paul Hardy/Corbis; **xxiii** (BR) ©José Fuste Raga/Corbis; **xxiv** (Bkgd) ©Craig Tuttle/Corbis; **xxv** (BR) ©Ron Watts/Corbis, (BL) Corbis

1 (TR) ©Philip Scalia/Alamy Images; **3** (T) Odilon Dimier/Altopress/NewsCom, jolopes/Fotolia (5) Rido/Fotolia **8** (B) SuperStock; **13** (B) Bridgeman Art Library; **15** (C) Morton Beebe/Corbis **16** ©Pedro Armestre/Getty Images; **17** ©DK Images; **18** (R, L, CR, CL) SuperStock; **19** (L) ©Gordon R. Gainer, ©Ramon Berk/Shutterstock, (CL) Getty Images, (CR) Photo Researchers, Inc.; **20** (BL) ©Sharon Day/Shutterstock, (TL) Comstock/Thinkstock, (TL, BL) DDB Stock Photography, NASA; **24** (Bkgd) ©Imagestate Media Partners Limited—Impact Photos/Alamy Images; **25** (R) Art Resource, NY; **28** (T) Roberto M. Arakaki/ImageState; **29** (T) Bettmann/Corbis, (BC) SuperStock; **30** (R) Buddy Mays/ImageState; **33** Arch White/Alamy Images; **35** (TR) Alamy Images, (L) Ernest Manewal/SuperStock; **40** (T) Museo Bellapart; **41** (TL) Niko Guido/Getty Images (TR) Blaine Harrington Photo, (BL) Latin Focus, (RC) PhotoEdit, (BR) ZUMApress/NewsCom; **46** (B) Marisol Díaz/Latin Focus, (T) Hola Images/Corbis **47** (T) Jimmy Dorantes/Latin Focus, (B) PhotoEdit; **48** Alamy Images; **49** (B) Kathy Ferguson-Johnson/PhotoEdit; **50** (Bkgd) Bettmann/Corbis; **51** (C) Bettmann/Corbis, (T) Bettmann/Corbis, (B) José Fuste Raga/Corbis; **54** (Bkgd) ©imagebroker/Alamy Images; **55** (R) Art Resource, NY; **57** (B) Panos Pictures; **63** (TCR) ©Jan A. Csernoch/Alamy Images, (TR) jackmicro/Fotolia (TL) ©Radius Images/Alamy, (BCL) Alamy Images, (BL) Getty Images, (BCR) Image Source/Glow Images, (TCL) Image Source/SuperStock, (BR) Newstock-images/SuperStock; **(66)** Blend Images/Alamy **68** (BR) Blend Images/Alamy, (T) Simón Bolívar (1783–1830) (chromolitho)/Private Collection/Archives Charmet/Bridgeman Art Library; **73** (B) ©Gary Bogdon/NewSport/Corbis, (T) Gary Bogdon/Gary Bogdon,

(B) H. Huntly Hersch/D. Donne Bryant Stock Photography; **75** Alamy Images; **77** Cindy Miller Hopkins/NewsCom; **78** (TL) micromonkey/Fotolia, (BR) DDB Stock Photography, (TL) Tony Arruza/Tony Arruza; (TL) Rido/Fotolia (BR) Ian Shaw/Alamy; **80** (Bkgd) Bettmann/Corbis; **81** (T, B) Bettmann/Corbis, (C) Linda Whitwam/©DK Images; **84** (Bkgd) ©dbimages/Alamy Images; **85** (Inset) Courtesy Marlborough Gallery, NY; **95** NewsCom; **97** (TL) Corbis Bridge/Alamy Images, (T) Rolf Adlercreutz/Alamy **99** (BCR) ©Andy Dean/Fotolia, (TCL) ©holbox/Shutterstock, (TL) ©Tetra Images/Getty Images, (BR) Alamy Images, (BL) Creatas/Thinkstock, Panos Pictures; (TCR) Barry Lewis/Alamy (BCL) MBI/Alamy (BR) Rob/Fotolia **102** DDB Stock Photography; **103** Paul Conklin/PhotoEdit; **104** (R, L) Lucky Dragon USA/Fotolia **105** (R, L) diego cervo/Fotolia **107** Panos Pictures; **108** (Bkgd) Bettmann/Corbis, (Inset) Martin Shields/Alamy Images; **109** (Inset) ©National Geographic Image Collection/Alamy Images, (T) ©Ron Niebrugge/Alamy Images; **110** (T) ©Hector Rio/EFE/NewsCom, (B) ©John Vizcaíno/Reuters/Landov LLC; **111** Jeff Greenberg/PhotoEdit; **112** (Bkgd) José Fuste Raga/Corbis; **113** (B) ©Randy Faris/Corbis, (C) Danny Lehman/Corbis, (T) Lindsay Hebberd/Corbis; **116** (Bkgd) Carlos S. Pereyra/DDB Stock Photography; **117** (Inset) SUN/NewsCom; **125** ©Greg Balfour Evans/Alamy Images; **127** (C) Jeff Greenburg/PhotoEdit, Inc.; **134** (TL) ©flashover/Alamy Images; **137** (B) Getty Images, (T) Bubbles Photolibrary/Alamy **138** (B) Jeremy Horner/Panos Pictures, (CL) National Geographic Image Collection/Alamy Images; **139** (BR) Jean-Leo Dugast/Panos Pictures, (TL) Jeremy Horner/Panos Pictures, (BC) Jon Spaull/Panos Pictures, (TR) Panos Pictures, (BL) Sean Sprague/Panos Pictures; **140** (TR) ©Bill Bachmann/Alamy Images, (B) John Birdsall/Alamy **141** (B) Alamy Images; **142** (Inset) Bettmann/Corbis, (Bkgd) Getty Images; **143** (B) ©J. A. Murillo, (C) Bettmann/Corbis, (T) Corbis; **146** (Bkgd) ©Blend Images/SuperStock; **147** (Inset) Art Resource, NY; **160** (BR) ©Dorothy Alexander/Alamy Images; **161** ©Corbis/SuperStock; **163** ©Slim Plantagenate/Alamy; **165** (CR) ©Jimmy Durantes/Latin Focus, Getty Images; **166** (BL) Cindy Miller Hopkins/NewsCom; **169** (B) ©imagebroker/Alamy; **170** (T, C) raptorcaptor/Fotolia **171** (T) Tomas Rodriguez/Corbis; **172** Bettmann/ Corbis; **173** (T, C) Bettmann/Corbis, (B) Corbis; **176** (Bkgd) ©imagebroker/SuperStock; **177** (Inset) The Great City of Tenochtitlán, detail of a woman selling vegetables, 1945 (mural), Rivera, Diego (1886–1957)/Palacio Nacional, Mexico City, Mexico/Giraudon/Bridgeman Art Library; **185** (T) ©David R. Frazier Photolibrary, Inc./Alamy; **(186)** Golden Pixels LLC/Alamy **187** (B) Alamy Images; **189** Laurence Mouton/PhotoAlto/Corbis **193** (B) eStock Photo, (T) James Nelson/Getty Images; **195** ImageState; **197** (T) ©Associated Press; **199** (BL) ANTONIO SCORZA/AFP/Getty Images/NewsCom, (TL) NewsCom; **200** (T) ©Alison Wright/Photo Researchers, Inc., (B) NewsCom; **201** ©Jimmy Dorantes/Latin Focus; **202** (Bkgd) Corbis; **203** (C) ©Prisma/SuperStock, (T, B) Bettmann/Corbis; **206** (Bkgd) ©imagebroker/Alamy Images; **207** (Inset) Art Resource, NY; **215** NewsCom;

219 (CR) ©Jimmy Dorantes/Latin Focus, AFP/Getty Images/ NewsCom; **221** ©Jack Hollingsworth/Corbis; Erin Ryan/ Corbis **226** Alamy; **228** (T) ANDRES LEIGHTON/AP Photo **229** (T) Alamy Images, (C) PhotoLibrary Group, Inc.; **230** (BL) Jon Bursnall/Latin Focus, (BR) Malcolm Fife/eStock Photo; **231** (B) ©Dave G. Houser/Corbis, (TL) Exactostock/SuperStock, (TR) NewsCom; **232** (TR) ©GoGo Images Corporation/ Alamy; **233** (CR) ©Jimmy Dorantes/Latin Focus, (T) Latin Focus; **234** (CL) ©Randy Faris/Corbis, (R) Bettmann/Corbis, (TR) Medioimages/Photodisc/Thinkstock; **235** (Bkgd) Alamy; **238** (Bkgd) Getty Images; **239** (Inset) Getty Images; **247** (BR)

Secretaría de Turismo y Desarrollo/Latin Focus; **255** (C) gekaskr/Fotolia (TR) Shutterstock, (T) Tony Cordoza/Alamy; **257** (B) Peter Chartran/D. Donne Bryant Stock Photography; **258** (B) PhotoEdit, (T) Reuters NewMedia, Inc./Corbis; **259** (L) ©Michael Taylor/Lonely Planet Images; **260** (L) Chris Trotman/DUOMO/©PCN Photography; **261** (T) Cspa/CSPA/ Cal Sport Media/ZUMAPRESS/NewsCom, (B) Darrell Walker/ UTHM/Icon SMI/NewsCom; **262** (B) ©Jimmy Dorantes/Latin Focus; **263** ZUMA Press,Inc./Alamy **264** (Bkgd) ©Nik Wheeler/ Corbis, (L) NASA; **265** (R) Bettmann/Corbis, (TL) Kevin Fleming/Corbis; **269** (B) Alamy Images, (T) ImageState